FLORA EXOTICA OF JAMMU AND KASHMIR

FLORA EXOTICA OF JAMMU AND KASHMIR

B.L. BHELLUM
RANI MAGOTRA
VIR JEE

GYAN

Flora Exotica of Jammu and Kashmir

ISBN : 978-81-212-1151-2

Published in 2013 in India by
Gyan Publishing House
23, Main Ansari Road, Daryaganj,
New Delhi - 110002
Phones : 23282060, 23261060
Fax : (011) 23285914
E-mail: books@gyanbooks.com
website: gyanbooks.com

Laser Type Setting : Rajender Vashist, Delhi
Printed at : G. Print Process.Delhi

Contents

Foreword

Flora Exotica of Jammu and Kashmir State enumerated by Dr. B. L. Bhellum, Prof. Rani Magotra and Dr. Vir Jee is a good attempt at enriching the knowledge about plant elements which have come over from the other areas of the world and naturalized in J & K State.

J & K State is well known for its diverse cultures as also the phytogeographic ranges offered. Variations in the topography, climate and geography have created a variety of agroclimatic zones vis-a-vis ecological niches in the state. These niches offer habitats in aquatic as also the terrestrial limits offering a variety of abode for naturalization of plants from various parts of India and also from across the seas and oceans.

Biological spectrum of the floristic elements encountered in the state indicates the mutualistic relationship between the plants and the variety of habitats. Many elements from different floristic zones of the world have migrated through land and oceanic routes and settled in these diverse niches and blended so intimately with local elements making it difficult to differentiate between the exotic and the indigenous. It seems that a bold attempt has been made by the authors in identifying these elements which exist currently as ornamentals, food crops and even weeds.

The book form presentation with illustrations and short taxonomic descriptions will prove useful for the students indulging in biodiversity investigation of the state and such studies need to be encouraged and highlighted.

Prof. B. L. Sapru

Jammu

12.06.2012

Preface

Since long, it has been our ardent desire to produce a book which will provide basic information about the exotic flora of this State. Besides, it was also envisaged to meet the requirement of students, researchers, foresters and teachers etc. who are interested in this field of botany. In general, the history of exotic flora in India is poorly known; nevertheless, some Exotics instead of them date back to the Moughal and British periods. In the present communication, an attempt has been made to identify the exotic species of Jammu and Kashmir State and to document the relevant data regarding their taxonomy, nativity and general distribution. This exercise is an outcome of a vast field experience of the authors together with a wide range of literature consultation. Some selective illustrations and photographs have been incorporated to facilitate their identification at a glance. Although a great care has been taken in the present compilation yet errors if any along with the suggestions for further improvement will be duly appreciated.

Authors

Acknowledgements

Special thanks are due to Prof. A. K. Koul, Dean Academics, BGSB University Rajouri and to Dr. B. M. Sharma (Ex Scientist) Floristic Division, IIIM, Jammu for rendering some fruitful suggestions. The senior author is also highly thankful to his elder brother Dr. R. L. Bhellum for constant encouragement. Dr. B. L. Bhellum and Dr. Vir Jee are thankful to Department of Higher Education for encouragement and to respective College Principals for inspiration and moral support. We also gratefully acknowledge the help and co-operation rendered by M/s Gyan Publishing House, New Delhi for completing this task.

1

Introduction

The state of Jammu and Kashmir bordering the country in the north, is aptly regarded as the "Crown of India". It conforms to the geographical boundries of 32.17 – 36.58 N latitude and 73. 26 – 80.26 E latitude and spans over an approximate area of 2,28,070 sq. km. which is distinctly divided into the three political provinces of Jammu, Kashmir and Ladakh.These subdivisions further discern a strong intrinsic individuality in their geographical, climatic, socio-economic, religeo-cultural and biotic characterstics.

Botanically, the area being situated at the cross roads of various phytogeographic regions, reveals a considerable admixture in its floristic wealth. The latter is amply documented in the monumental treatise of the Hooker's "Flora of British India" (1872 – 1897). Since then, many notable contributions have been made on the subject with respect to the study area; these include: Parker (1918), Rao (1960), Wali and Tiku (1964), Stewart (1916-17, 1967a, 1967b, 1972, 1982), Singh and Gohil (1972), Singh and Kachroo (1973), Singh and Wafai (1973), Rau (1975), Kachroo (1980), Anonymous (1982), Hartmann (1984, 1987) and Seybold and Kull (1985). Besides, several local floras have been published to complement diverse vegetational wealth of this state viz. Singh and Kachroo (1976), Kachroo *et. al.* (1977), Sharma and Kachroo (1981, 1983), Dhar and Kachroo (1983) and Swami and Gupta (1998), etc.

Compared to the rich repository of data concerning local flora, little information is available about the exotic flora of this state which includes Singh and Kachroo (1976) and Vidyarthi (2003). Together with the indigenous flora, the present attempt could prove very fruitful in analyzing and evaluating the overall floristic wealth of the state.

(i) Exotic flora – a historical perspective

In general, the history of exotic flora in India stands poorly documented; nevertheless it seems plausible to infer that most of the exotics date back to the Moughal and British periods. Although the quest for the beautiful plants and gardens has remained a vibrant endeavour in India since ancient times yet its renaissance has led to the introduction and improvement of many ornamental and horticultural plants from various parts of the world (Colthurst, 1937; Jindal, 1970; Swarup, 1971; Khoshoo, 1974 and Randhawa, 1976).

The state of Jammu and Kashmir being bestowed with a rich array of picturesque spots also did not lag in getting influenced by various exogenous elements. It's awe – inspiring scenic beauty together with compelling charm of parks and gardens; lakes and rivers; meadows and mountains; peaks and glaciers, etc. have traditionally attracted various shades of people from all across the globe. These include: tourists and travelers; amateurs and artists; adventurers and explorers; pilgrims and poets; philanthropists and nature lovers; missionaries and servicemen etc. Besides, kings and rulers have also undertaken keen interest towards garden building in this region. Many plants or their propagules having ornamental, economic or medicinal attributes have been introduced by these people which subsequently got acclimatized with local environmental conditions and today adorn various parks and gardens thereby adding grace to the grandeur of this state. Randhawa (1976) held that the romantic beauty of Kashmir gardens has significantly contributed to aesthetic reputation of the Moughals especially Jahangir and Shah Jahan. The grand avenue chinar tree (*Platanus orientalis*) mostly abounding the parks and gardens of Kashmir is also a Moughal introduction. In addition to chinars, roses, jasmines, carnations, irises, lilies, daffodils, tulips etc. were also introduced during this period. Together with these introductions, some garden escapes and obnoxious weeds too found their way (though inadvertently) into this state.

(ii) Geology and Climate

Geologically, the state of Jammu and Kashmir enjoys its own significance. Being situated in transverse Himalayan segment of the Punjab and Kashmir Himalaya, about 70% of the states physical area is held by Ladakh; 19% by Jammu and remaining 11% by Kashmir (Kanth, 1985). Despite small geographical size of Kashmir, a fine stratified sequence of all ages from Archean and Pre-cambrian onwards to Tertiary and recent times is encountered in this region. Koul (1977) suggests that " the geological evolution of Kashmir is akin to that of the Himalaya though of course with some local variations".However a remarkable event in geology of Kashmir has been the Pleistocene ice age. The repeated glacial and interglacial periods have given final touches to physiography of Kashmir.

The Jammu hills lying outside the Pir Panjal and between the Jhellum and Ravi possess two distinct geoglacial formations, namely the shiwalik and alluvium. The former extends mainly north of Tawi, while latter represents north-west extensions of Indo-gangetic plains. The shiwalik system comprising hills of moderate elevation, dips generally to the south and is of sedimentary character. Its lower divisions correspond closely to the Murrees, while middle and upper parts reveal lithological analogy with those of adjacent salt range and Potwar area (Wadia, 1953).

Ladakh is situated in highland crystalline mass of the Trans-Himalayan zone. Wadia, while commenting upon the geology of Ladakh stated that " the great insulation and absence of any water action in Ladakh has led to the accumulation of abundant detrital products on the dry uplands and valleys forming a mantle rock or rigolith of fresh, undecomposed fragments. The bare mountains thus exhibit the exquisite desert coloration of rocks due to peculiar sloar weathering".

de Terra and Peterson (1939) held that the main Himalaya around the upper Indus belongs to the same tectonic unit as Kashmir and the succession of events in pleistocene records must in these regions, generally be identical". Earlier, many workers including Godwin –Austen (1862 – 1880); Lydekker (1883); Destreich (1906); Dainelli (1922-35) and Trinkler (1932) etc. have collected data and contributed to the geological history of this state.

A great diversity in altitude and physiography of the study area fosters a blend of subtropical-temperate –cold arid type of climate. Jammu, situated mainly in subtropical part, is characterized by a periodic climate of hot dry season from March to June followed by a warm monsoon period from July to September, cold weather from October to December with little rainfall in January and February.

The temperate valley is essentially Mediterranean, characterized by a mild winter, hot and dry summer and rains during the cool season (Meher–Homji, 1971). The Pir Panjal acts as a barrier to south-west monsoon while, north and north -east mountains check the influence of cold blasts of Ladakh. Conversely, Ladakh is typified by great extremes of heat and cold together with excessive dryness. During summer, the temperature usually rises up to 35°C, while, the winter temperature may dip down as low as – 40°C. The rainfall is scant ranging annually from 100 to 600 mm. Drass experiences a heavy snowfall in this region.

2

The Vegetational Spectrum

The vegetational spectrum of the state is quite diverse, ranging from subtropical (Jammu) to temperate (Kashmir) followed by cold arid desert type in Ladakh.

Sharma and Kachroo (1981) analysed natural vegetation of Jammu into three types – level land, Kandi and Foot hills. The level land is largely under cultivation as well as colonization thereby restricting the natural forests to foot-hills and the kandi belt. Barring some local variations, the general profile of vegetation in Kashmir discerns a transition from temperate to sub-alpine – alpine type. In sharp contrast to the flora of Jammu and Kashmir, natural forests are altogether lacking in Ladakh. In view of spatial features, no distinct profile is visualized in this region. Stewart (1916-17), however, recognized oastic, desert and alpine floristic elements in its vegetation, while Dhar *et. al.* (1994) categorized this region into the transitional mountain system (T.M.S.), Ladakh mountain system (L.M.S.) and Zanaskar mountain system (Z.M.S.) on the basis of altitude and vegetation types.

Some characteristic exotics encountered in the study area include:

Argemone mexicana, Ageratum conyzoides, A. houstonianum, Anaphalis nepalensis, Artemisia japonica, Aster falconeri, Caesalpinia pulcherrima, Centaurea cyanus, Chenopodium ambrosioides, Chloris barbata, Chrysanthemum cinerarifolium, Conyza bonariensis, C. Canadensis, Erigeron swatensis, Euphorbia heterophylla, Euphorbia serpens, Galinsoga parviflora, G. quadriradiata, Gnaphalium purpureum, Guizotia abyssinica, Ipomoea fistulosa,Ipomoea pes-tigridis, Lantana camgra, Lindernia parviflora, Mimosa pudica, Opuntia dillenii, Oxalis corniculata, Parthenium hysterophorus, Sclerocarpus africanus, Silybum marianum and Xanthium strumarium etc.

American elements : *Argemone mexicana, Cassia occidentalis, Cissampelos pariera, Clitoria ternatea, Coronopus didymus, Cosmos bipinnata, Eclipta prostrata, Eruca sativa,Galinsoga parviflora, Hamelia patens, Leucaena leucocephala, Magnolia grandiflora, Mimosa pudica, Opuntia dillenii, Parkinsonia aculeata, Pentas lanceolata, Stigmaphylon ciliata, Tamarindus indica.*

Asiatic elements : *Allium cepa*, *Medicago sativa, Lepidium sativum, Punica granatum.*

Australian elements : *Acacia auriculaeformis, Emex australis*

European elements : *Avena sativa, Bellis perennis, Calendula officinalis, Coriandrum sativa, Delphinium ajacis, Foeniculum vulgare, Iberis amara, Lathyrus aphaca, odoratus, Medicago lupulina, M. polymorpha, Oxalis cornicuata, O. corymbosa, Spergula arvensis, Vacaria pyramidata, Vicia hirsuta, Viola tricolor.*

Sino-Japanese elements : *Campsis grandiflora, Chrysanthemum indicum, Rosa chinensis, Gardenia jasminoides.*

A variety of fruit trees are grown in Jammu and Kashmir which do not survive in the plains of India. The supply of the fruits to the rest of the country has paid dividends in maintaining the good number of exotics in Kashmir. These are generally grown in the orchards and gardens. Besides some species including *Castanea sativa, Cercis siliquastrum, Prunus amygdalus, Magnolia grandiflora, Magnolia kobus, Malus pumila, Diospyros kaki, Eriobotrya japonica, Catalpa bignonioides Prunus armeniaca, P. avium, P. domestica, Pyrus communis, Robinia pseudo-acacia, Salix babylonica, Syringa vulgaris Tamarix parviflora, Viburnum opalus, Wiegela florida* are also grown as ornamentals. Presence of pollen grains of *Morus alba* from postglacial sediments of Kashmir indicate their earlier introduction in Kashmir (Sharma and Vishnu-Mitre, 1968). The references of the presence of the cultivated species of the state which migrated from different regions have also been found in works of Brandis 1906 and Parker 1918. Our approach is based exclusively on identification of the species upon morphological and their distribution considerations. Some exotic climbers quite common in Jammu and Kashmir state include *Clematis florida, Jasminum officinale, Lonicera japonica, Parthenocissus inseta, P. tricuspidata, Lagerstroemia indica, Rosa chinensis, Vitis riparia* The number of genera and species of exotics have been evaluated by visiting numerous pockets of the state and by consulting available taxonomic works which has led to the present compilation.

3

Floristic Analysis and Taxonomic Description

The present work comprises of 547 exotic species representing 397 genera belonging to 113 families of flowering plants. All these families are arranged according to Bentham and Hooker's system of classification with slight modifications wherever necessary.

Ten families of the exotics in the order of dominance are as follows:

Table I : Break up of genera and species in the 10 dominant families of flowering plants in the present work

Family	*No. of genera*	*No. of Species*
1. Brsssicaceae	38	64
2. Asteraceae	29	50
3. Fabaceae	18	29
4. Rosaceae	11	20
5. Boraginaceae	11	19
6. Euphorbiaceae	05	17
7. Caryophyllaceae	08	13
8. Convolvulaceae	05	13
9. Malvaceae	05	13
10. Fumariaceae	02	13

Taxonomic Description

Each species studied is described briefly followed by flower colour, locality, nativity and flowering and fruiting period. Metric system has been followed for all meaurements provided. Arrangement of taxa follows alphabetical sequence. Nomenclature is updated in accordance with ICBN (ed. 1988). The macroscopic features have been given priority over microscopic characters. The illustrations/photographs of selected species have been provided as visual aid.

Ranunculaceae

Delphinium ajacis L.

A spring annual, ornamental, herb, about 70 cm tall; leaves alternate, much dissected to the base into narrow segments softly and minutely hairy; flowers pretty, blue and white or reddish in terminal racemes; bracts foliaceous; sepals terminating into a long, conical, hollow, spur; petals united, 1 produced into a spur within calyx; stamens many; carpel 1, softly pilose; fruit a follicle with numerous ovules in two rows, splitting one side.

Commonly cultivated in gardens and parks.

Flower colour : Purple or blue

Specimens examined : Bhellum 10617

Locality : Ramban and Jammu

Nativity : Europe

Flrs. and Frts. : Feb. – April

Distribution : India, Europe, Pakistan and Afghanistan

Delphinium ajacis L.

Nigella damascena L.

Annual glabrous, erect herbs, 30 – 45 cm in height; leaves much dissected; flower terminal, white, or blue, 2.5 – 3.5 cm across; carpels

5 almost united throughtout their length; fruit a globular capsule; planted in gardens and parks.

The plant is commonly named as love in mist or Devil in a bush. Some authors are of the openion that the plant is of Mediterranean origin.

Flower colour: Pale blue or white

Specimens examined : Bhellum 10615

Locality : Natha Top.

Nativity : Mediterranean region and Europe

Flrs. and Frts. : Feb. – March

Distribution : India, Pakistan, Afghanistan, Europe and Mediterranean region.

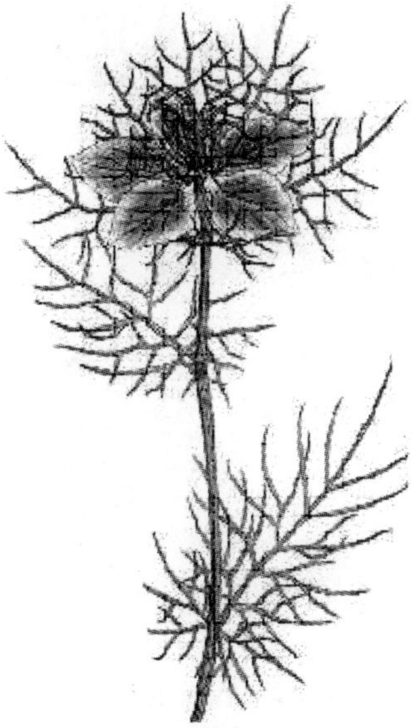

Nigella damascena L.

N. sativa L.

An erect annual herb; leaves alternate, 2.5 – 5 cm long, 2 – 3 pinnatisect, segments linear or linear- lanceolate; flowers terminal long, peduncled, pale blue or white; sepals clawed, ovate, acute; carpels 3 to 5, styles 5, persistent.

Cultivated and also grows wild.

Flower colour: Pale blue or white

Specimens examined : Bhellum 10540

Locality : Srinagar

Nativity : Mediterranean region

Flrs. and Frts. : Feb. – March

Distribution : India, Pakistan, Afghanistan, Europe and Mediterranean region.

Nigella sativa L.

Ranunculus asiaticus L.

Annual or perennial herb; leaves long stalked, ovate, deeply 3 – lobed; flowers of variable colours.

Flower colour : pink, red or yellow with dark centre.

Specimens examined :

Locality : Srinagar

Nativity : Persian

Flrs. and Frts. : March - April

Distribution : India, Persia

Ranunculus asiaticum

Paeoniaceae

Paeonia suffruticosa Haw.

Annual or perennial herb; leaves lobed in elliptic to lanceolate segments, green above and pale and hairy beneath; flowers solitary, rose-coloured or white; stalk stout; planted for its ornamental, showy and fragrant flowers; stamens numerous; carpels 3-5, free.

Paeonia suffruticosa Haw.

Flower colour: Rose coloured or white

Specimens examined : Bhellum 15534

Locality : Srinagar

Nativity : China

Flrs. and Frts. : May - August

Distribution : India, China Pakistan, Afghanistan

Magnoliaceae

Liriodendron tulipifera L.

A large deciduous tree; leaves 15-20 or more, as long as broad, 4-lobed; flowers about 5 cm across, greenish; sepals and petals deciduous; fruits a narrow cone.

Flower colour: Pale green

Specimens examined : Bhellum 14574

Locality : Srinagar

Nativity : United States

Flrs. and Frts. : May - August

Liriodendron tulipifera L.

Magnolia grandiflora L.

An ornamental handsome tree; leaves elliptic oblong, coriaceous shining, planted in gardens for showy flowers; buds enclosed in silky spathaceous bracts; Fruits a woody cone, seeds bright red.

Flower colour: White

Specimens examined : Bhellum 10703

Locality : Srinagar and Jammu

Nativity : North and Southern America

Flrs. and Frts. : May – August

Distribution : India, Pakistan, N. America

Magnolia grandiflora L.

M. kobus DC.

An ornamental tree; flowers showy; sepals 3, petals 6 or more, 2- or more seriate, anthers bithecous, introse; ovaries many.

Planted in gardens.

Flower colour: White

Specimens examined : Bhellum 12341

Locality : Srinagar

Nativity : Japan *Magnolia kobus* DC.

Flrs. and Frts. : March –July

Distribution : India, Pakistan, Japan.

M. liliflora Desrouss.

An ornamental tree, flowers showy, sepals 3; petals 6 or more seriate; anthers bithecous; ovaries many, cohering in an ovoid head; ovules 6 or more.

Planted in gardens for its beautiful flowers.

Flower colour: White and purple without

Specimens examined : Bhellum 15641

Locality : Srinagar

Nativity : China

Flrs. and Frts. : May-July

Distribution : India, China

Magnolia liliflora Desrouss.

Anoniaceae

Artabotrys odoratissima R. Br.

A large evergreen tree; leaves oblong-lanceolate, shortly acuminate, glabrous, shining; flowers pale yellow, highly fragrant, solitary or in pairs; sepals 3; petals 6; fruit yellow, obovoid, of many carpels, aromatic.

Flower colour: Pale yellow

Specimens examined : Bhellum 14703

Locality : Jammu

Nativity : China, Tenasserim and Ceylon

Flrs. and Frts. : May-July

Distribution : India, Ceylon, China and *Tenasserim*

Artabotrys odoratissima R. Br.

Polyalthia longifolia Benth. & Hook.

An ornamental large evergreen tree; leaves 20 cm long or more, lanceolate, shining, glabrous, margin undulate; flowers yellowish-green, in fascicles or in shortly pedunculate umbels.

Planted in gardens as an avenue tree.

Flower colour: Yellowish green

Specimens examined : Bhellum 10543

Locality : Srinagar

Nativity : China

Flrs. and Frts. : May-July

Polyalthia longifolia Benth. & Hook.

Distribution : India, China and Ceylon

Menispermaceae

Cissampelos pariera L.

Twining shrubs with grey- tomentose branches, leaves orbicular or reniform 4-15 cm across; flowers greenish- yellow, male flowers in axillary corymbose cymes, female flowers racemose, crowded in the axil of the foliaceous bracts; drupe compressed, scarlet when ripe.

Cissampelos pariera L.

Climber, grows on bushes and hedges.

Flower colour: Pale yellow

Specimens examined : Bhellum 10805

Locality : Peera

Nativity : South America

Flrs. and Frts. : March-April

Distribution : India, Cosmopolitan in warm tropical and subtropical countries of the world.

Berberidaceae

Mahonia aquifolium (Pursh) Nutt.

An evergreen shrub, branches stout; leaves pinnate, bright green, leaflets upto 9, oblique-ovate, toothed; turning red-purple in winter; flowers minute, yellow, in 7.5 cm long clustered racemes; fruits bluish purple.

Flower colour: Yellow

Specimens examined : Bhellum 13330

Locality : Srinagar

Nativity : Columbia and Oregon

Flrs. and Frts. : May-August

Distribution : India and Columbia

Mahonia aquifolium (Pursh) Nutt.

M. japonica Thunb.

An evergreen shrub; stem and branches stout; leaves pinnate, dark green, about 45 cm long or more, margin sharply toothed; flowers pale-yellow; berries bluish purple.

Flower colour: pale yellow

Specimens examined : Bhellum 13875

Locality : Srinagar

Nativity : Japan

Flrs. and Frts. : May - August

Distribution : India, Japan

M. napaulensis DC.

An evergreen shrub; stem and branches bark corky; leaves pinnate, dark green, coriaceous, shining, about 45 cm long or more, margin sharply toothed; bracts persistent; flowers pale-yellow; sepals 6 in two series; petals 6 in two series; berries bluish purple.

Flower colour: pale yellow

Specimens examined : Bhellum 13875

Locality : Srinagar

Nativity : Nepal

Flrs. and Frts. : May – August

Distribution : India, Nepal

Mahonia napaulensis DC.

Nandina domestica Thunb.

Erect, Shrubs, about 1.4 m tall; leaves alternate, tripinnate, leaflets lanceolate, rhomboid-lanceolate, entire; flowers white, in large terminal panicles; berries red.

Nandina domestica Thunb.

Cultivated as an ornamental in gardens and parks.

Flower colour: *White*

Specimens examined : Bhellum 13230

Locality : Srinagar

Nativity : Japan and China

Flrs. and Frts. : May-August

Distribution : India, Japan and China

Papaveraceae

Argemone mexicana L.

Erect, prickly 50 -125 cm tall herbs; leaves nearly amplexicaule, sinuate-pinnatifid, variegated; flowers yellow, capsule ellipsoid; seeds black.

Grows on waste places, now naturalized.

Flower colour: Yellow

Specimens examined : Bhellum 10102

Locality : Jammu

Nativity : Mexico, Central America and West Indies.

Flrs. and Frts. : April-June

Distribution : India, Mexico, Jamaica, Carribies, South Europe, west Indies and now naturalized in most of the warm countries of the world.

Argemone mexicana L.

A. ochroleuca Sweet

Herbs, deep-bluish green, tinged with faint purplish, stem; flowers white or cream coloured.

Grows on waste places and now introduced and natrualised.

Flower colour: White tinged with pale yellow

Specimens examined : Bhellum 10209

Locality : Jammu

Nativity : Mexico

Flrs. and Frts. : April-May

Distribution : India, Britain, Mexico and most of the warm countries of the world.

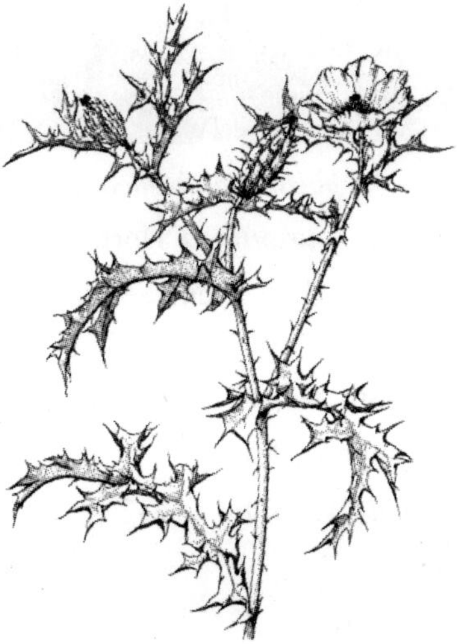

Argemone ochroleuca Sweet

Eschscholzia californica Cham.

Annual, 30-60 cm tall herbs; leaves ternately dissected, into linear or oblong segments,petiole long; flowers opening in sunshine, yellow-orange to deep orange at the base of the petals; capsule strongly ribbed.

Cultivated in the gardens and parks for its showy flowers.

Flower colour: orange yellow

Specimens examined : Bhellum 14331

Locality : Jammu

Nativity : North America

Flrs. and Frts. : Feb. – April

Distribution : India, Pakistan and North America.

Eschscholzia californica Cham.

E. californica Cham. var. *aurantiaca* Hort.

Annual herbs, flowers 5 -7.5 cm across, yellow orange to deep orange at the base of the petals;

Cultivated in the gardens and parks for its showy flowers.

Flower colour: orange yellow

Specimens examined : Bhellum 14232

Locality : Jammu

Nativity : North America

Flrs. and Frts. : Feb. – April

Distribution : India, Pakistan, North America.

***Papaver dubium* L.**

Annual herbs, 10 – 90 cm in height, green parts of the plant glaucous, covered with appressed hairs towards base and spreading hair above; leaves oblong deeply lobed, 1-2 pinnatipartite, lower ones petiolate, bluish-green, clothed with spreading hairs; flowers pink or scarlet; petals narrow to broadly obovate,with dark purple base, caducous; anthers bithecous, bluish, oblong, filament slender; ovary superior, stigma sessile, stigmatic rays 6-12; capsule oblong, ovoid, glabrous.

Cultivated for its showy flowers.

Flower colour: Pink or scarlet with basal dark spot

Specimens examined : Bhellum 12231

Locality : Jammu

Nativity : Switzerland and Britain

Flrs. and Frts. : March-April

Distribution : India, Britain and other countries of the Asia, France, Spain, Belgium, Switzerland, Poland, Denmark, Morocco, Czechoslovakia, Italy, Tunesia and Canary Islands.

Papaver dubium L.

P. hybridum L.

Annual, hairy herbs, springly branched, 20-40 cm tall or more; leaves oblong, lobed, 2-3 pinnatifid, segments lobed, lobes acute, sparsely hairy on both surfaces; flowers pink-red with blackish spot at the base; fruit a capsule, 1-2 cm long, stigmatic rays 4-8, disc convex; capsule ovate, oblong, setose or hispid.

Cultivated for its ornamental flowers.

Flower colour: Pink red with blackish spot at the base

Specimens examined : Bhellum 13451

Locality : Jammu

Nativity : South Europe

Flrs. and Frts. : March-April

Distribution : India, Afghanistan, W. Pakistan, South Europe, N. Africa and Central Asia.

Papaver hybridum L.

P. macrostomum Boiss. Huet ex Boiss.

Annual herbs, 30-40 cm tall; leaves 1-pinnatisect, usually with distant linear-lanceoalte or oblong-lanceolate lobes, lobes acute; flowers purple or pink, 3-6 cm across; petals obovate, orbicular; stamens longer than the ovary; Capsule oblong or ellipsoid, glaucous or glabrous, stigmatic rays 5-10.

Cultivated for ornamental flowers and also found as naturalized.

Flower colour: Purple or pink with or without a basal blotch

Specimens examined : Bhellum 12450

Locality : Jammu

Nativity : South America

Flrs. and Frts. : March-April

Distribution : India, Turkey, Armenia, W. Asia, Afghanistan and West Pakistan.

P. nudicaule L.

Annual, sometimes tufted herbs; scape 10–40 cm long; leaves rosulate, radical only, somewhat glaucous, bristly or ciliate; pinnately 3-lobed; flowers yellowish or reddish orange, rarely whitish with yellowish base; Capsule oblong or obovoid–oblong.

Papaver nudicaule L.

Cultivated for ornamental flowers and also found as an escape.

Flower colour: yellowish orange

Specimens examined : Bhellum 10621

Locality : Srinagar

Nativity : Siberia

Flrs. and Frts. : March – April

Distribution : India, Sieberia, N. and C. Asia, W. Pakistan and Afghanistan.

P. rhoeas L.

Annual, branched herbs, 30-60 cm in height; leaves pinnately divided, segments narrow, awned; scape with spreading or appressed hairs; flowers scarlet; petals in equal pairs; anthers blue; capsule smooth, stlaked, subglobose to obovoid, stigmatic rays 10-12.

Cultivated for ornamental flowers.

Flower colour: Red or scarlet violet

Specimens examined : Bhellum 13667

Locality : Jammu

Nativity : Asia and Europe

Flrs. and Frts. : March – April

Distribution : India, Europe and N. Africa

Papaver rhoeas L.

P. somniferum L.

Annual herbs, 60-130 cm tall; leaves oblong, lobed, flowers of variable colours, drooping in buds but get straightended at maturity, petals orbicular or entire, caducous; Capsule 2.5 cm across, seeds black or white.

Cultivated for ornamental flowers.

Flower colour: Red

Specimens examined : Bhellum 10625

Locality : Doda and Banihal

Nativity : Mediterranean region

Flrs. and Frts. : Feb. – March

Distribution : India, Europe and Asia. Cultivated or found as an escape in W. Pakistan and nauturalised in eastern Angola

Papaver somniferum L.

Fumariaceae

Corydalis alpestris C. A. Mey.

Annual or perennial herbs ; root stock like a scaly tuber; radical leaves 1-2, similar but smaller than cauline leaves, cauline leaves 2 - 4 alternate, scattered, ternate, segments oblong, mucronate; flowers bluish or violet-white; capsule 10 – 15 cm long; oblong narrowly obovate; Grows wild at high altitude.

Flower colour: Bluish or violet- white

Specimens examined : Bhellum 10621

Locality : Jammu

Nativity : South America

Flrs. and Frts. : June – August

Distribution : India, Caucasus, Turkey, C. Asia, Kashmir and Alaska

Corydalis alpestris C.A. Mey.

C. diphylla Wall. var. *diphylla*

Annual 15-30 cm or more, unbranched glabrous Nochangi, often mottled with red - purple; radical leaves absent, cauline leaves 2, opposite or whorled, glabrous on both the surfaces; racemes; flowers purple-red or bright orange yellow in 5-15 cm; stamens 6, in two opposite groups; style shorter than the ovary; capsule ovate, oblong, 5 – 7 cm long.

Grows wild, flowers pretty, beautiful.

Flower colour: Yellow and purple-red

Specimens examined : Bhellum 11621

Locality : Padder

Nativity : Nepal

Flrs. and Frts. : March – April

Distribution : India, Throughout the Himalaya and Pakistan.

C. pulchella Aitch. ex Hemsley

An erect perennial herb 15 – 25 cm tall, glabrous or subglacous; racemes terminal not exceeding the leaves; flowers yellow, 12 – 18 mm long; capsule about 13 mm long with deflexed pedicel.

Grows wild at high altitude.

Flower colour: yellow

Specimens examined : Bhellum 10621

Locality : Kashmir

Nativity : Afghanistan

Flrs. and Frts. : March–April

Distribution : India, Afghanistan and Pakistan

C. longipes DC.

Delicate, perennial; 20–40 cm long or more; leaves 3 or more ternate; flowers small, in short simple racems; 10–12 mm long, yellow, spur short conical; capsule oblong-obovate or obovate 6–10 mm long.

Grows wild at high altitude.

Flower colour: Pale yellow or yellow

Specimens examined : Bhellum 15621

Locality : Jammu

Nativity : Nepal

Flrs. and Frts. : March – May

Distribution : India, Nepal and throughout the Himalaya

C. govaniana Wall. var. *swatensis* (Kitam.) Jafri

Annual, glabrous herbs; stem glabrous, 20–50 cm tall; radical leaves as long as the stem, bipinnate, leaflets wedge-shaped, apiculate, cauline leaves similar but smaller, glabrous on both surfaces;inflorescence 5–10 cm long, terminal racemes dense ; flowers yellow, 2–2.5 cm long; capsule 1–1.5 cm long.

Grows wild at high altitude.

Flower colour: Pale yellow

Specimens examined : Bhellum 10621

Locality : Jammu

Nativity : Pakistan

Flrs. and Frts. : March – April

Distribution : India, North West Himalaya and Pakistan

C. pakistanica Jafri

A diffuse or ascending perennial herb; lower leaves similar to radical leaves but smaller; racemes short, 15 – 20 flowered, becoming slightly lax later on; flowers yellow, 15 – 18 mm long including spur; capsule 8 – 10 mm long, acute or subacute.

Grows wild at high altitude.

Flower colour: Pale yellow

Specimens examined : Bhellum 12923

Locality : Srinagar

Nativity : Pakistan

Flrs. and Frts. : March – April

Distribution : India and Pakistan

C. hendersonii Hemsl.

A short, tufted perennial herb, with stout cylindrical rootstock; radical leaves glabrous, or minutely glandular; cauline leaves similar but smaller; flowers yellow. Grows wild at high altitude.

Flower colour: Pale yellow

Specimens examined : Bhellum 10671

Locality : Kashmir

Nativity : Tibet and Afghanistan

Flrs. and Frts. : March – April

Distribution : India, Afghanistan and W. Tibet

C. meifolia Wall.

Erect or suberect perennial herbs, 15 – 30 cm tall; rootstock thick; radical leaves usually 3- pinnatisect, pinnae opposite or subopposite; inflorescence 10 – 20 cm long; flowers yellow with purple or violet tips; capsule oblong-ellipsoid, 7 – 10 mm long.

Grows wild at high altitude.

Flower colour: yellow with purple tinge

Specimens examined : Bhellum 11821

Locality : Srinagar

Nativity : Nepal

Flrs. and Frts. : March – May

Distribution : India, Nepal and Himalaya

C. rupestris Kotschy ex Boiss.

Perennial herbs, 7 – 10 cm tall, glabrous or glaucous; rootstock thick; leaves narrow elongated, bipinnatisect, lobes minute; scape naked, 5 – 10 flowered, with flowers often turned to one side; flowers yellow 15 – 20 cm long, spur subglobose or sac-like; capsule 15 mm long, elliptic, acute.

Grows wild at high altitude.

Flower colour: Pale yellow

Specimens examined : Bhellum 10431

Locality : Srinagar

Nativity : Iran

Flrs. and Frts. : March – May

Distribution : India, Iran and Pakistan

C. schelesnowiana Regel & Schmalh. ex Regel

Perennial herbs, 15 – 30 cm tall, glabrous or glaucous; radical leaves 3 – 4 ternate, trilobed, lobes obovate; racemes born on terminal branches; flowers small, 5 – 12 mm long, yellow or golden yellow; capsule linear.

Flower colour: Yellow or Golden Yellow

Specimens examined : Bhellum 10334

Locality : Ladakh

Nativity : Turkestan

Flrs. and Frts. : March – May

Distribution : India, Iran Pakistan and Turkestan

C. tibetica Hooer f. & Thoms.

Perennial diffuse herb; stem leafless, rarely 1-leaved; racemes simple, hardly exceeding the radical leaves; flowers 15 – 20 mm long including the spur; sepals minute, denticulate; capsule 7 – 12 mm long.

Flower colour: Yellow

Specimens examined : Bhellum 10334

Locality : Ladakh

Nativity : Srinagar, Poonch

Flrs. and Frts. : March – May

Distribution : India, W. Tibet and Pakistan

Fumaria indica (Hausskn.) Pugsley

Annual delicate herbs, much branched, 5 – 25 cm long, glabrous, glaucous; leaves much dissected 2 – 3 pinnatisect, decompound, racemes shortly peduncled or subsessile; flowers white or pale pink, 5 – 6 mm long; fruit suborbicular with rounded apex; grows in cultivated fields as a weed.

Flower colour: Pale Pinkish or white

Specimens examined : Bhellum 13611

Locality : Jammu

Nativity : Central Asia

Flrs. and Frts. : March – April

Distribution : India, Afghanistan, Pakistan, C. Asia, Persia, Turkestan and introduced elsewhere

Fumaria indica (Hausskn.) Pugsley

F. vaillantii Loisel.

Annual small delicate herbs, leaves upto 9 cm long, much dissected, segments flat, often finely lobed; inflorescence 15 – 30 cm long; very similar to the above species but flowers pinkish violet; sepals lanceolate, obovate; petals 4 – 6 mm long, pinkish violet or pale pink; fruits often subglobose, apiculate.

Grows in cultivated fields as a weed.

Flower colour: Pinkish violet

Specimens examined : Bhellum 10621

Locality : Jammu

Nativity : France

Flrs. and Frts. : March – April

Distribution : India, Europe Temperate Asia, France and N. Africa

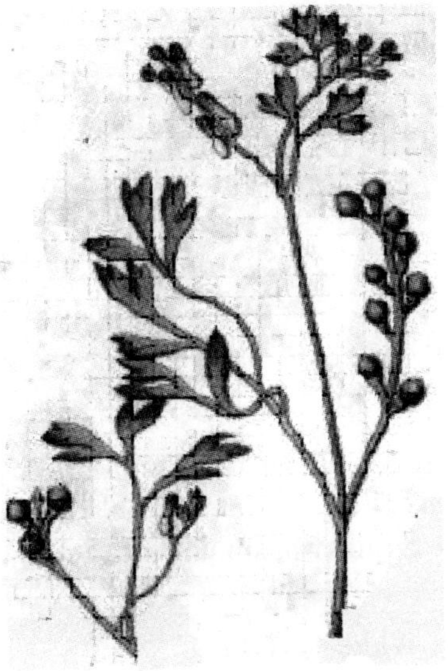

F. vaillantii Loisel.

Brassicaceae

Alliaria petiolata (M. Bieb.) Cavara & Grande

Annual herbs, 20 – 40 cm tall or more, usually glabrous or subglabrous; leaves simple, cordate, or ovate, lyrately pinnatipartite, lower petiolate, petiole long, ovate cordate, upper sessile, margin dentate; racemes upto 30 cm long, flowers white, nearly 5 mm across; siliquae linear, terete, bilocular, dehiscent.

Flower colour: White

Specimens examined : Bhellum 14054

Locality : Kashmir

Nativity : Siberia

Flrs. and Frts. : April-August

Distribution : India, Pakistan, Europe, North Africa, and cooler parts of the Asia.

Alliaria petiolata (M. Bieb.) Cavara & Grande

Aphragmus oxycarpus (Hooker f. & Thoms.) Jafri

Perennial herbs, 3 – 7 cm in height, sparsely hairy; basal leaves rosulate, upper ones oblong – elliptic, to oblong linear, glabrous; flowers 5 mm across, white or pinkish; siliquae lanceolate to elliptic, 5 – 10 mm long, glabrous.

Flower colour: White

Specimens examined : Bhellum 14732

Locality : Srinagar

Nativity : West Tibet

Flrs. and Frts. : April-August

Distribution : India, Pakistan, Afghanistan and Tibet

Arabidopsis russelliana Jafri

Annual erect herbs, sparely hairy below, glabrous above; lower leaves pinnatifid, upper ones linear oblong; racemes 20 cm long; flowers pink about 3 mm across, pink; siliquae linear, compressed, recurved, glabrous.

Flower colour: white

Specimens examined : Bhellum 14279

Locality : Srinagar

Nativity : Pakistan

Flrs. and Frts. : April-August

Distribution : India, Pakistan, Afghanistan.

A. taraxacifolia (T. Anders.) Jafri

Annual or biennial herbs; basal leaves petioled, lyrately pinnatifid, terminal lobe larger, lateral shorter; cauline leaves sessile, lanceolate; racemes 10 – 20 flowered; flowers about 4 mm across, white or pale rose; siliquae linear, 4 – 6 mm long, glabrous.

Flower colour: white or pale rose

Specimens examined : Bhellum 13449

Locality : Kashmir

Nativity : Pakistan

Flrs. and Frts. : April-August

Distribution : India, Pakistan, Afghanistan.

Arabis fruticulosa C. A. Mey

Perennial 10 -20 cm tall herbs, densely pubescent with minute stellate hairs; radical leaves rosulate, often congested, very variable in size; racemes about 10 flowered; flowers 6 – 8 mm across, violet or pale rose-coloured; siliquae oblong, linear compressed.

Flower colour: white

Specimens examined : Bhellum 14398

Locality : Srinagar

Nativity : Central Asia

Flrs. and Frts. : April-August

Distribution : India, Pakistan, Afghanistan, North and Central Asia

A. tibetica Hooker f. & Thoms.

Perennial 5 – 20 cm tall herbs, clothed with forked hairs, rarely glabrescent; basal leaves oblanceolate, sinuate dentate, upper ones toothed, lobed; racemes 15 – 20 flowered; flowers pale white or yellowish tinged with pink, 5 – 6 mm across; siliquae 30 – 60 mm long, compressed, glabrous.

Flower colour: white yellowish tinged with pink

Specimens examined : Bhellum 14545

Locality : Srinagar

Nativity : Tibet

Flrs. and Frts. : April-August

Distribution : India, Pakistan, Afghanistan and Central Asia.

Barbarea vulgaris R. Br.

Biennial or perennial glabrous herbs, 30 – 60 cm tall or more; leaves rosulate, lyrate, 3 – 5 ternate, terminal one larger than the lateral one; racemes upto 40 flowered; flowers5 – 7 mm across, yellow; siliquae 15 – 30 cm long, erect, glabrous.

Flower colour: Pale yellow or white

Specimens examined : Bhellum 14129

Locality : Srinagar

Nativity : Europe and Britain

Flrs. and Frts. : April-August

Distribution : India, Pakistan, Afghanistan, Europe and Asia.

Barbarea vulgaris R. Br.

Brassica campestris (L.) Clapham

An erect annual herb, 30 – 90 cm tall; leaves glaucous, radical hispid, upper glabrous; flowers yellow; petals persistent till the corymb elongate; siliquae cylindrical, elongated, terete or angled.

Flower colour: Yellow

Specimens examined : Bhellum 12646

Locality: Jammu

Nativity : Europe

Flrs. and Frts. : Feb. – March

Distribution : India, Pakistan, Afghanistan and Europe

Brassica campestris (L.) Clapham

B. juncea (L.) Czern. Coss.

Annual herbs, stem erect, rarely glacuous or hispid; lower leaves oblong-lanceolate, toothed; upper narrow, lanceolate, toothed, subsessile; flowers bright yellow; siliquae linear lanceolate; cultivated as a vegetable and the flowers are showy.

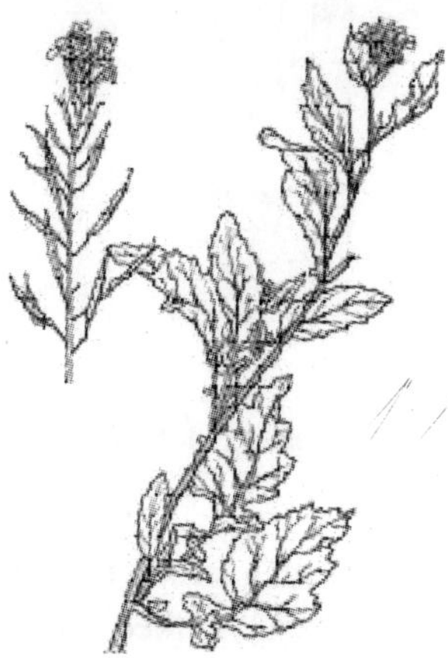

Brassica juncea (L.) Czern. Coss.

Flower colour: orange yellow

Specimens examined : Bhellum 12341

Locality : Jammu

Nativity : Tibet

Flrs. and Frts. : Feb. – April

Distribution : India, Pakistan and Tibet

B. nigra (L.) Koch

Annual, rigid, glabrous or hispid herbs; leaves all petiolate, lower ones lyrate, the upper nearly entire; flowers yellow arranged in long racemes; sepals spreading; petals bright yellow; widely cultivated for its volatile oil and seeds.

Flower colour: Bright yellow

Specimens examined : Bhellum 14638

Locality : Jammu

Nativity : Europe

Flrs. and Frts. : Feb. – March

Distribution : India, Pakistan, Europe and North Africa

B. nigra (L.) Koch

B. oleracea L. var. *botrytis* L.

Annual or biennial herbs with a strong but not tuberous root system; leaves glabrous or glaucous, basal stalked, upper ones narrow sessile, sometimes clasping; flowers in long racemes, yellow.

Cultivated as a vegetable and flowers are showy.

Flower colour: orange yellow

Specimens examined : Bhellum 12741

Locality : Jammu

Nativity : Europe

Flrs. and Frts. : Feb. – April

Distribution : India, Pakistan, Greece to Great Britain, Southern Europe or Mediterranean regions.

B. oleracea L. var. *botrytis* L.

Annual or biennial herbs, glabrous or glacuous; basal leaves stalked, upper sessile; flowers yellow borne on long racemes.

Brassica oleracea L. var. *capitata* L.

Cultivated as a vegetable.

Flower colour: orange yellow

Specimens examined : Bhellum 12541

Locality : Jammu

Nativity : India, Pakistan, Afghanistan, West and Southern Europe.

Flrs. and Frts. : Feb. – April

Distribution : India, Pakistan, West and Southern Europe.

B. oleracea L. var. *gonyloides* L.

Annual or biennial, herbs, leaves glabrous or glaucous; flowers borne in long racemes; siliquae elongate, terete.

Cultivated as a vegetable.

Flower colour: orange yellow

Specimens examined : Bhellum 14425

Locality : Jammu

Nativity : India, Pakistan, Afghanistan, West and South Europe.

Flrs. and Frts. : Feb. – April

Distribution : India, Pakistan, West and Southern Europe.

Brassica oleracea L. var. *gonyloides* L.

B. rapa L.

Biennial with tuberous roots; stem upto 100 cm tall; leaves lyrate pinnatifid, usually 5 ternate, 10 - 30 cm long; racemes upto 40 flowered; flowers 6 – 10 mm across, dull yellow or golden yellow; siliquae upto 80 mm long.

Cultivated as a vegetable.

Flower colour: Orange yellow

Specimens examined : Bhellum 12342

Locality : Jammu

Nativity : Central and Southern Europe and Western Siberia

Flrs. and Frts. : Feb. – April

Distribution : India, Pakistan, Afghanistan, Central and Southern part of Europe around Mediterranean regions and Western Siberia.

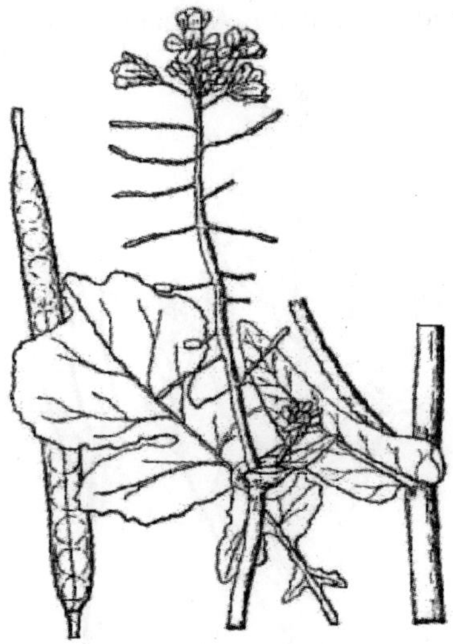

B. rapa L.

Braya tibetica Hooker f. & Thoms.

Perennial caespitose, 4 – 8 cm tall herbs; stem much branched from the base,often pilose; radical leaves, rosulate, linear- oblong, 20 – 40 cm long, 1 – 2mm broad, entire or shallowly toothed; flowers about 2 mm across, whit or pinkish; siliquae ellipsoid, hairy or glabrous.

Flower colour: white or Pinkish

Specimens examined : Bhellum 14139

Locality : Ladakh

Nativity : Tibet

Flrs. and Frts. : April-August

Distribution : India, Pakistan, Afghanistan and Tibet.

Camelina sativa (L.) Crantz

Annual or biennial herbs; stem 30 – 60 cm tall; branches mostly from the base glabrous or sometimes sparsely hairy; flowers about 3.5 cm across; fruit siliqulae with distinct midrib.

Flower colour: Yellow

Specimens examined : Bhellum 14349

Locality : Ladakh

Nativity : Europe

Flrs. and Frts. : April-August

Distribution : India, Pakistan, Afghanistan Europe and Asia.

Camelina sativa [L.] Crtz.

Cardamine impatiens L.

Annual or perennial herbs, 20 – 60 cm tall, erect or suberect, glabrous or hairy ; leaves variable in length, pinnate, usually with 5 – 8 pairs of leaflets, terminal one stalked; lower ovate, oblong; flowers 3 – 4 mm across, white; siliquae linear compressed.

Flower colour: white

Specimens examined : Bhellum 14549

Locality : Poonch

Nativity : Europe

Flrs. and Frts. : April-August

Distribution : India, Pakistan, Afghanistan, Europe and Asia.

Cardamine impatiens L.

C. flexuosa With.

Annual or biennial herb, 10 – 30 cm tall; branches many from the base; basal leaves 2 – 7 jugate, glabrous or hairy, leaflets ovate-orbicular, terminal one slightly larger; flowers white.

Flower colour: white

Specimens examined : Bhellum 14190

Locality : Srinagar

Nativity : Britain

Flrs. and Frts. : April-August

Distribution : India, Pakistan, Afghanistan, Europe, Asia and introduced in North America.

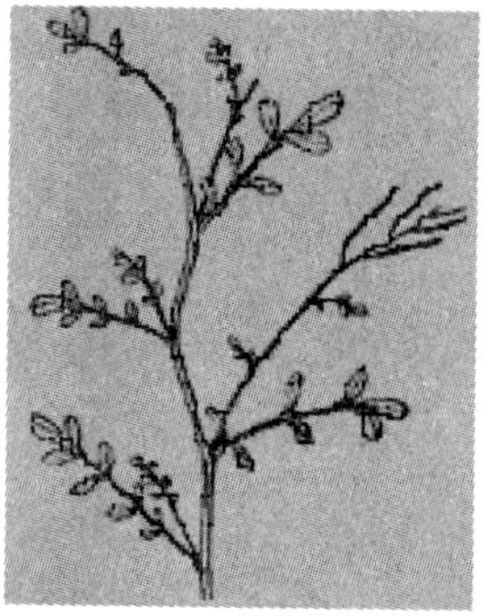

Cardamine flexuosa With.

Chorispora tenella (L.) DC.

Annual, erect, 15 – 35 cm tall, branched from the base, glabrous or sparsely glandular; basal leaves rosulate, oblanceolate, sinuate toothed, 3 – 8 cm long, upper ones shortly stalked or sessile; flowers about 10 mm across, pinkish or violet sometimes white; siliquae 25 – 35 mm long beaked.

Chorispora tenella (L.) DC.

Flower colour: Pink or Violet sometimes white

Specimens examined : Bhellum 14634

Locality : Kashmir and Chenab Valley

Nativity : Siberia

Flrs. and Frts. : April - July

Distribution : India, Pakistan, Europe, Asia and Introduced in North America.

C. sibirica (Pallas) DC.

Annual herbs, 10 – 20 cm tall, often branched from the base, sparsely hairy; basal leaves rosulate, oblanceolate, pinnatifid, lobes narrow, upper ones similar but smaller, sessile or subsessile; racemes 10 – 20 flowered; flowers about 8 mm across; siliquae 15 – 25 mm long, often curved, beaked.

Flower colour: Yellow

Specimens examined : Bhellum 14364

Locality : Kashmir and Chenab Valley

Nativity : Trans-Casparian region

Flrs. and Frts. : April - July

Distribution : India, Pakistan and Central Asia

Chorispora sibirica (Pallas) DC.

Christolea crassifolia Camb.

Perennial, suberect, much branched herb, 20 – 40 m tall; leaves variable in size, shape and pubescence, obovate-oblong, 5 – 25 cm long, usually toothed towards apex; racemes about 10 mm long, 10 – 20 flowered; flowers 5 – 7 mm across, white with purple base, or turning mauve or yellow when dried; siliquae linear to oblong, 10 – 30 mm long.

Flower colour: White with purple base, turning pale yellow

Specimens examined : Bhellum 14421

Locality : Ladakh

Nativity : Tibet

Flrs. and Frts. : April-August

Distribution : India, Pakistan, Afghanistan, Iran and Central Asia.

Conringia planisiliqua Fisch.& Mey.

Annual, erect, branched, glabrous or glaucous herbs, 10 – 50 cm tall; leaves oblong, ovate, glabrous, somewhat glaucous, entire; basal obovate, shortly stalked, obtuse, entire, upper ones usually oblong ovate, sessile, amplexicaule, 2 – 10 cm long; racemes usually many flowered; flowers small, about 5 mm across, yellow or white; siliquae linear compressed.

Flower colour: Pale yellow or white

Specimens examined : Bhellum 14367

Locality : Srinagar

Nativity : East Caucasus

Flrs. and Frts. : April-August

Distribution : India, Pakistan, Afghanistan, Iran and Central Asia.

Coronopus didymus (L.) Lesser

Annual or biennial hairy glabrous, prostrate, foetid herbs; stem about 30 cm in height, clothed with simple or 2-fid, hairs; basal and lower leaves stalked, deeply pinnatisect; upper leaves narrow and entire; flowers minute white; sepals ovate, green; petals absent, when present linear; siliquae emarginate above and below, 1-seeded.

Grows in cultivated fields as a weed and on waste places..

Flower colour: Yellow

Specimens examined : Bhellum 12464

Locality : Srinagar

Nativity : Pakistan

Flrs. and Frts. : April-August

Distribution : India and tropical S. America

Coronopus didymus (L.) Lesser

Descurainia sofia (L.) Webb. & Berth.

Annual or biennial herbs 30 – 60 cm tall or more, hairs simple or stellate and often glandular ; leaves 2- 3-pinnatisect, lobes linear oblong; flowers 2-3 mm across, yellow; stamens 6; style short, stigma depressed, capitate; siliquae linear, 15 – 35 mm long; seeds reddish-brown, 1 – 2 seriate.

Flower colour: Yellow

Specimens examined : Bhellum 12337

Locality : Ladakh

Nativity : Europe

Flrs. and Frts. : April-August

Distribution : India, Pakistan, Afghanistan, Africa and Europe.

Dontostemon glandulosus (Kar. & Kir.) O. E. Schulz

Erect or spreading herbs 4 – 15 cm tall; leaves linear, 10 – 25 mm long, 3 – 5 mm broad, margin entire or minutely toothed; racemes 10 – 25 flowered; flowers 3 – 4 mm across, white or Pink; siliquae linear subcylindrical, glandular.

Flower colour: White or Pinkish

Specimens examined : Bhellum 13664

Locality : Srinagar

Nativity : Central Asia

Flrs. and Frts. : April-August

Distribution : India, Pakistan and West China

Draba nemorosa L.

Annual, erect, herbs, 5 – 25 cm tall or more, simple or branched from the base; basal leaves rosulate, oblong, obovate, 8 – 35 cm long; cauline leaves absent or a few, distant, oblong or ovate; racemes many flowered; flowers about 2 mm across, pale yellow; siliquae oblong-elliptic, 5 – 10 mm long.

Flower colour: Pale yellow

Specimens examined : Bhellum 14680

Locality : Srinagar

Nativity : Europe and Switzerland

Flrs. and Frts. : April – August

Distribution : India, Pakistan, Asia, Arctic and temperate Europe

D. tibetica Hooker f. & Thoms.

Perennial, caespitose herbs; leaves upto 2 or aphyllous, when present rosulate, oblong-lanceolate; flowers yellow 5 mm across; siliqulae 16 – 18 mm long.

Flower colour: Yellow

Specimens examined : Bhellum 13652

Locality : Srinagar

Nativity : Tibet

Flrs. and Frts. : April – July

Distribution : India, Pakistan, Central Asia, Afghanistan and Tibet.

Drobopsis verna C. Koch

Erect or suberect, annual herbs, 5 – 15 cm tall; radical leaves oblong obovate, spathulate or oblong –lanceolate, 5 – 15 mm long and 2 – 6 mm broad, sessile; racemes lax, flowers ebracteate; yellow often turning white, about 3 mm across; siliquae linear oblong, 15 – 25 mm long.

Flower colour: Pale yellow or white

Specimens examined : Bhellum 14673

Locality : Srinagar

Nativity : Armenia

Flrs. and Frts. : April-August

Distribution : India, Pakistan, Afghanistan, Turkey and Asia.

Eruca sativa L.

Annual somewhat foetid herbs, 30 – 60 cm in height; leaves lyrately pinnatifid, lower ones subrosulate, flowers of variable colours, pale yellow, dull-yellow or dirty white; siliquae 15 – 30 mm long erect or appressed to the stem; seeds biseriate.

Cultivated for vegetables and found as an escape.

Flower colour: Pale yellow

Specimens examined : Bhellum 10621

Locality : Jammu

Nativity : South America

Flrs. and Frts. : March – April

Distribution : India, S. America and Pakistan

Erucastrum gallicum (Willd.) O. E. Schultz.

Annual, erect, more or less hairy herbs, hairs retrose; leaves alternate, petiolate, irregularly pinnate; racemes elongate; flowers yellow; siliquae elliptic compressed, minutely pitted reticulate.

Grows wild on waste places.

Flower colour: Yellow

Specimens examined : Bhellum 13612

Locality : Srinagar

Nativity : Europe

Flrs. and Frts. : March – June

Distribution : India, Pakistan, Nepal and Europe

Erysimum aitchisonii O. E. Schulz

Annual or biennial, robust, 30-60 cm tall; branches appressed, canescent; basal leaves rosulate, oblanceolate, 5 -8 cm long, 5 – 10 mm broad; racemes 30 – 50 flowered much longer at maturity; flowers 10-12 mm across; siliquae subcylindric, terete, 40-55 mm long.

Flower colour: Yellow

Specimens examined : Bhellum 14654

Locality : Kashmir

Nativity : Afghanistan

Flrs. and Frts. : April-August

Distribution : India, Pakistan and Afghanistan

E. hieraciifolium L.

Biennial or perennial herbs, 30 – 50 cm tall or more appressed hairy; stem often simple, subangular, rarely branched; basal leaves rosulate, very variable, elliptic toothed or subentire; racemes upto 40 cm long in fruiting; flowers 10 mm across, yellow; siliquae linear – terete, erect, 30 – 60 mm long.

Flower colour: Yellow

Specimens examined : Bhellum 14554

Locality : Kashmir

Nativity : Europe

Flrs. and Frts. : April-July

Distribution : India, Pakistan, Europe and temperate Asia

E. schlagintweitianum O. E. Schulz

Biennial or perennial erect upto 10 cm tall herb; stem brached from the base; radical leaves rosulate, narrowly oblanceolate, 20 – 30 mm long; cauline leaves a few linear almost entire; racemes 10 – 20 flowered; flowers about 5 mm across, yellow; siliquae 35 mm long 1mm broad, subcylindrical linear, appressedly hairy.

Flower colour: Yellow

Specimens examined : Bhellum 12354

Locality : Kashmir

Nativity : Tibet

Flrs. and Frts. : April-July

Distribution : India, Pakistan and Tibet

Euclidium syriacum (L.) R. Br.

An annual, rigid, diffuse, much branched, pubescent herb; leaves entire, 2.5 – 3.6 cm long, coarsely toothed, or pinnatifid, clothed with forked hairs on both the surfaces; flowers small, ebracteate white, in terminal or lateral cymes; sepals spreading equal at the base; siliquae 4 – 6 mm long, subglobose, indehiscent

Flower colour: White or cream-coloured

Specimens examined : Bhellum 14712

Locality : Srinagar, Banihal and Batote

Nativity : Syria

Flrs. and Frts. : April– June

Distribution : India, Pakistan, Afghanistan, South west Asia, South Russia.

Goldbackia laevigata (M. Bieb.) DC.

An erect, annual herb, upto 60 cm in height or more, shining; leaves petioled radical ovate-oblong; upper auricled slightly toothed; flowers pale-rose, siliquae pendulous, covered with reticulate veins; seeds oblong.

Flower colour: White or Pale-Pinkish

Specimens examined : Bhellum 14498

Locality : Kashmir

Nativity : Astrachan

Flrs. and Frts. : April-August

Distribution : India,Pakistan, Turkey and Trans-Caspian regions

Iberis amara L.

Annual or perennial herbs, mostly branched from the base, glabrous or hairy; leaves simple or entire, scattered, lower spathulate, upper ones lanceolate or oblong, sparsely dentate towards apex; flowers 10 mm across, white, petals unequal outer two petals twice as long; siliquae about 5 mm across.

Cultivated in gardens as an ornamental.

Flower colour: White

Specimens examined : Bhellum 10123

Locality : Jammu

Nativity : Europe

Flrs. and Frts. : March – April

Distribution : India and Europe

Iberis amara L.

I. umbellata L.

Annual herbs; stem 15 – 30 cm tall; leaves lanceolate, 5 – 10 cm long; flowers purple pink or white,minute; inflorescence in corymbs.

Flower colour: White or purple pink

Specimens examined : Bhellum 13103

Locality : Jammu

Nativity : South Europe

Flrs. and Frts. : March – April

Distribution : India and Europe

Iberis umbellata L.

Lepidium sativum L.

Annual, erect, rarely decumbent herbs, 30 – 60 cm tall; mostly glabrous rarely pilose; basal leaves long petioled, pinnatisect or lyrate-pinnate, cauline leaves varying, upper sessile, glabrous or nearly so; flowers white rarely pinkish; siliquae obovate to oblong. Naturalized and cultivated in the wheat fields.

Flower colour: White
Specimens examined : Bhellum 14687
Locality : Batote
Nativity : West Asia and Egypt
Flrs. and Frts. : Feb. – March
Distribution : India, Pakistan and Egypt.

L. viriginicum L.

Annual herbs 30 – 50 cm tall; stem erect, minutely hairy or downy with long appressed simple hairs; basal leaves lyrate or pinnately lobed, with large rounded terminal lobe and numerous lateral lobes clothed with appressed hairs on both the surfaces; racemes 5 – 10 cm long; flowers minute, 1 - 2 mm across; siliquae 3 – 4 mm across almost orbicular with a broad but a shallow notch at apex.

Flower colour: White

Specimens examined : Bhellum 14460

Locality : Srinagar

Nativity : Virginia and North America

Flrs. and Frts. : April-August

Distribution : India, Pakistan, Afghanistan,and North America

Lobularia maritima Desv.

Perennial erect or suberect herbs, 12 – 35 cm tall; stem branched from the base, silvery hairy; leaves oblanceolate, 20 – 40 mm long, entire or slightly toothed; racemes 20 – 30 flowered, upto 20 cm long; flowers about 5 mm across, white or pinkish; siliquae ovate, oblong or obovate or suborbicular compressed.

Flower colour: White

Specimens examined : Bhellum 10238

Locality : Batote

Nativity : Mediterranean region

Flrs. and Frts. : Feb. – March

Distribution : India, Mediterranean region

Lunaria annua L.

Annual or biennial, 30-100 cm tall; leaves simple, lower ones long stalked, broadly cordate, acuminate; racemes many flowered, lax; flowers nearly 3 cm across; fruits siliculae elliptic oblong to almost orbicular, rounded at both the ends.

Flower colour: Purple, Violet, Pink or White

Specimens examined : Bhellum 14892

Locality : Srinagar

Nativity : South-east Europe

Flrs. and Frts. : May – October

Distribution : India, Pakistan, South east Europe and Germany

Malcolmia africana (L.) R. Br.

Annual polymorphic herbs; stem 30 – 60 cm in height, or more, branched, branches forked, hairy; leaves petioled, 2.5 – 15 cm long; flowers of variable colours, near the end of the branches, white, pink or purple; siliquae 4 – 7 cm long, narrow linear, straight or spreading.

Flower colour: White, Violet or Pink

Specimens examined : Bhellum 14354

Locality : Srinagar

Nativity : Algeria

Flrs. and Frts. : April-August

Distribution : India,Pakistan, South Europe, North Africa, Asia and China.

M. intermedia C. A. Mey

Annual herbs, leaves variables, racemes 5 – 8 flowered.

Flower colour: White

Specimens examined : Bhellum 13153

Locality : Kashmir

Nativity : Trans-Caspian region

Flrs. and Frts. : April - July

Distribution : India,Pakistan, Iran, Iraq, Afghanistan and Trans-Caspian region

Matthiola incana R. Br.

Biennial or perennial herbs 30 – 60 cm tall, pubescent; leaves long, oblong to lanceolate; flowers in terminal racemes; flowers of different colours in cultivated forms; siliquae 3 – 8 cm long, erect, thick. Grown in the gardens for its showy flowers.

Flower colour: White

Specimens examined : Bhellum 10633

Locality : Batote

Nativity : Europe

Flrs. and Frts. : Feb. – March

Distribution : India.

M. flavida Boiss.

Perennial herbs, 15 – 100 cm tall, tomentose, with stellate hairs; basal leaves oblanceolate, elliptic ovate, sinuate, lobulate, dentate or entire, very variable in size, upper ones oblanceolate to linear,shortly stalked or sessile; flowers 10 – 15 mm across, brownish mauve to purple, fragrant; siliquae linear oblong, straight, compressed.

Flower colour: Mauve or Purplish

Specimens examined : Bhellum 14364

Locality : Kashmir

Nativity : Iran

Flrs. and Frts. : April-August

Distribution : India, Pakistan Iran, Afghanistan and Turcomania.

Nasturtium officinale R. Br.

Perennial rhizomatous, procumbent herbs, 15 – 70 cm tall, rooting from the node; leaves lyrately pinnate, lower stalked, upper sessile, auricled at the base, leaflets 5 – 9, terminal leaflet larger, suborbicular or cordate; racemes 10 – 25 flowered; flowers about 4 mm across, white; siliquae oblong, subcylindrical, 10 – 20 mm long, seeds biseriate.

Flower colour: white

Specimens examined : Bhellum 14476

Locality : Srinagar and Jammu

Nativity : Europe and America

Flrs. and Frts. : April-August

Distribution : India, Pakistan, Afghanistan, Europe, America and Asia.

Neslia apiculata Fisch.

An annual erect herb, 15 – 45 cm tall, clothed with simple or forked hairs rarely somewhat glabrous or glandular; radical leaves 2.5 – 5 cm long, oblong, lanceolate; cauline leaves shorter, stem clasping, auricles sagittate; flowers, yellowish-green or golden yellow, many, petals golden yellow; siliquae 1.5 - 4 mm across with a fine network of wrinkles.

Flower colour: Yellow or Golden yellow

Specimens examined : Bhellum 14382

Locality : Srinagar and Padder

Nativity : East Caucasus

Flrs. and Frts. : May – October

Distribution : India, Pakistan, Nepal, South Europe, North West Africa and West Asia.

Notoceras bicorne (Aiton) Amoy.

A stiff, profusely branched, annual herb, branched from the base; leaves narrow oblong, entire; racemes many flowered, short; flowers with sepals of appressed hairs; siliquae 4 – 8 mm long, stiff erect, ndehiscent, subsessile; seeds 4 – 8.

Flower colour: White

Specimens examined : Bhellum 13454

Locality : Kashmir

Nativity : Canary Islands

Flrs. and Frts. : April-August

Distribution : India, Pakistan and westwards to Mediterranean region

Parrya nudicaulis (L.) Regal

Perennial, sparsely glandular herb; radical leaves rosulate, pinnatipartite, lanceolate, 5 – 15 cm long; racemes 10 – 15 flowered or more; flowers about 20 mm across lilac, violet or white; siliquae 30 - 60 mm long, oblong, compressed, erect and glandular.

Flower colour: White or lilac-violet

Specimens examined : Bhellum 14474

Locality : Zanskar

Nativity : Siberia

Flrs. and Frts. : April-August

Distribution : India, Pakistan, Afghanistan, Arctic Europe, Central and North Asia,

Raphanus sativa L.

Annual or biennial herbs, glabrous or with scattered hairs; root thick fleshy of different forms; leaves lyrate, pinnate, or pinnatifid, roughly pilose; flowers large yellow, veined with purple; siliquae indehiscent, long, terete, beak long.

Flower colour: White, yellow with purple veins or violet

Specimens examined : Bhellum 12364

Locality : Srinagar and Jammu

Nativity : Mediterranean region and Western Asia

Flrs. and Frts. : Feb. – March

Distribution : India, Pakistan, Europe, Mediterranean region and western Asia

Rorippa islandica (Oeder.) Borbas

Annual or biennial, herbs 10 – 50 cm tall with slender roots; stem erect or ascending, shoot glabrous, or puberulous; inflorescence racemes;

flowers ebracteate, yellow or pale yellow; petals with long claw, siliquae linear, or elliptic much flattened, seeds 1 -2 seriate.

Usually found on waste places.

Flower colour: Yellow

Specimens examined : Bhellum 13552

Locality : Srinagar

Nativity : Europe and Denmark

Flrs. and Frts. : April – October

Distribution : India, Pakistan, Nepal, Europe, Denmark and temperate Asia

R. montana (Wall. ex Hooker f. & T. Anders.) Small

Perennial herbs, 15 – 30 cm tall; leaves simple, 5 – 12 cm long, margin entire or slightly toothed, lower ovate, oblong, upper ones linear or obovate, racemes upto 10 cm long; flowers yellow; siliquae glabrous linear, 15 – 20 cm long.

Grows on waste places.

Flower colour: Yellow

Specimens examined : Bhellum 11562

Locality : Srinagar

Nativity : Nepal Himalaya

Flrs. and Frts. : May – October

Distribution : India, Pakistan, Nepal, Europe, East Asia and introduced in N. America.

R. sylvestris L.

Annual, erect or decumbent herbs, 15 – 50 cm tall; leaves pinnate, deeply pinnatisect, lobes obovate, or oblong, cuneate; flowers 4 – 5 mm across, yellow, arranged in racemes; siliquae cylindrical, linear-oblong, glabrous, seeds many.

Grows on waste and moist places.

Flower colour: Yellow

Specimens examined : Bhellum 11562

Locality : Srinagar

Nativity : Europe and Asia

Flrs. and Frts. : May – October

Distribution : India, Pakistan, Nepal, Europe, Asia and introduced in N. America and temperate Eurasia.

Sinapis alba L.

Annual, erect, branched, hairy herbs, upto 90 cm tall; lower leaves 5 – 15 cm long, lyrate hispid, upper leaves shortly stalked, subequal, sinuate, crenate; racemes many flower; flowers 10 mm across yellow; siliquae 20 – 40 mm long, compressed.

Flower colour: Pale yellow or white

Specimens examined : Bhellum 123643

Locality : Srinagar

Nativity : Europe and Britain

Flrs. and Frts. : Feb. – March

Distribution : India, Pakistan, Europe, North America

S. arvensis L.

Annual, erect, branched, hispid, herbs, 20 – 50 cm tall; leaves lyrately pinnate, terminal lobe large, coarsely toothed; racemes, many flowered; flower ebracteate 10 mm across, yellow; siliquae, 20 – 40 mm long;

Flower colour: Pale yellow

Specimens examined : Bhellum 127643

Locality : Srinagar

Nativity : Europe

Flrs. and Frts. : Feb. – March

Distribution : India, Pakistan, Europe, North Africa and Mediterranean region.

Sisymbrium altissinum L.

Annual or biennial, erect, branched, herbs, 20 – 80 cm tall; basal leaves loosely rosulate, shortly petioled, runcinate, pinnatifid, 6 – 15 cm long, 3 – 8 cm broad, terminal lobe larger, upper leaves 5 – 7 jugate, with linear lobes; flowers 5 – 6 mm across; yellow; siliquae 50 – 80 mm long, linear subcylindrical, usually straight, glabrous.

Flower colour: Yellow

Specimens examined : Bhellum 14682

Locality : Srinagar

Nativity : Europe

Flrs. and Frts. : April-August

Distribution : India, Pakistan, Afghanistan, Tibet and South West Asia

S. irio L.

Annual, erect, brached, 20 – 60 cm tall herbs; leaves petioled, very variable, 2 – 6 jugate, cauline leaves similar 1 – 3 jugate, smaller; racemes many flowered, 30 cm long in fruiting; flowers about 3 mm across, yellow; siliquae 30 – 45 mm long, linear.

Flower colour: yellow

Specimens examined : Bhellum 14732

Locality : Srinagar and Jammu

Nativity : West Europe

Flrs. and Frts. : April-August

Distribution : India, Pakistan, Afghanistan and Tibet

S. loeselii L.

Annual or biennial, upto 100 cm tall, branched, hispid below; basal leaves lyrate, pinnatipartite, terminal lobe elongate, lateral lobes 3 – 4 paired, dentate, upper ones similar but smaller; racemes many flowered, upto 40 cm long in fruiting; flowers 6 – 8 mm across, bright yellow; siliquae 20 – 40 cm long or more linear subcylindrical, erect.

Flower colour: Yellow

Specimens examined : Bhellum 14582

Locality : Srinagar

Nativity : Europe

Flrs. and Frts. : April-August

Distribution : India, Pakistan, Afghanistan, Tibet and most of the Asia and distributed elsewhere

S. officinale L.

Annual, erect, stiff, branched, hairy herb, 20 – 50 cm tall; basal leaves rosulate, deeply pinnatisect, terminal lobe stalked, irregurly toothed, cauline leaves smaller; racemes branched, 20 – 30 flowered; flowers 4 mm across, yellow; siliquae short, 10 – 15 mm long.

Flower colour: Yellow

Specimens examined : Bhellum 14572

Locality : Srinagar

Nativity : Europe

Flrs. and Frts. : April-August

Distribution : India, Pakistan, Afghanistan, Europe, Asia and Africa.

Thlaspi arvense L.

Annual hairy herbs, 50 – 70 cm tall, rarely glabrous; basal leaves oblanceolate, 2 – 8 cm long, upper leaves lanceolate, oblong, 2 – 6 cm long, sessile; racemes many flowered; flowers 3 – 5 mm across, white; siliquae orbicular, deeply notched at the apex.

Flower colour: White

Specimens examined : Bhellum 14848

Locality : Srinagar

Nativity : Sweeden

Flrs. and Frts. : April-August

Distribution : India, Pakistan, Afghanistan, Sweden and throughout the northern hemisphere.

T. cochleariforme DC.

Perennial herbs, mostly branched from the base, glabrous or subglaucous; radical leaves rosulate, spathulate, or oblong–obovate, shortly stalked, 2.5 – 5.5 cm long, apex rounded, margin entire; cauline leaves ovate, cordate, amplexicalue, 1 – 2 cm long margin entire or obscurely toothed; flowers 5 mm across, white; siliquae 4 – 10 mm long, oblong, obovate, apex emarginate, rarely subentire, glabrous.

Flower colour: White

Specimens examined : Bhellum 13738

Locality : Srinagar

Nativity : North Asia

Flrs. and Frts. : April-August

Distribution : India, Pakistan, Afghanistan and North Asia.

T. coclearioides Hooker f. & Thoms.

Perennial decumbent branched herbs, mostly branched from the base, glabrous; basal leaves rosulate, spathulate, 1.5 – 3 cm long, apex rounded, upper ones elliptic-ovate, 5 – 20 mm long, glabrous; racemes 10 – 15 flowered; flowers 4 – 5 mm across, white; siliquae 8 – 11 mm long, slightly curved, subcontorted, flattened, apex subemarginate.

Flower colour: White

Specimens examined : Bhellum 13435

Locality : Srinagar

Nativity : Eastern Himalaya

Flrs. and Frts. : April-August

Distribution : India, Pakistan, Afghanistan and Eastern Himalaya.

T. kotschyanum Boiss. & Hohen.

Annual herbs, 15 – 25 cm tall, usually branched from base, glabrous or glaucous; basal leaves ovate, oblong, 10 – 30 mm long, 5 – 10 mm broad, base amplexicaule, apex obtuse or rounded; racemes many flowered; flowers 2 mm across, white; siliquae obcordate-orbicular, about 11 mm across.

Flower colour: White

Specimens examined : Bhellum 14438

Locality : Srinagar

Nativity : Iran

Flrs. and Frts. : April-August

Distribution : India, Pakistan, Afghanistan, South and West Asia.

Turritis glabra L.

Annual or biennial herbs, glabrous or glaucous; radical leaves 5 – 15 cm long, oblong – obovate, shortly stalked, cauline leaves oblong – ovate, sagittate-amplexicaule, glabrous; racemes many flowered; flowers white or pale yellow; siliquae long, slender, erect, bilocular dehiscent; seeds 1 – 2 seriate.

Flower colour: Pale yellow or white

Specimens examined : Bhellum 14740

Locality : Srinagar

Nativity : Europe and Britain

Flrs. and Frts. : April-August

Distribution : India, Pakistan, Afghanistan, Europe and Asia. Introduced elsewhere in the world.

Violaceae

Viola odorata L.

Root stock stout; herbs caulescent, 15 – 20 cm tall, stoloniferous, stolons slender; leaves ovate-cordate, 1.5 – 3.5 cm long, 2 – 4 cm broad, obtuse, crenate; stipule lanceolate, subulate, toothed, glandular; flowers violet, tinged with white, fragrant; petals obovate, orbicular, spur cylinder, obtuse, 4.5 mm long; capsule globose, hirsute.

Flower colour : White streaked purple

Specimens examined : Bhellum 10121

Locality : Srinagar

Nativity : Europe, Africa and Asia

Flrs. and Frts. : March-May

Distribution : India, Europe, Africa and Asia

V. tricolor L.

Annual herbs, 15 – 30 cm tall, stem simple or branched, branches glabrous; leaves variable, basal rounded or cordate, upper ones ovate to oblong or lanceolate, margin crenate or serrate; stipule palmatifid to pinnatifid; flowers 2.5 – 5 cm across blue, whitish, or yellow spotted dark purple; sepals subulate, mucronate; petals orbicular, obovate, lateral petal bearded at the base.

Grows as an ornamental for flowers.

Flower colour: Yellow spotted dark purple

Specimens examined : Bhellum 10627

Locality : Jammu

Nativity : Europe

Flrs. and Frts. : March – April

Distribution : India and Europe

Caryophyllaceae

Arenaria griffithii Boiss.

Annual or perennial, tufted herbs, glabrous to pubescent; leaves densely crowded, 5 – 8 mm long, ciliate, straight or recurved, one nerved, becoming lax upwards; flowers white; sepals ovate, acute, shorter than petals; capsule 6-valved, shorter than the sepals.

Grows wild on grassy slopes.

Flower colour: White

Specimens examined : Bhellum 10827

Locality : Jammu

Nativity : Afghanistan

Flrs. and Frts. : March – May

Distribution : India, Afghanistan and Pakistan

A. leptoclados (Reichb.) Guss.

Annual, decumbent or ascending herbs, 10 – 25 cm tall; leaves obovate to spathulate, especially the lower ones mucronate, flowers white, calyx gradually narrow above; seeds without tubercles.

Grows wild on grassy slopes.

Flower colour: White

Specimens examined : Bhellum 10426

Locality : Jammu

Nativity : Silicy

Flrs. and Frts. : March – May

Distribution : India, C. Europe, Asia, Turkey, China and N. W. Africa.

Dianthus barbatus L.

Annual glabrous herbs, upto 45 cm tall or more, stem 4-angled; leaves lanceolate to ovate – lanceolate; flowers in desne cymes; flowers red spotted white; bracts 4, pointed, equaling the calyx; petals red or of different colours, toothed; broad, flat.

Planted in the gardens for its showy flowers.

Flower colour: Red or different coloured spotted white

Specimens examined : Bhellum 12426

Locality : Jammu

Nativity : Russia to China

Flrs. and Frts. : March – May

Distribution : India, C. Europe, Russia and China

D. chinensis L.

Annual herbs, leaves linear; flowers pink; calyx 5-toothed; corolla with long claw; stamens 10, ovary 1-celled, styles 2; capsule, cylindrical.

Ornamental, planted in the gardens.

Flower colour: Pink

Specimens examined : Bhellum 11626

Locality : Jammu

Nativity : China and Japan

Flrs. and Frts. : March – May

Distribution : India, China and Japan

Gypsophila elegans Bieb.

Annual glabrous herbs; leaves 2 – 6 cm long, oblanceolate, lanceolate, or linear-lanceolate; flowers in lax panicles; pedicel, slender; calyx broadly campanulate, nerves green with scarious margins.

Planted as an ornamental particularly on the margins of the beds

Flower colour: white with purple veins

Specimens examined : Bhellum 12306

Locality : Jammu

Nativity : Silicy

Flrs. and Frts. : March – May

Distribution : India and C. Europe,

Holosteum umbellatum L.

Annual, viscid, herbs, 10 – 25 cm tall; stem erect, simple or many from the base; basal leaves spathulate, oblanceolate, apex subacute; cauline leaves sessile, glabrous, glandular on margins; flowers white, included when young; capsule exceeding the sepals; seeds minutely tuberculate.

Grows wild on dry places.

Flower colour: White

Specimens examined : Bhellum 11127

Locality : Jammu

Nativity : Afghanistan and Pakistan

Flrs. and Frts. : March – May

Distribution : India, Turkey, Iran, Afghanistan, Syria, Arabia, Cyprus and Pakiatan.

Leptodiclis holosteoides (C. A. Mey.) Fenzl.

Annual glandular or pubescent herbs, 80 cm tall or more; leaves linear or linear- lanceolate, 3 – 7 cm long, acute or acuminate; flowers solitary axillary, sepals linear-lanceolate, ciliate, glabrous or glandular; petals white, spathulate, obovate; capsule globose.

Grows wild on dry places.

Flower colour: White

Specimens examined : Bhellum 10697

Locality : Jammu

Nativity : Russia.

Flrs. and Frts. : March – May

Distribution : India, Iran, Caucasus, Turkey, Afghanistan, Nepal, W. Tibet, Mongolia and N. W. China.

Spergula arvensis L.

Annual herbs, branched from near the base, pubescent or glandular; stem geniculate; leaves green to grey green, fleshy, convex above; flowers 4 – 8 mm across, arranged in forked or subumbellate cymose or panicles; pedicel 1 – 3 cm long, slender, spreading or deflexed; bracts small or scarious; sepals ovate, with scarious margin; petals obovate, slightly longer than sepals; capsule ovoid-conical longer than calyx.

Grows wild on waste places and in cultivated fields as a weed.

Flower colour: White

Specimens examined : Bhellum 11202

Locality : Ramgarh

Nativity : Europe

Flrs. and Frts. : March-April

Distribution : India and grows as cosmopolitan.

Stellaria alsinoides Boiss. & Buhse

Annual glabrous or sparsely hairy herbs, stem 5 – 10 cm tall; leaves linear glabrous, acute; flowers in dichasial cymes; sepals lanceolate, glabrous, margin scarious; petals shorter than sepals, white, shortly bilobed into linear lobes.

Grows wild on waste places and in cultivated fields.

Flower colour: White

Specimens examined : Bhellum 10527

Locality : Jammu

Nativity : Iran

Flrs. and Frts. : March – May

Distribution : India, Iran, Afghanistan, Central Asia and Pakistan.

S. media (L.) Vill.

Annual decumbent, 20 – 50 cm tall herb; lower leaves ovate, cordate, base cuneate, apex acute, or shortly acuminate; upper sessile, ovate or elliptic; flowers in terminal cymes; pedicel glandular pubescent; sepals 5 ovate, lanceolate, subacute; petals 5, white, shorter than sepals; capsule ovate, oblong, longer than calyx.

Grows wild on waste places and in cultivated fields.

Flower colour: White

Specimens examined : Bhellum 10720

Locality : Udhampur

Nativity : Europe

Flrs. and Frts. : March-April

Distribution : India, Europe and grows as cosmopolitan.

S. tibetica Kurz

Densely glandular pubescent herbs 10 – 15 cm tall; leaves oblong, apex acute to subacute, sessile; flowers in cymes; bracts coriaceous; sepals elliptic, 5 – 6 mm long, margin scarious; petals bifid, lobes obtuse; stamens shorter than sepals; capsule ovoid.

Flower colour: White

Specimens examined : Bhellum 12880

Locality : Ladakh

Nativity : Tibet

Flrs. and Frts. : March-April

Distribution : India and Tibet.

S. uliginosa Murr.

Annual procumbent or suberect, 20 – 50 cm tall, glabrous, herbs;

stem slender 4-angled,glaucous; leaves ovate, lanceolate to linear, apex acute or acuminate; sepals lanceolate, subulate; petals white, small or absent.

Grows wild on waste places and in cultivated fields.

Flower colour: White

Specimens examined : Bhellum 10877

Locality : Srinagar

Nativity : Germany

Flrs. and Frts. : March – May

Distribution : India, Europe, Balkans, N. Armenia and Temperate and Alpine Himalayas.

Vaccaria pyramidata Medik

Annual 30 – 50 cm tall herbs; leaves cordate, apex acute, glabrous, sessile; flowers in loose dichasial cymes; calyx tubular, tube inflated, 5-angled; petals pink coloured; capsule globular, 4-valved.

Grows wild on waste places and in cultivated fields.

Flower colour: Pink

Specimens examined : Bhellum 10560

Locality : Batote

Nativity : Europe

Flrs. and Frts. : April-May

Distribution : India Europe, Siberia, America and Pakistan.

Portulacaceae

Portulacca oleracea L.

Annual glabrous, ascending, succulent, prostrate herbs, about 30 cm tall; leaves fleshy, spathulate, subsessile, alternate or subopposite; flowers yellow, few in subterminal heads; sepals unequal; petals 5, obovate, yellow; stamens 8 – 12 ; styles 3 – 8 ; capsule ovoid; seeds many.

Found in cultivated fields and on moist situations in gardens and parks.

Flower colour: Yellow

Specimens examined : Bhellum 103035

Locality : Jammu

Nativity : North America

Flrs. and Frts. : April-May

Distribution : India, N. America and throughout warm countries of the world.

Portulacaria afra Jacq.

Shrub, semievergreen, usually 2.5- 4.5 cm tall; stem red; leaves small, rounded, succulent; flowers pink, arranged in panicles; sepals persistent, fruit berry pinkish, indehiscent, 1-seeded, 3 mm long, 3-winged.

Flower colour: Pink

Specimens examined : Bhellum 13426

Locality : Jammu

Nativity : South Africa

Flrs. and Frts. : March – May

Distribution : India, C. Europe, North Africa

Talinum calycinum Engelm.

Succulent herbs; leaves flat, exstipulate; flowers racemed or panicled; petals 5; stamens many; capsule 2 – 3 valved; seeds, subglobose.

Grown as an ornamental for flowers.

Flower colour: Pink

Specimens examined : Bhellum 13196

Locality : Jammu

Nativity : Mexico

Flrs. and Frts. : March – May

Distribution : India, C. Europe and North Africa

Tamaricaceae

Tamarix parviflora DC.

Deciduous shrubs or small trees, 2- 7 m tall, branches numerous, slender, arching; leaves alternate, scale- like, bright green, tiny, glands secrete salts; flowers tiny, rose-pink, arranged in spike-like racemes; fruits capsule

Flower colour: Pink

Specimens examined : Bhellum 10122

Locality : Srinagar

Nativity : Europe

Flrs. and Frts. : April – June

Distribution : India, Pakistan, Europe, Burma.

Malvaceae

Abutilon crispum (L) Medik.

Diffuse, annual, pubescent or hairy; leaves cordate, base rounded, apex acuminate, margin crenate; petioled or nearly sessile; flowers small, yellow; calyx tubular below, sepals 5, lanceolate; petals 5, yellow; carpels obtuse, nearly glabrous, 2 – 3 seeded.

Flower colour: Yellow

Specimens examined : Bheilum 12486

Locality : Jammu

Nativity : Tropical America

Flrs. and Frts. : March – May

Distribution : India, Tropical America

A. pictum

Evergreen, erect shrubs; leaves alternate, ovate, 3 – 5 lobed, margins dentate; flowers orange yellow, streaked with purple veins; calyx valvate, tubular below; petals 5, connate below, free above; staminal tube divided at apex into numerous stamens, anther monothecous; carpels 5 – many, styles as many as carpels.

Flower colour: Orange yellow with dark purple veins

Specimens examined : Bhellum 13426

Locality : Jammu

Nativity : South Africa

Flrs. and Frts. : March – May

Distribution : India, C. Europe and North Africa

Althaea rosea (L.) Cav.

Biennial arborescent shrubs, pubescent or villous, erect; leaves cordate, margin toothed; infloresum racemose, flowers terminal, bracteoles foliaceous, deciduous; flowers upto 10 cm across, white or pink on first in the morning, deep red during night.

Planted for its ornamental flowers.

Flower colour: Rose coloured

Specimens examined : Bhellum 10544

Locality : Batote

Nativity China

Flrs. and Frts. : May – August

Distribution : India and China

Hibiscus mutabilis L.

A shrub, without prickles; leaves about 10 cm long, base cordate, margin toothed; peduncle upto 15 cm long, jointed near the top; bract shorter than the calyx; flowers about 10 cm across, white or pink; sepals ovate, lanceolate, connate below the middle; capsule globose, flattened, hairy.

Planted in the gardens for its ornamental and showy flowers.

Flower colour: Pink

Specimens examined : Bhellum 12476

Locality : Jammu

Nativity : China

Flrs. and Frts. : June. – October

Distribution : India and China,

H. rosa-sinensis L.

Shrubs, evergreen, leaves ovate, lanceolate, 3-nerved at the base, more or less acuminate, coarsely serrate, glabrous, shining; bracteoles 5 – 7 lanceolate, connate at base and shorter than the calyx; flowers solitary axillary, about 10 mm across; calyx campanulate, divided almost upto the middle; cultivated in gardens for ornamental flowers.There are several varieties with single or double flowers varying in colour from crimson to red and pale.

Cultivated in the gardens for its ornamental flowers.

Flower colour: Red

Specimens examined : Bhellum 10691

Locality : Jammu

Nativity : China

Flrs. and Frts. : March – August

Distribution : India, Pakistan and China

H. schizopetalus (Mast.) Hooker f.

A shrub, branches drooping; leaves alternate, ovate-elliptic apex acute, margin toothed; flowers orange red, 5 – 8 cm across, pendulous.

Flower colour: Orange red

Specimens examined : Bhellum 12407

Locality : Jammu

Nativity : Tropical East Africa

Flrs. and Frts. : March – May

Distribution : India and Tropical East Africa

H. syriacus L.

A small, ornamental shrub; leaves upto 5 cm long or more, lower ovate, upper ones more or less 3-lobed, dentate or crenate, glabrous, cuneate at the base, 3-nerved; bracteoles 6 – 8, linear; flowers 5 cm across; corolla lilac with a red – purple eye.

Cultivated in the gardens for its beautiful flowers.

Flower colour: Bluish white or Purplish

Specimens examined : Bhellum 12522

Locality : Jammu

Nativity : Syria

Flrs. and Frts. : March – May

Distribution : India and Syria,

Malva parviflora L.

Annual spreading herbs, branches many from the base, slightly downy; leaves orbicular, lobed, peduncles short, bracteoles, linear; flowers 5 – 10 mm across, white or pale pink in axillary or solitary clusters; sepals broad, acute; petals notched, scarcely exceeding the sepals; carpels wrinkled; fruits 5 – 6 mm across; seeds brown; grows as weed.

Flower colour: Pale pink

Specimens examined : Bhellum 10155

Locality : Jammu

Nativity : South Europe

Flrs. and Frts. : May-June

Distribution : India, Pakistan, Afghanistan, S. Europe, Persia, Arabia and Mediterranean region.

Malvastrum coromandelianum (L.) Garcke

Perennial herbs, 60 – 80 cm, usually gregarious; leaves ovate, elliptic, 3.6 cm long, sparsely hairy on both surfaces, serrately toothed; bractioles 3 linear; flowers solitary or axillary, often in groups; flowers yellow, 1.5 – 2 cm across; petals pale yellow somewhat longer than sepals; fruits 5 – 7 mm across; grows wild on shady places.

Flower colour: Yellow

Specimens examined : Bhellum 10490

Locality : R.S.Pura

Nativity : South America

Flrs. and Frts. : May-June

Distribution : India, America,Tropics of both the hemispheres and Australia

Malvastrum coromandelianum (L.) Garcke

Malvaviscus arboreus Cav.

Shrubs, evergreen ornamental, leaves ovate, lanceolate, 3-nerved at the base, more or less acuminate, coarsely serrate, glabrous, shining; bracteoles 5 – 7, lanceolate, connate at base and shorter than the calyx; flowers solitary axillary; calyx campanulate, divided almost upto the middle.

Cultivated in gardens for ornamental flowers.

Flower colour: Pink

Specimens examined : Bhellum 10621

Locality : Jammu

Nativity : Tropical America

Flrs. and Frts. : March – April

Distribution : India, Pakistan and Tropical America

Urena lobata L.

Perennial tomentose erect, undershrub, 1 – 1.5 m tall; leaves alternate, long petioled, cordate, grayish green, upper ones elliptic, irregularly serrate; bractioles 5, equaling or slightly exceeding the calyx; flowerw solitary axillary or in clusters, yellow, 2 – 2.5 cm across; fruits 1 cm across.

Common on waste places, now found as naturalized in the local flora.

Flower colour: Yellow

Specimens examined : Bhellum 10265

Locality : Ramban

Nativity : Probably Africa

Flrs. and Frts. : April-May

Distribution : India, Africa and all tropical regions of the world.

Bombacaceae

Chorisia speciosa St. Hil.

A medium sized tree; stem and branches usually armed; leaves palmately compound; leaflets ovate, lanceolate, acumiante, usually serrate, fllowers pinkish-white or pink. Grown as avenue tree in gardens.

Flower colour: White tinged with pink

Specimens examined : Bhellum 12626

Locality : Jammu

Nativity : Tropical Africa, Argentina and Brazil

Flrs. and Frts. : March – May

Distribution : India, Tropical Africa, Ceylon

Bombax malabaricm DC.

A tall deciduous tree, bark grey covered with sharp conical prickles; leaves digitate, large spreading, glabrous, leaflets lanceolate, acuminate, cuneate at the base; flowers large, numerous, crimson-coloured occasionally yellow and white; Capsule 12 – 15 cm long.

Flower colour: Crimson-coloured

Specimens examined : Bhellum 13720

Locality : Jammu and Udhampur

Nativity : Tropicla America

Flrs. and Frts. : March – May

Distribution : India and Tropical America

Sterculiaceae

Dombeya calantha Schum.

Evergreen shrub, stem hairy; leaves alternate, broad ovate, cordate, lobed or unlobed, hairy; flowers pink red in axillary cymes; petals flat, persistent; staminal tube antheriferous at the margin.

Flower colour: Pinkish-red

Specimens examined : Bhellum 13926

Locality : Jammu

Nativity : Central Africa

Flrs. and Frts. : March – May

Distribution : India and C. Europe.

Sterculia alata Roxb.

A large tree, young shoots covered with dense golden pubescence; leaves ovate cordate, acute, glabrous, clustered at the end of the branches, 7-nerved; flowers a few axillary; bracteoles caducous; calyx campanulate, deeply tomentose; 5-parted, segments linear-lanceolate; follicles, globose, woody; cultivated in gardens for shade.

Flower colour: Pale yellow within greenish without

Specimens examined : Bhellum 10295

Locality : Jammu

Nativity : Burma & South India

Flrs. and Frts. : April – June

Distribution : India, Burma, Pakistan

Tiliaceae

Corchorus aestuans L.

Annual, pubescent herbs, upto 60 cm tall, often purple tinged; leaves suborbicular to ovate, lanceolate, 2.5 – 10 cm long; flowers yellow; capsule 2 – 3 cm long; seeds dark-brown.

Grows on waste places.

Flower colour: Yellow

Specimens examined : Bhellum 10280

Locality : Jammu

Nativity : Tropical America, Asia and Africa

Flrs. and Frts. : May-August

Distribution : India, Ceylon Malaya, Paninsular Australia, West Indies and Africa

Tilia platyphylos Scop.

Deciduous, large trees upto 40 m tall; bark grey, fissured; leaves simple, alternate, hairy on nerves beneath, margin serrate; flowers white, fragrant; peduncle of inflorescence persists in fruits; sepals 5; petals 5; stamens numerous; fruit rounded, cream-coloured nutlets, 1 cm across. Planted as avenue tree.

Flower colour: White

Specimens examined : Bhellum 12452

Locality : Srinagar

Nativity : Europe

Flrs. and Frts. : April – May

Distribution : India and Europe

Linaceae

Linum grandiflora Desf.

Annual erect upto 60 cm tall herb; stem branched, glabrous; leaves sessile, alternate, broadly lanceolate, margin entire; flowers red arranged in cymose clusters; sepals free, enlarging in fruiting; petals free, obovate, red; stamens 5, united at the base; ovary ovoid, styles 5, connate at the base; capsule subglobose, brown, compressed

Flower colour: Rose-pink or Red

Specimens examined : Bhellum 14729*Locality* : Jammu

Nativity North Africa

Flrs. and Frts. : March – May

Distribution : India and North Africa

Linum grandiflora Desf.

Linum usitatissimum L.

Erect annual herbs; stem slender, branched; flowers blue; sepals 5, lanceloate; petals 5, connate at the base, blue; fruiting capsules contain sharp pointed seeds. The seeds are used for the preparation of oil and nutritive tonic.

Flower colour: Purple

Specimens examined : Bhellum 12466

Locality : Jammu

Nativity : Mediteranean region

Flrs. and Frts. : March – May

Distribution : India, C. Europe, Mediterranean region

Geraniaceae

Geranium pusillum L.

A small beautiful wild annual herb, stem diffuse slender glandular-pubescent annual. leaves suborbicular or reniform, 10-28 mm broad, plamatipartite; segments 5-7, terminally 2-3-lobed, lobes obtuse, mucronate. stipules 1.5-2 mm long, ovate-lanceolate, sometimes 2-fid, hairy, peduncles 2-flowered, glandular. flowers c. 4 mm broad, bracts ovate-lanceolate, 1-1.5 mm long, hairy. sepals 1.5-3 mm long, ovate or oblong-ovate, long ciliate, glandular-pubescent. petals slightly exceeding sepals, obovate, lilac or pink, base sparsely ciliate, filament base dilated, ciliate. beak 6-8 mm long, glandular-pubescent. mericarps appressed, pubescent, not wrinkled. seed oblong, glabrous c. 1.5 mm long.

Flower colour: Purplish pink

Specimens examined : Bhellum 12632

Locality : Banihal

Nativity : Asia

Flrs. and Frts. : April – July

Distribution : India, Pakistan, Nepal, Europe and introduced in N. America

Balsaminaceae

Impatiens sulcata Wallich

Plants annual, (20-)60-120 cm tall, stem erect, terete, robust, conspicuously grooved, simple or branched in upper part, sparsely glandular at nodes, leaves opposite or verticillate in upper part of stem; petiole (0.5-)1.5-3.5 cm, sparsely glandular or without glands; leaf blade elliptic-ovate or ovate-lanceolate, (4-) 6-20 × 2-5.5 cm, with red or purple stipitate basal glands, lateral veins 8-12 pairs, base cuneate or subrounded, slightly inequilateral, margin crenate-serrate, apex acuminate or long acuminate, inflorescences subcorymbose-racemose, many flowered; peduncles 3.5-9 cm. pedicels swollen at apex, bracteate at base; bracts pink or purple-red, lanceolate or ovate-lanceolate. Flowers purplish pink, large, 3-3.5 cm across, capsule pendulous, clavate, 2-2.5 cm. seeds obovoid, rugose.

Flower colour: purplish-pink

Specimens examined : Bhellum 11612

Locality : Srinagar

Nativity : Nepal

Flrs. and Frts. : May – October

Distribution : India, Pakistan and Nepal

Oxalidaceae

Oxalis corniculata L.

Annual or perennial, hairy, stoloniferous herbs; stems procumbent, 15 – 45 cm tall, rooting at joints; leaves with 3 leaflets, alternate or long stalked; stipule, small, adnate to the stalk; flowers bisexual, solitary or in small umbels; sepals 5, free; petals 5, twisted in bud; stamens 10, in two groups of 5 each, filaments united at the base.

Common on waste places.

Flower colour: Yellow

Specimens examined : Bhellum 10607

Locality : Srinagar

Nativity : South Europe

Flrs. and Frts. : Feb.-Dec.

Distribution : Cosmopolitan throughout the warmer parts of the world.

Oxalis corniculata L.

O. corymbosa DC

Annual, acaulescent herbs; bulbils clustered, sheathed in scales; leaves erect, 8 – 30 mm long, 3-foliate, leaflets cuneate at the base, apex obcordate, upper surface pubescent, punctuate; scape upto 27 cm long; inflorescence in subumbellate clusters; flowers purple; ovary glabrous, style pubescent.

Cultivated in the gardens for its beautiful flowers.

Flower colour: Purple

Specimens examined : Bhellum 10775

Locality : Batote

Nativity : South America

Flrs. and Frts. : August-October

Distribution : India, Pakistan and S. America

O. latifolia H.B. & K.

Puberulous herbs; bulbils clustered or solitary; leaflets triangular, 1.5 – 4 cm across; glabrous; many flowers on scape, subumbellate; pedicel 1 – 1.5 cm long or more; sepals lanceolate, 3.5 mm long; filaments unequal.

Cultivated in the gardens and waste places.

Flower colour: Pink

Specimens examined : Bhellum 10230

Locality : Ramban

Nativity : Mexico

Flrs. and Frts. : May-August

Distribution : India and Mexico

Simaroubaceae

Ailanthus altissima (Mill.) Swingle

A tall deciduous tree, producing abundant root suckers; leaves upto 80 cm long; leaflets usually with 1-3 pairs of glandular teeth; petals woolly-tomentose within; filaments longer than anthers; samara twisted at the top; planted along the roadsides.

Flower colour: Pale yellow

Specimens examined : Bhellum 13234

Locality : Srinagar

Nativity : China

Flrs. and Frts. : May-August

Distribution : India, Pakistan and China.

Meliaceae

Azadirachta indica A. Juss.

Deciduous, moderate-sized, trees;leaves bipinnate, sometimes tripinnate, pinnae usually opposite, lanceolate, margin serrate, apex acuminate, the lateral more or less oblique; flowers lilac-blue in numerous axillary cyme bearing panicles; calyx deeply 5-lobed; petals linear oblanceolate; staminal tube purple, anthers at the mouth of the tube; ovary 5-celled; drupe globose, yellow when ripe, smooth at first, become wrinkled later; cultivated for shade and medicinal value.

Flower colour: Pale yellow

Specimens examined : Bhellum 10341

Locality : Jammu

Nativity : Persia and Asia Minor

Flrs. and Frts. : May-July

Distribution : India, Pakistan, Persia and Asia Minor

Melia azedarach L.

A deciduous tree; bark dark grey; leaves 2- or 3-pinnate, more or less opposite, leaflets ovate, acuminate, serrate; flowers fragrant, bisexual, petals lilac, staminal tube purple; disc annular; ovary glabrous 5-celled, ovules 2 in each cell; fruit a drupe 5-seeded or fewer by abortion; remaining on the tree longer after ripening; planted as avenue tree for shade and commonly called pride of India.

Flower colour: Lilac

Specimens examined : Bhellum 10341

Locality : Jammu

Nativity : South West Asia

Flrs. and Frts. : April-July

Distribution : India, Pakistan, China, Burma Turkey and Iran.

Celastraceae

Euonymus japonicus L. f.

Evergreen shrubs; stem much branched, strongly columnar; leaves small, broadly ovate, lustrous, dark green; flowers axillary, small, inconspicuous, greenish white; The plant is grown as ornamental.

Commonly grown as hedge plant.

Flower colour: Greenish white

Specimens examined : Bhellum 10629

Locality : Srinagar

Nativity : Japan

Flrs. and Frts. : April – August

Distribution : India, Pakistan and Japan,

Vitaceae

Parthenocissus inserta (Kern.) K Fritsch.

A woody climber, 20- 30 m tall bearing tendrils with twining tips; leaves palmately compound, leaflets 5, margins toothed; flowers green, arranged in clusters; berries purplish-black, 5-7 mm across. Grows ususlly on the walls.

Flower colour: green

Specimens examined : Bhellum 12760

Locality : Srinagar

Nativity : Britain

Flrs. and Frts. : May-August

Distribution : India and Britain

P. tricuspidata Planch.

Climber upto 20 m tall; tendrils much branched having adhesive disc; leaves simple 5-6 cm long, usually 3-lobed, orbicular or ovate, margin crenate-serrate, accuminate, base cordate; ovary 5-lobed; berry bluish black; seeds 6-8 mm long.

Commonly grown on the walls of the houses.

Flower colour: Pale green

Specimens examined : Bhellum 11160

Locality : Srinagar

Nativity : Japan and C. China

Flrs. and Frts. : May-August

Distribution : India, Japan and China

Parthenocissus tricuspidata Planch.

Vitis vinifera L.

Deciduous woody, climber; leaves simple, 1 – 9 foliate; flowers cymose, bisexual or polygamous; calyx 5-lobed; petals 5, free; ovary usually 2-celled, with 2 ovules in each cell; fruits seedless or 1 – 4 seeded, berry; commonly grown for fruits.

Flower colour: Green

Specimens examined : Bhellum 10240

Locality : Jammu

Nativity : S. Europe and W. Asia

Flrs. and Frts. : May-August

Distribution : India, S. Europe and W. Asia

Aceraceae

Acer negundo L.

A handsome deciduous tree, flowers appearing before leaves, It is distinguished from all the indigenous species by pinnate compound leaves. A small tree of the United States. Planted as avenue tree.

Flower colour: Pale green

Specimens examined : Bhellum 11341

Locality : Srinagar

Nativity : N. America

Flrs. and Frts. : April-July

Distribution : India, Pakistan and N. America.

A. palmatum Thunb.

Deciduous upto 15 m tall; bark greenish-grey or light brown; stem glabrous; leaves sub-orbicular, 3-6 x 4-8 cm, pubescent; flowers pale-yellow to pinkish-white; fruits somewhat with wings, glabrous.

Grown as an avenue tree in gardens.

Flower colour: Pale yellow or pinkish white

Specimens examined : Bhellum 10381

Locality : Srinagar

Nativity : Japan

Flrs. and Frts. : April-July

Distribution : India, Pakistan and Japan.

Malphigiaceae

Mascagnia macroptera (DC.) Nied

Shrubs, fast-growing vine that reaches 10-12 feet high. It produces clusters of bright-yellow flowers. This plant is often listed as being from Central America but it grows as far south as Brazil.

It's a fast grower, reaching 10-12 feet high, and also grows in partial shade.Grown in the gardens.

Flower colour: Yellow

Specimens examined : Bhellum 14516

Locality : Srinagar

Nativity : China

Flrs. and Frts. : April – November

Distribution : India, Pakistan and China.

Sapindaceae

Koelreuteria paniculata Laxm.

Deciduous Trees or shrubs, bark greyish brown to black, stout, fissured when dry; lenticels gray to dark brown, small; branches tuberculate, appressed pubescent or glabrous, leaves fascicled on young branches, spreading, pinnate, imperfectly bipinnate, or sometimes bipinnate, to 50 cm; leaflets 7-18 (terminal one sometimes connate with uppermost pair below middle), sessile or very shortly petiolate, opposite or alternate, ovate or broadly ovate to ovate-lanceolate, 3-10 × 3-6 cm, papery, abaxially barbate on vein axils, sometimes tomentose, or densely pale yellow pubescent, adaxially scattered appressed pubescent on midvein, base obtuse to subtruncate, apex acute or shortly acuminate, thyrses 25-40 cm, densely pilosulose, branches spreading and long, cymes on last branches 3-6-flowered, densely arranged and capitate; bracts narrowly lanceolate, scabrous-hairy, flowers pale yellow, slightly fragrant; capsules conical, 4-6 cm, 3-ridged, apex acuminate; carpels ovoid, abaxially reticulate veined, adaxially smooth and slightly shiny, seeds subglobose, 6-8 mm in dia.

Grown as avenue tree.

Flower colour: Yellow

Specimens examined : Bhellum 14516

Locality : Srinagar

Nativity : China

Flrs. and Frts. : April – November

Distribution : India, China, Japan and Pakistan .

Koelreuteria paniculata Laxm.

Sapindus mukorossi Gaertn.

A deciduous, handsome tree; bark grey; leaves alternate, paripinnate 30 – 65 cm long, leaflets 5 – 10 pairs, aternate or opposite, graduall smaller towards apex, acuminate, coriacious; inflorescence in termina thyrsus; flowers small, regular, polygamous; calyx lobes somewha unequal, ciliate; petals, white or purplish, alternating with the calyx lobes; stamens inserted in the centre of the disc, filament, white woolly ovary 3-celled, fruit a drupe, fleshy, 1-seeded; grows wild.

Flower colour: Greenish-yellow

Specimens examined : Bhellum 14906

Locality : Jammu

Nativity : China

Flrs. and Frts. : April – July

Distribution : India, Pakistan and China.

Sapindus mukorossi Gaertn.

Anacardiaceae

Pistacia atlantica Desf.

Pistacia atlantica is a deciduous tree growing up to 7 m tall with branches spreading and growing erect to form a dense crown. The trunk is stout and covered in fissured bark;leaflets usually 9 lance-shaped, monoecious and hermaphrodite trees have been seen but are unusual. The fleshy, oily fruit oblong, borne by the female tree is 6- 8 mm long and pink in color, ripening blue. It is planted as an ornamental shady bearing and drought tolerant.

Rarely cultivated for seeds.

Flower colour: pale-yellow

Specimens examined : Bhellum 10553

Locality : Srinagar

Nativity : Afghanistan

Flrs. and Frts. : April – November

Distribution : India, Pakistan and Afghanistan

Pistacia atlantica Desf.

P. khinjuk Stocks

A deciduous tree or shrub up to 6 m tall. Young shoots puberulous; leaves imparipinnate, leaflets 3-7 in number, coriaceous, opposite to subopposite, subsessile, ovate to ovate-oblong, glabrous,apiculate or subacuminate, base often oblique; terminal leaflet larger than the laterals. panicles extra-axillary, suberect; drupe 4-6 mm long, suborbicular.

Grows wild.

Flower colour: White

Specimens examined : Bhellum 11612

Locality : Assar in district Doda

Nativity : Baluchistan and Pakistan

Flrs. and Frts. : May – October

Distribution : India and Pakistan,

P. vera L.

A dioecious, deciduous shrub or middle sized tree; leaves compound, imparipinnate, leaflets lanceolate, acuminate; flowers minute. Pistacea species are disdtributed for their nuts.

Planted in gardens.

Flower colour: Yellow or reddish

Specimens examined : Bhellum 10123

Locality : Srinagar

Nativity : Mediterranean region

Flrs. and Frts. : April – November

Pistacea vera L.

Coriariaceae

Coriaria nepalensis Wall.

glabrous shrubs; branches long, spreading, reddish-brown, branchlets quadrangular; leaves elliptic, 2.5 – 5 cm long, acute, entire or obscurely serrate; flowers one or many in axillary clusters; petals 5, smaller stamens and style red or purplish; fruit dark brown or black.

Grows wild, fairly common among shrubby vegetation on hill-sides and ravines

Flower colour: Greenish yellow

Specimens examined : Bhellum 12453

Locality : Jammu, between Batote and Ramban

Nativity : Nepal

Flrs. and Frts. : April - July

Distribution : India, Nepal and Pakistan and China

Fabaceae

Aeschynomene indica L.

An annual or shrubby glabrous, herb, stem 50 – 100 cm tall; leaves odd pinnate, stalked, leaflets 41 – 61 sensitive, narrowly oblong, obtuse, diminishing in size towards the end of branches; flowers yellow aften streaked with purple, about 1.3 cm across; bracts and bracteoles small, lanceolate; stamens all united near the base, ultimately divided into two bundles of five each; pods stalked, flattend, smooth, upper margin nearly straight, lower indented, dividing the pod into 7 – 9 indehiscent, 1-seeded joints. Grows wild.

Flower colour: Yellow

Specimens examined : Bhellum 10686

Locality : Jammu

Nativity : America

Flrs. and Frts. : July – August

Distribution : India now pantropical

Aeschynomene indica L.

Amorpha fruticosa L.

Deciduous shrub with straight branches; leaves imparipinnate, leaflets 11-25, opposite, pellucid-punctate; flowers dark-purple; clayx teeth unequal, the upper one shorter; corolla twice as long as calyx; stamens 10, monadelphous; ovules 2, glandular, curved at the top.

Flower colour: Dark purple

Specimens examined : Bhellum 11875

Locality : Srinagar

Nativity : North America

Flrs. and Frts. : April -June

Distribution : India, Mexico and N. America

Amorpha fruticosa L.

Arachis hypogea L.

Herbs, annual climbing plant, growing to a height of 1–2 meters, where suitable support is available, leaves pinnate with two leaflets and a terminal tendril, which twines around supporting plants and structures helping the sweet pea to climb, flowers are purple, 2-3.5 cmsbroad, in the wild plant, larger and very variable in colour in the many cultivars.Cultivated for its edible kernel.

Probably cultivated throughout the world.

Flower colour:Usually purple, variable

Specimens examined : Bhellum 10561

Locality : Jammu

Nativity : Probably a native of Brazil

Flrs. and Frts. : April – June

Distribution : India, Pakistan and Brazil

Arachis hypogea L.

Clitoria ternatea L.

Perennial climber, summer-growing perennial climber with a woody base, climbing on tall grasses and crops. Leaves with 5-7 leaflets elliptic to narrowly lanceolate 3-5 cm long, shortly pubesent underneath, flowers solitary, attractive, deep blue, occasionally pure white, very shortly pedicellate, 4 to 5 cm long, pod flat, linear, beaked, about 10 cm long, slightly pubescent. Cultivated for ornamental value, throughout the world.

Flower colour: Blue

Specimens examined : Bhellum 10281

Locality : Jammu

Nativity : Tropical America

Flrs. and Frts. : April – June

Distribution : India, Pakistan,

Clitoria ternatea L.

Indigofera linnaei Ali

Prostrate, appressed pubescent herbs; stem upto 60 cm tall, arising numerous from the root-stock; leaves small, acute; flowers small, red in sessile axillary heads; Pods 5 mm long, densely white-pubescent.

Flower colour: Pink

Specimens examined : Bhellum 13026

Locality : Jammu

Nativity : Tropical Africa

Flrs. and Frts. : May – September

Distribution : India and Tropical Africa

Indigofera linnaei Ali

Laburnum anagyroides Med.

A small deciduous tree; leaves 3-foliate, leaflets elliptic lanceolate, or ovate; flowers yellow, arranged in pedulous racemes; calyx 2-lipped; corolla yellow; stamens 10, monadelphous, 4 nearly twice as long as the remaining 6; fruits pods; seeds poisonous.

Laburnum anagyroides Med.

Flower colour: yellow

Specimens examined : Bhellum 13299

Locality : Srinagar

Nativity : S. & C. Europe

Flrs. and Frts. : April – November

Distribution : India and S. & C. Europe

Lathyrus aphaca L. f.

Annual herbs, climbing or trailing, upto 45 cm tall; apparent leaves are really stipules, stipule-foliaceous, triangular, hastate, 3.5 cm long, 2 cm broad, in pairs, opposite, appressed to stem; flowers solitary, about 1 cm long, pale yellow; bracts minute, caducous; calyx 5-toothed, equally lobed; corolla papilionaceous; stamens diadelphous; pods linear-oblong, yellow or brown at maturity.

Grows wild as a weed in wheat fields and on margins.

Flower colour: Pale yellow

Specimens examined : Bhellum 10451

Locality : Udhampur

Nativity : Europe

Flrs. and Frts. : March-April

Distribution : India S. W. and C Asia, Pakistan, and N. Africa

Lathyrus aphaca L. f.

L. odoratus L.

Herbs, climbing with the tendrils; stem hollow, weak; leaves pinnately compound, terminal leaflets modified into tendrils; flowers with papilionaceous corolla; fruits pods.Cultivated for its ornamental value, flowers showy and fragrant.

Cultivated throughout the world.

Flower colour: Pink and Purple

Specimens examined : Bhellum 12553

Locality : Jammu

Nativity : Italy

Flrs. and Frts. : April – June

Distribution : India and Pakistan.

Lathyrus odoratus L.

Lupinus albus L.

Annual, thickly pubescent throughout, hairs appressed, white; stems few, up to 2 m long, leaf palmately compound, leaflets 7-9, 25-35 mm long, c. 14-18 mm broad, obovate, mucronate, glabrous above, pubescent below; stipules adnate, inflorescence subsessile, few flowered, pedicel

1-2 mm long. calyx 8-9 mm long, both lips shallowly lobed. Corolla 8-14 mm long, white to dark, fruit 8-11 cm long, sub cylindric, 5-6-seeded.

Flower colour: White

Specimens examined : Bhellum 12325

Locality : Jammu and Kashmir

Nativity : Silicy

Flrs. and Frts. : March – May

Distribution : India and Central Europe

Lupinus albus L

L. polyphyllus Lindley

Perennial herbaceous herb with stout stems growing to 1.5 m tall; leaves palmately compound with (5-) 9-17 leaflets 3-15 cm long; the flowers born on a tall spike, each flower 1-1.5 cm long, most commonly blue to purple in wild plants; the polyphyllus variety in particular make up a great number of the hybrids which are generally grown as garden lupins.

Flower colour: Deep blue or purple

Specimens examined : Bhellum 14676

Locality : Jammu

Nativity : South Africa

Flrs. and Frts. : March – May

Distribution : India and Central Europe

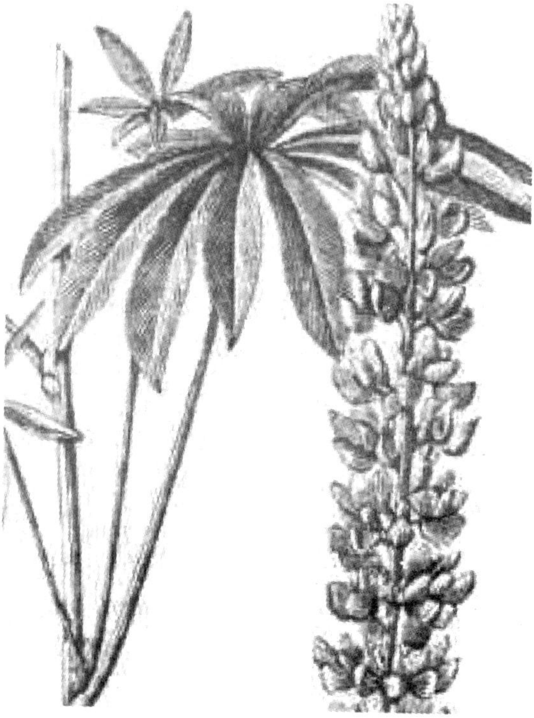

Lupinus polyphyllus Lindley

Medicago lupulina L.

Annual herbs, stem erect or procumbent, leaves trifoliate, leaflets obovate, upper part toothed lower one entire; terminal one stalked, lateral sessile; flowers small, yellow, crowded in globose or ovoid heads; pods smooth, minute, strongly curved when ripe, tip coiled; seeds solitary; Grows at the open places.

Flower colour: Yellow

Specimens examined : Bhellum 10572

Locality : Ramban

Nativity : Europe

Flrs. and Frts. : March-April

Distribution : India, Sieberia, Europe, Abyssinia and Afghanistan

Medicago lupulina L.

M. polymorpha L.

Annual herbs, procumbent, stem nearly glabrous, 10 – 60 cm tall; leaves trifoliate, leaflets 3, obovate, upper part toothed, lower one entire; flowers in 2 – 6 in axillary peduncles; pods spirally twisted in 2 or 3 coils, net-veined.

Grows as a weed in wheat fields.

Flower colour: Yellow

Specimens examined : Bhellum 12108

Locality : R.S.Pura

Nativity : Europe

Flrs. and Frts. : March-May

Medicago polymorpha L.

Distribution : India, China, Sieberia and Abyssinia

M. sativa L.

Annual prostrate herbs on open situation, stem herbaceous; leaves trifoliate, flowers yellow, fruits pods coiled.

Flower colour: Yellow

Specimens examined : Bhellum 11203

Locality : Campus, Srinagar University

Nativity : South-West Asia, Caucasian Mountains of Iran and Afghanistan

Flrs. and Frts. : May-August

Distribution : India, Nepal, Pakistan, Central Asia and Europe, Iran and Afghanistan

Medicago sativa L.

Melilotus alba Desr.

Annual herbs, pubescent or nearly glabrous; stem 30 – 100 cm tall; leaves of 3-leaflets, leaflets ovate or oblong, upper part toothed lower one entire, lateral leaflets sessile, terminal one stalked, veins parallel running out in small teeth; stipule narrowly lanceolate, long pointed, united to the leaf-stalk; flowers white, in long axillary racemes; calyx bell-shaped, teeth 5, distinct, lanceolate, nearly equal, acute; corolla papilionaceous; stamens diadelphous; pods indehiscent, ovoid, longer than the calyx, tipped with the persistent style; seeds 1 or 2 .

Found in waste places and as a weed in cultivated fields.

Flower colour: White

Specimens examined : Bhellum 10621

Locality : Jammu

Nativity : Europe and Western Asia

Flrs. and Frts. : March – April

Distribution : India, Burma, Bhutan, Tibet, Pakistan, Afghanistan, Arabia, Iran, Turkey, Europe, Central Asia and Russia.

Melilotus alba Desr.

M. indica (L.) All.

Annual, erect, nearly glabrous herbs; stem 15 – 50 cm tall; slender, solid, herbaceous, green; leaves 3-foliate, leaflets obovate, base cuneate, odd leaflet terminal, dentate in upper half, glabrous on both the surfaces; inflorescence elongated in axillary or terminal racemes; peduncle 2.5 – 3.5 cm long; bracts minute; fruits ovoid, ellipsoid, apiculate, 1 or rarely 2-seeded.

On waste places and mostly in wheat fields as weed.

Flower colour: Yellow

Specimens examined : Bhellum 10821

Locality : Jammu

Nativity : S. Europe

Flrs. and Frts. : March – April

Distribution : India, Burma, Bhutan, Europe, Pakistan and Afghanistan.

Melilotus indica (L.) All.

Phaseolus vulgaris L.

Annual climbing herbs on the bushes, leaves trifoliate, flowers white, corolla papilionaceous; pods edible when raw; seeds nutritious rich in proteins.

Cultivated throughout the world

Flower colour: White

Specimens examined : Bhellum 12121

Locality : Bhaderwah

Nativity : Mexico and Guatemala

Flrs. and Frts. : July – September

Distribution : India and Mexico

Phaseolus vulgaris L.

Pisum sativum L.

Annual herb, glabrous upto 1 m tall or more; leaves compound, pinnate, leaflets, 1 – 3 pairs, 2 – 7 cm long 1 – 4 cm broad, orbicular to elliptic oblong; stipule semicordate at the base; racemes 1 – 3 flowered, purple or white; legumes 3 – 12 cm long, yellow or brown, glabrous.

Pisum sativum L.

Cultivated in almost all parts of the state and most parts of the world.

Flower colour: White or purple

Specimens examined : Bhellum 11875

Locality : Assar

Nativity West Asia

Flrs. and Frts. : April – May

Distribution : India and W. Asia

Robinia pseudo-acacia L.

Deciduous shrub or small trees; stem solid woody, leaves pinnately compound, leaflets oblong, oval, rounded at apex; stipule spiny; inflorescence pendulous, 9 – 14 cm long racemes; flowers cream-coloured, tinged with pink; calyx 5-toothed, tinged with red; corolla papilionaceous; stamens 10, diadelphous, intruded; pods upto 15 cm long.

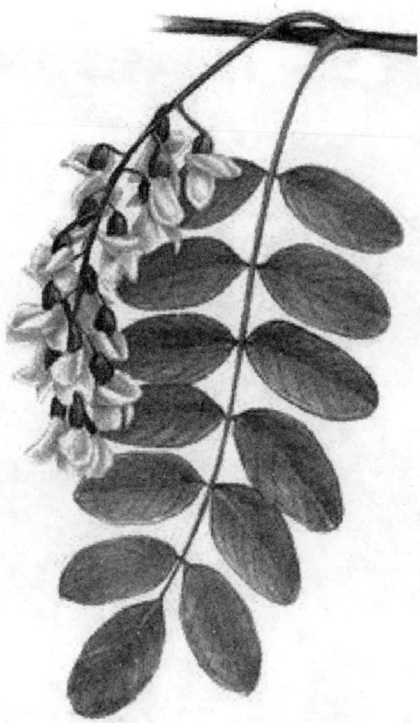

Robinia pseudo-acacia L.

Cultivated and now naturalised.

Flower colour: Cream-coloured

Specimens examined : Bhellum 10621

Locality : Srinagar

Nativity : South America

Flrs. and Frts. : April – June

Distribution : India and USA.

Sesbania grandiflora Pers.

Shrub or a tree that grows to 8-10 m in height; leaves pinnate, may be 30 cm long, with 12-20 pairs of oblong, rounded leaflets averaging 3-4 cm long and about 1 cm wide, leaves are borne at the terminals of branches, and the canopy is open, with a thin crown which produces light shade, racemes bear 2-3 flowers, flowers pink-red or white the pods usually 30-50 cm long by about 8 mm wide. fodder, food, and soil improvement are the principal uses of this species, leaves, seed pods, and flowers of grandiflora are prepared as food. the young, tender pods are edible. Planted as hedge.

Sesbania grandiflora Pers.

Flower colour: White

Specimens examined : Bhellum 11341

Locality : Jammu

Nativity : Malaya and N. Australia

Flrs. and Frts. : July – September

Distribution : India, Malaya and North Australia.

S. sesban L.

Common sesban is a small, often multi-stemmed tree, growing to 4-8 m high; leaves are pinnately compound, 2-18 cm long with 6-27 pairs of linear oblong leaflets; raceme with 2-20 pea-shaped flowers which are yellow with purple or brown streaks on the corolla; pods are subcylindrical, straight or slightly curved up to 30 cm long and 5 mm wide containing 10-50 seeds. Common sesban has a long history of use in India, primarily as a green manure and a source of cut and carry forage. Harvested leaves make a rich compost. Its leaves are a good source of protein for cattle and sheep.

Sesbania sesban L.

Flower colour: Yellow

Specimens examined : Bhellum 11681

Locality : Jammu

Nativity : South Africa

Flrs. and Frts. : July – September

Distribution : India, Throughout the Himalaya southwards – often cultivated, Pantropical.

Sophora japonica L.

Deciduous tree, crown spreading; leaves pinnately compound; flowers yellow; calyx tube 5-toothedl corolla 5-toothed; fruits pods; grows mostly on the hills.

Flower colour: Yellow or yellowish-white

Specimens examined : Bhellum 10111

Locality : Srinagar

Nativity : India, China and Japan

Flrs. and Frts. : May-August

Distribution : India, China and Japan

Sophora japonica L.

Sparteum junceum L.

Deciduous shrub up to 10-12 feet tall. Its long, slender stems are erect with few branches; stems are cylindrical and green when young; mature into woody branches with bark; plants have 1 to several trunks; leaves oval, small, 0.5-1 inch long, ephemeral, remaining on the plant for 4 months or less; inflorescence is an open raceme at the end of branches, with several flowers located on current-year shoots; flowers are large, pea-like, up to 1 inch long, and grow on short stalks on both sides of the main stem; fruit is a linear legume, 2-4 inches long and 5 mm wide, with 10-15 seeds. Spanish broom is native to the Mediterranean region in southern Europe, southwest Asia and northwest Africa, where it is found in sunny sites, usually on dry, sandy soils. Grown in gardens.

Flower colour: Bright yellow

Specimens examined : Bhellum 11141

Locality : Srinagar

Nativity : Mediterranean region

Flrs. and Frts. : May-October

Distribution : India, and Mediterranean region of the world.

Sparteum junceum L.

Trifolium alexandrianum L

Annual herbs, stem herbaceous, hollow ca 60 cm tall or more; leaves trifoliate, margin dentate; flowers dull-white tinged purple, arranged in racemose heads; fruits in pods; cultivated for fodder.

Flower colour : White tinged purple

Specimens examined : Bhellum 10453

Locality : Jammu

Nativity : South America

Flrs. and Frts. : March – April

Distribution : India, Pakistan, Bangladesh, Syria and S. America

T. hybridum L.

Annual or perennial, herbs; stem upto 60 cm tall, glabrous; leaves with 3 leaflets, obovate, rounded at the apex, about 2.5 cm long or more; flowers in axillary or terminal long stalked, globose heads, purple or pinkish-white; calyx lobes 5, awl-shaped glabrous; stamens 10, diadelphous.

Originally introduced for fodder and now found on common waste lands.

Flower colour: Purple or pinkish-white

Specimens examined : Bhellum 11561

Locality : Srinagar

Nativity : Europe and continental Asia

Flrs. and Frts. : April – June

Distribution : India, Europe and Continental Asia

T. tomentosum L.

Annual herbs, stem hollow, herbaceous, flowers purple, calyx inflated, bladder-like, often reddish in fruits; corolla papilionaceous; grows on open places.

Flower colour : Purple

Specimens examined : Bhellum 12461

Locality : Srinagar

Nativity : Europe

Flrs. and Frts. : April – June

Distribution : India, Europe and Continental Asia

Trifolium tomentosum L.

Vicia faba L.

A rigid, erect plant 0.5-1.8 m tall, with stout stems, leaves 10–25 cm long, pinnate with 2-7 leaflets, and of a distinct glaucous grey-green color; unlike most other vetches, the leaves do not have tendrils for climbing over other vegetation; flowers 1-2.5 cm long, with five petals, the standard petal white, the wing petals white with a black spot and the keel petals white, fruits broad leathery pod, green maturing to blackish-brown, with a densely downy surface; in the wild species, the pods are 5–10 cm long and 1 cm diameter, but many modern cultivars developed for food use have pods 15–25 cm long and 2–3 cm thick, each pod contains 3-8 seeds round to oval and 5–10 mm diameter in the wild plant, usually flattened and up to 20–25 mm long, 15 mm broad and 5–10 mm thick in food cultivars.

Flower colour: White with blue spots

Cultivated for vegetable as green pod.

Specimens examined : Bhellum 13451

Locality : Jammu

Nativity : West Asia or Mediterranean region

Flrs. and Frts. : March – April

Distribution : India, Pakistan, Mediterranean region and W. Asia

Vicia faba L.

V. hirsuta Gray

Annual herbs, stem weak, more or less hairy; stem 30 – 70 cm tall; leaves pinnate, the rachis ending in a tendril; leaflets 12– 20 narrowly oblong, obtuse; flowers in racemes, upto 6 in number, white tinged purple; or pale blue; pods oblong, acute, hairy, 2-seeded.

Common in cultivated fields.

Flower colour: White

Specimens examined : Bhellum 10241

Locality : Satwari

Nativity : Europe, West Africa and Continental Asia

Flrs. and Frts. : March-April

Distribution : India, Nepal, Bhutan, Pakistan N. Africa, Congo, Angola, Europe and naturalized in Australia and America.

V. hirsuta Gray

V. sativa L.

Annual herbs, stem weak, climbing; stem upto 60 cm tall or more; glabrous or obscurely puberulous; leaves pinnate,3 – 8 cm long, rachis ending into tendril; leaflets 4 – 6 pairs of upper leaves; flowers bluish-red, solitary rarey in pairs, sessile, in the leaf-axil; pods turgid, glabrous, upto 5 cm long; seeds 8 – 10, dark-brown;

Common in cultivated fields.

Flower colour: Purple pink

Specimens examined : Bhellum 12291

Locality : Satwari

Nativity : Europe, West Africa and Continental Asia

Flrs. and Frts. : March-April

Distribution : India, Nepal, Bhutan, Pakistan N. Africa, Continental Asia and Europe.

Vicia sativa L.

Wisteria sinensis (Sims.) Sweet

Deciduous woody climber; leaves pinnate, having 7 – 13 leaflets, margin entire; inflorescence in drooping racemes; flowers blue-violet; stamens diadelphus, anthers uniform; ovary stipitate, hairy with a lobed disc at the base of the stipe, climbs on walls and huts in the gardens and old houses. Cultivated and now found as an escape.

Flower colour: Mauve coloured

Specimens examined : Bhellum 10762

Locality : Srinagar

Nativity : China

Flrs. and Frts. : April – May

Distribution : India and China

Wisteria sinensis (Sims.) Sweet

Caesalpiniaceae

Bauhinia purpurea L

A medium-sized tree; leaves about 10 – 15 cm long, usually longer than broad, split at the tip into two lobes, the lobes pointed or rounded; flowers showy and rose-purple at the end of the branches; calyx sheath-like, split into two halves; corolla having 5 petals, 4 – 5 cm long, usually one of the petal deeply coloured than the rest; stamens usully 5, usually of these 3 bears anthers and the other two sterile; pods 15 – 25 cm long, flat, purplish at maturity.

Cultivated in most parts of the state for showy fragrant flowers.

Flower colour: Rose-like or Purple

Specimens examined : Bhellum 10781

Locality : Jammu

Nativity : South East Asia

Flrs. and Frts. : July – September

Distribution : India and S.E. Asia

Bauhania purpurea L

B. variegata L.

A medium sized deciduous, tree; leaves simple, cordate, suborbicular, 8 – 11 cm long, glabrous, 2-lobed at apex, lobing upto 1/ 3 of the length of leaf; inflorescence raceme; flowers bisexual, light purple; calyx tube cylindric, ovate, spathaceous, undivided or split into 2 or 3 segments; petals obovate or oblanceolate; stamens 5, well developed, rarely fewer; pods glabrous, 15 – 20 cm long.

Bauhania variegata L.

Cultivated all over the state in the gardens.

Flower colour: White or Purple

Specimens examined : Bhellum 10621

Locality : Jammu

Nativity : China

Flrs. and Frts. : March – April

Distribution : India, Burma, China and Pakistan

Caesalpinia pulcherima Swartz

Shrubs, unarmed, glabrous, erect; leaves 10 – 16 cm long; flowers 3.2 cm across, yellow or red; filaments very long, bright-red; pods, smooth, flattened, dehiscent.

Cultivated as an ornamental.

Flower colour: Yellow or red

Specimens examined : Bhellum 14116

Locality : Ramban

Nativity : Probably America

Flrs. and Frts. : April – November

Distribution : India, Pakistan and America

Caesalpinia pulcherima Swartz

Cassia corymbosa (Lamk.) Irwin & Barneby

Glabrous shrubs or small trees upto 4 m tall; leaves pinnate, leaflets oblong-lanceolate, acute, shortly stalked, glandular pubescent between the lower pairs of leaflets; flowers few in corymbs; petals golden yellow, 1-1.5 cm; pods cylinderic.

Flower colour: Yellow

Specimens examined : Bhellum 14710

Locality : Jammu

Nativity : South America

Flrs. and Frts. : April – November

Distribution : India, Pakistan and South America

Cassia corymbosa Lamk.

C. javanica L.

Perennial medium sized, deciduous trees; btanchlets drooping; leaves pinnate, obtuse.

Flower colour: Yellow

Specimens examined : Bhellum 13506

Locality : Jammu

Nativity : Java and Sumatra

Flrs. and Frts. : April – August

Distribution : India, Pakistan, Java and Sumatra

Cassia javanica L.

C. laevigata Willd.

Shrub 2-3 m high with yellow flowers and pinnate leaves consisting of three or four pairs of ovate leaflets. The pods are cylindrical, 7-10 cm long containing shiny seeds. Widespread in the tropics and extensively browsed by cattle.

Flower colour: Yellow

Specimens examined : Bhellum 14436

Locality : Ramban

Nativity : America

Flrs. and Frts. : April – November

Distribution : India, Pakistan, America, from Mexico to Brazil

C. occidentalis L.

Annual or perennial herbs, unarmed, erect, foetid; stem angular, 0.5 – 1.5 m tall; leaves unipinnately compound, leaflets 6 – 12 ovate or ovate-oblong, cuneate, acuminate; glabrous; flowers in axillary or terminal racemes, yellow; bracts lanceolate, acuminate; pods upto 16 cm long, compressed laterally. Grows wild, common on wastelands.

Flower colour: Yellow

Specimens examined : Bhellum 10685

Locality : Jammu

Nativity : South America

Flrs. and Frts. : May-August

Distribution : India and S. America

Cassia occidentalis L.

Parkinsonia aculeata L.

Shrub or evergreen small tree; bark, thin, smooth,branches green, glabrous armed with spines; leaves vigorous, usually with 2 pairs of pinnae, congested at he base of the rachis, crowed on dwarf axillary shoots, leaflets 25 – 30 pairs, minute to 5 cm long, oblong, obovate, or obovate; flowers yellow in lax axillary racemes; calyx 5 lobed, cleft deep, segments, oblong, deciduous; petals broadly obovate, or suborbicular; ovary stipitate, silky villous; pods 2.5 - 10 cm long.

Cultivated for bright showy flowers and graceful foliage.

Flower colour: Bright yellow

Specimens examined : Bhellum 10386

Locality : Chakrohi, Jammu

Nativity : America

Flrs. and Frts. : May – August

Distribution : India, Pakistan, America

Parkinsonia aculeata L.

Delonix regia Raf.

A large elegant tree; leaves compound, pinnate, upto 50 cm long or more, pinnae 10 – 20 pairs each pinna bears bears 20 – 30 light green leaflets; flowers in large racemes at the end of the braches each flower reach 10 – 12 cm across; calyx encloses the petals before opening, the inside of the calyx bright scarlet; petals bright scarlet, the standard slightly larger in size and variegated red and yellow in colour, spoon-shaped with crinkled margins; stamens 10, filament unequal, anther yellow; fruit a large pod.

Flower colour: Bright scarlet.

Flower colour: Red and yellow or bright scarlet

Specimens examined : Bhellum 10621

Locality : Jammu

Nativity : Madagascar

Flrs. and Frts. : March – April

Distribution : India, Pakistan and Madagascar.

Delonix regia Raf.

Cercis siliquastrum L.

Deciduous shrub or small tree; leaves reniform, upto 15 cm across, often broader than long; flowers from the old wood, dark purple; pods about 10 cm long, upper suture narrowly winged.

Grown as a novelty, flowers emerging from the bark.

Flower colour: Purple

Specimens examined : Bhellum 11930

Locality : Srinagar

Nativity : South Europe and Orient

Flrs. and Frts. : May-August

Distribution : India, Pakistan and Europe

Cercis siliquastrum L.

Tamarindus indica L.

Deciduous shrub or small evergreen, tree; leaves paripinnate, leaflets 10 – 12 pairs, oblong; flowers in lax 10 – 12 flowered racemes; flowers variegated yellow or pale yellow tinged with red; calyx tube turbinate, teeth lanceolate; petals pale yellow tinged with red; stamens monadelphous, 3 perfect, the others reduced to bristles; pods 7 – 20 cm long, compressed, curved, brown, indehiscent.

A beautiful, roadside plant.

Flower colour: yellow or pale yellow tinged with red

Specimens examined : Bhellum 11201

Locality : Miran Sahib

Nativity : Tropical Africa

Flrs. and Frts. : July-November

Distribution : India, Tropical Africa

Tamarindus indica L.

Mimosaceae

Acacia auriculiformis A. Cann.

A tree; phyllode 12 – 20 cm long, and about 1.4 – 5 cm broad, falcate, narrowed at both the ends, veins parallel; flowers yellow, arranged in spikes, panicled at the tips of the branches; pods springly curved.

Acacia auriculiformis A. Cann.

Flower colour: Yellow

Specimens examined : Bhellum 14516

Locality : Jammu

Nativity : Temperate Australia

Flrs. and Frts. : April – November

Distribution : India, Australia,

A. farnesiana (L.) Willd.

An evergreen shrub; bark dark-grey, smooth, branches slightly zig-zag, marked with pale grey or pale brown dots, young twigs glabrescent; spines stipular in pairs below the petiole; leaves compound, 2 – 8 pairs leaflets linear, oblong, acute, glabrous; flowers yellow, fragrant, in globose paniculate heads; calyx campanulate; corolla yellow; pods subcylindric 5 – 7.5 cm long, turgid, black-brown.

Flower colour: Yellow

Specimens examined : Bhellum 10624

Locality : Jammu

Nativity : Tropical America

Flrs. and Frts. : March – April

Distribution : India and Tropical America.

Acacia farnesiana (L.) Willd.

A. nilotica (L.) Willd. Ex Delile

Large deciduous armed trees; bark dark-brown, rough fissures longitudinal; stipular spine straight; leaves compound, bipinnate, pinnae of first order upto 7 pairs, pinnules 18 – 25 pairs, linear acute; flowers in globose heads, golden coloured; fruits distinctly stalked tomentum grey-pubescent, constricted between the seeds.

Flower colour: yellow

Specimens examined : Bhellum 10690

Locality : Jammu

Nativity : North America, North Africa & Arab

Flrs. and Frts. : July-August

Distribution : India, North America, Africa and Arab

Acacia nilotica (L.) Willd. Ex Delile

Albizia julibrissin Durazz.

Deciduous unarmed, small tree; bark dark-grey; leaves compound, 15 – 30 cm long; leaflets in 6 – 12 pairs or more, oblique, oblong, base rounded, apex acute; flowers in globose heads, pink; calyx tubular shortly toothed; stamens monadelphous, far protruded, tinged pink; pods 7 – 12 cm long, linear, thin, 8 – 12 seeded.

Flower colour: Pink

Specimens examined : Bhellum 14841

Locality : Batote

Nativity : Persia, Central China and Asia

Flrs. and Frts. : May-October

Distribution : India, Persia, Central China and Asia.

Albizia julibrissin Durazz.

Leucaenia latisiliqua (L.) Gilles

Shrubs or trees, 2-5 m tall; branches grey-green; leaves ca. 9-20 pairs, leaflets linear-oblong to lanceolate; petals crreamy white; inflorescence in axillary 4-10 heads; legumes 10-15 cm long.

Flower colour: Cream coloured

Specimens examined : Bhellum 10621

Locality : Jammu

Nativity : South America

Flrs. and Frts. : March – May

Distribution : India, Pakistan and S. America

Mimosa pudica L.

An undershrub; leaves pinnate, pinnae 1 or 2 pairs, sensitive, arising at the ends of the rachis so as to appear digitate; flowers pink or purplish pink

Grown as an ornamental in the gardens. The species has run wild in many parts of the country.

Flower colour: Purple

Specimens examined : Bhellum 10345

Locality : Jammu

Nativity : Tropical America

Flrs. and Frts. : April – August

Distribution : India, Pakistan, Tropical America

Mimosa pudica L.

Rosaceae

Agrimonia nepalesis D. Don

Perenial hairy herbs; leaves pinnately compound; stipule adnate with the base of the tube; flowers in terminal spike-like racemes; calyx-tube with top-shaped; corolla with 5 petals.

Flower colour: White

Specimens examined : Bhellum 12655

Locality : Srinagar

Nativity : Nepal

Flrs. and Frts. : April – May

Distribution : India, Pakistan, Nepal, Thailand, China (Tibet), Japan, and Korea

Cotoneaster acuminatus Lindl.

A large shrub; with slender branches; leaves crowded, lanceolate, long pointed; flowers white arranged cymes on short flattened leafy branchlets; fruits onlong, red when ripe.

Flower colour : White

Specimens examined : Bhellum 11389

Locality : Srinagar

Nativity : Nepal

Flrs. and Frts. : April – May

Distribution : India, Pakistan, Nepal, Bhutan, Burma and West China

Cotoneaster acuminatus Lindl.

C. afghanicus Klotz.

Perennial erect, shrubs; leaves simple, margin entire; flowers white, sepals 5; petals 5; stamens numerous; fruits yellow turning black.

Flower colour: White

Specimens examined : Bhellum 12678

Locality : Srinagar

Nativity : China and Japan

Flrs. and Frts. : April – May

Distribution : India, Pakistan and Afghanistan

C. kaganensis Klotz.

Perennial shrubs; leaves simple, margin entire; flowers white; sepals 5; petals 5; stamens numerous.

Flower colour: White

Specimens examined : Bhellum 12438

Locality : Srinagar

Nativity : Pakistan

Flrs. and Frts. : April – May

Distribution : India

C. integrrimus Medik.

Perennial, erect, bushy shrubs; leaves ovate, pubescent; cymes short, few flowered; fruits glabrous, black or red.

Flower colour: White

Specimens examined : Bhellum 11458

Locality : Srinagar

Nativity : Europe

Flrs. and Frts. : April – May

Distribution : India

Cotoneaster integrrimus Medik.

C. microphyllus Wall. ex Lindl.

A small shrub; branches many, dense; leaves hard, very variable in size, ovate, acute or obtuse, usually coriaceous, shining above and glabrous beneath except in nerves; flwers white; fruits globose, bright red.

Flower colour: White

Specimens examined : Bhellum 11646

Locality : Srinagar

Nativity : Nepal

Flrs. and Frts. : April – May

Distribution : India, Nepal, Bhutan, Burma and China

Cotoneaster microphyllus Wall. ex Lindl.

C. pruinosus Klotz.

Perennial shrubs; branches many from the base; flowers white; fruits globose.

Flower colour: White

Specimens examined : Bhellum 10689

Locality : Srinagar

Nativity : India and North Pakistan

Flrs. and Frts. : April – May

Distribution : India

Cydonia oblonga Mill.

A large deciduous, shrub; young shoots tomentose; leaves simple, 5 – 10 cm long, ovate or ovate-elliptic, base rounded or cordat, entire, dark-green, glabrous above and tomentose beneath; flowers 5 cm across, white or pinkish; calyx tomentose; corolla with 5 petals; stamens many; fruit a pome, pyriform, ribbed, depressed at the apex, clothed with grey or wooly tomentum.

Flower colour: White or pinkish

Specimens examined : Bhellum 10641

Locality : Srinagar

Nativity : South Europe and Asia; however Parker is of opinion that it is probably indigenous to Persia and Turkestan.

Flrs. and Frts. : April-July

Distribution : India, S. Europe and Asia

Cydonia oblonga Mill.

Eriobotrya japonica (Thunb.) Lindley

A small, evergreen tree; leaves narrowly oblanceolate, apex acuminate, margin serrate; inflorescence in terminal panicles; flowers 1.2 cm across, white, fragrant; ovary 2 – 5 celled, styles 5, connate and wooly below; fruit succulent, pyriform, yellow; seeds 2 – 5 large, anguar.

Cultivated for its fruits in the plains of Jammu region.

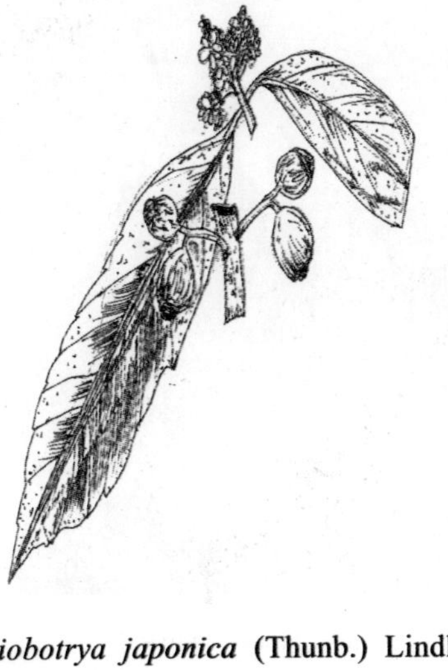

Eriobotrya japonica (Thunb.) Lindley

Flower colour: White

Specimens examined : Bhellum 10289

Locality : Banihal

Nativity : Japan and China

Flrs. and Frts. : April – November

Distribution : India, Japan and China

Fragaria vesica L.

Erect or ascending perennial, stoloniferous herbs; leaves 3-foliate; leaflets sessile, or petiolulate, sparsely hairy or glabrescent above, pubescent beneath, margin toothed; petioles 4 – 10 cm long or more; covered with spreading or appressed hairs; flowers yellow, 1 – 3, pedicellate, bracteoles entire or toothed; calyx 5-lobed, silky-hairy; petals rhomboic-ovate, slightly longer than calyx; berries reddish brown.

Flower colour: Yellow

Specimens examined : Bhellum 10725

Locality : Batote

Nativity : Temperate Europe, Western Asia and East of North America

Flrs. and Frts. : May-June

Distribution : India, W. Asia, Europe and N. America

Fragaria vesica L.

Kerria japonica (L.) DC.

A deciduous shrub; branches slender, straight, green; leaves 3.5 – 7.5 cm long, ovate, lanceolate, coarsely biserrate, apex acuminate; flowers yellow about 2.4 cm across.

Commonly grown along hedges for its foliage and branches.

Flower colour: Orange yellow

Specimens examined : Bhellum 10750

Locality : Srinagar

Nativity : Japan

Flrs. and Frts. : April -July

Distribution : India and Japan

Kerria japonica (L.) DC.

Malus pumila Mill.

Small, deciduous trees; leaves ovate, elliptic, margin crenate or serrate, apex acuminate; flowers in umbels or fascicles on leafy shoots; fruits globose.

Apple is found under cultivation in Kashmir.

Flower colour: White-pinkish

Specimens examined : Bhellum 10121

Locality : Srinagar

Nativity : Caucasus

Flrs. and Frts. : April-July

Distribution : India, Pakistan, Caucasus and Afghanistan

Malus pumila Mill.

Rosa chinensis Jacquin

Erect shrubs, 1–2 m tall. Branchlets purple-brown, terete, robust, subglabrous; prickles abundant to absent, curved, stout, flat, leaves including petiole 5–11 cm; stipules mostly adnate to petiole, free parts auriculate, margin entire, often glandular-pubescent, apex acuminate; rachis and petiole sparsely prickly and glandular-pubescent; leaflets 3–5, rarely 7, greenish abaxially, dark green adaxially, broadly ovate or ovate-oblong, 2.5–6 × 1–3 cm, both surfaces subglabrous, adaxially often shiny, base subrounded or broadly cuneate, margin acutely serrate, apex long acuminate or acuminate; flowers 4 or 5 and fasciculate, rarely solitary, slightly fragrant or not, 4–5 cm in diam.; Petals 5, red, pink, white, or purple, obovate, base cuneate, apex emarginate. Styles free, exserted, nearly equaling stamens, pubescent. fruit ovoid or pyriform, 1–2 cm in diam., glabrous.

Flower colour: Pink, white or purple

Specimens examined : Bhellum 12567

Locality : Jammu

Nativity : China

Flrs. and Frts. : March – September

Distribution : India, Pakistan and China

R. laevigata Mchx.

An evergreen scandant shrub, armed with curved prickles; leaflet on flowering shoot 3, dark-green, glabrous and shining above; flowers solitary, white, 4 – 7 cm across.

Flower colour: White

Specimens examined : Bhellum 11356

Locality : Jammu

Nativity : China

Flrs. and Frts. : March – August

Distribution : India, Pakistan and China

Rosa laevigata Mchx.

Prunus armeniaca L.

A medium sized tree; leaves broadly ovate, acuminate, margin crenate, glandular hairy on the nerves beneath, when young, sometimes sparsely hispid above; stipule lanceolate, glandular on margins; flowers appearing, before the leaves, solitary, or in fascicles, pinkish at first turning white with age; calyx tube campanulate, lobes rounded, pubescent; petals suborbicular; stamens inserted on the mouth of the corolla tube; drupe downy or glabrous, yellow tinged with red.

Cultivated and occasionally self-sown and still not naturalized.

Flower colour: Pinkish at first turning white with age.

Specimens examined : Bhellum 13230

Locality : Ramban

Nativity : China

Flrs. and Frts. : May-August

Distribution : India, Pakistan, China and Afghanistan

Prunus armeniaca L.

P. avium L.

A deciduous tree; leaves flaccid, coarsely serrate; petioles with two large glands near the top; flowers appear before the leaves; calyx-lobes 5, entire; fruits red berries turning black later.

Cultivated in the hilly areas.

Flower colour: White

Specimens examined : Bhellum 10255

Locality : Srinagar

Nativity : S. Europe and W. Asia

Flrs. and Frts. : May-August

Distribution : India, Pakistan and Afghanistan

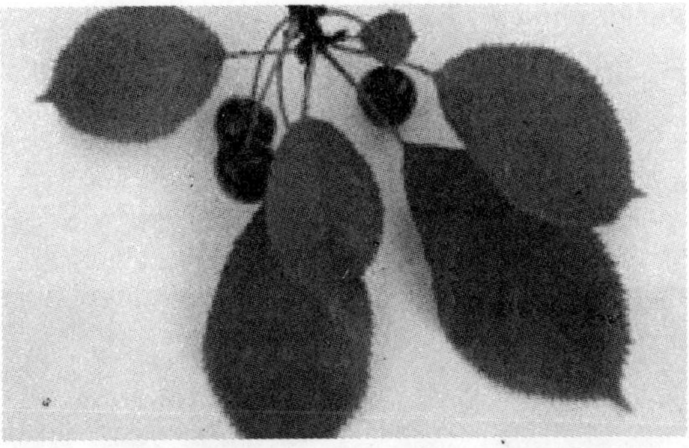

Prunus avium L.

Sorbus domestica L.

A deciduous spreading tree; leaves pinnate, leaflets serrate, floccose tomentose beneath; flowers white; fruits 1.5-3 cm long, pyriform.

Flower colour: White

Specimens examined : Bhellum 13221

Locality : Srinagar

Nativity : S. Europe, W. Asia and N. Africa

Flrs. and Frts. : July. – August

Distribution : India, S. Europe, W. Asia and N. Africa

Sorbus domestica L.

Spiraea cantoniensis Lour.

A deciduous shrub with arching branching; flowers white about 3 – 4 mm across arranged in dense umbels; pedicel slender 1.2 cm long.

Flower colour: White

Specimens examined : Bhellum 10689

Locality : Srinagar

Nativity : China and Japan

Flrs. and Frts. : April – May

Distribution : India, China

Spiraea cantoniensis Lour.

S. gracilis Maxim.

A slender nearly glabrous herb; branches terete; leaves elliptic-oblong, rounded, glabrous; flowers white, bisexual, arranged in simple corymbs; stamens longer than the petals; disc conspicuous.

Flower colour: White

Specimens examined : Bhellum 12580

Locality : Srinagar

Nativity : Nepal

Flrs. and Frts. : April – May

Distribution : India and Nepal

S. prunifolia L.

Shrubs; leaves ca 2.6 cm long, elliptic, bright glossy green above, finely and sharply serrate; flowers in sessile umbles; flowers white.

Flower colour: White

Specimens examined : Bhellum 12632

Locality : Srinagar

Nativity : China

Flrs. and Frts. : April – May

Distribution : India and China

Spiraea prunifolia L.

Saxifragaceae

Astibe rivularis Ham ex D. Don

Erect, hairy herbs; rootstock perennial; leaves alternate, irregularly 2-pinnate; stipule large membranous; leaflets ovate, sometimes lobed, cordate, sharply and unequally toothed; flowers minute, bisexual sometimes unisexual, greenish yellow; stamens 5, opposite the sepals; capsule small, 2-beaked.

Flower colour: greenish-white

Specimens examined : Bhellum 10442

Locality : Srinagar

Nativity : Nepal

Flrs. and Frts. : April – August

Distribution : India, Western Himalaya and Bhutan.

Astibe rivularis Ham. ex D. Don

Bergenia ciliata (Haw.) Sternb. f. *ciliata*

Rootstock very thick; stem short, thick, very fleshy; leaves ovate or orbicular, margin entire, fringed with short stiff hairs; flowers white or pinkish-purple arranged in a spreading terminal scape about 4-10 cm long.

Flower colour: Pinkish tinged purple

Specimens examined : Bhellum 10123

Locality : Srinagar

Nativity : Nepal

Flrs. and Frts. : April – November

Distribution : India and other temperate Himalayan regions.

B. ciliata (Haw.) Sternb. f. *ligulata*

Rootstock very thick; stem short, thick, very fleshy; leaves ovate or orbicular, margin entire, fringed with short stiff hairs; flowers white or pinkish-purple

Flower colour: Pinkish tinged purple

Specimens examined : Bhellum 10293

Locality : Srinagar

Nativity : Nepal

Flrs. and Frts. : April – August

Distribution : India, temperate Himalaya, Bhutan and Afghanistan

Bergenia ciliata (Haw.) Sternb. f. *ligulata*

Saxifraga afghanica Aitch. & Hemsl.

Plants many branched, with crowded shoots forming cushions, flowering stem 0.8-2.5 cm, glandular hairy; leaves aggregated into a rosette, oblong to subspatulate, 4-7 × 1.3-2 mm, leathery, both surfaces glabrous, chalk glands 5, margin denticulate-ciliate proximally or glabrous, apex recurved, obtuse, Cauline leaves lanceolate-oblong, 3.5-5 × ca. 1 mm, chalk gland 1, margin glandular hairy proximally, apex obtuse or acute. Cyme (2-4-flowered, rarely flower solitary; branches ca. 1 cm. Sepals erect, purple, oblong to sublanceolate, 2-3 × 1-1.4 mm, abaxially and marginally sparsely glandular pilose, veins 3, not confluent at apex, apex acute, petals usually pink, obovate, ca. 5 × 2.5-3.3 mm, 5-veined, base gradually narrowed into a short claw, apex obtuse. Stamens 3-3.5 mm. Ovary semi-inferior; styles 1.5-2.2 mm.

Flower colour: Grey - Purple

Specimens examined : Bhellum 10293

Locality : Srinagar

Nativity : Afghanistan and Pakistan

Flrs. and Frts. : April – August

Distribution : India, Afghanistan and Pakistan

S. androsacea L.

Caespitose, herb, 2-7 cm high. Leaves 5-10 mm long, obovate, spathulate to oblanceolate, entire or tri-lobed apically, sparsely glandular-ciliate;. Scape 1-2.5 cm long, erect, sparsely glandular, with 0-2 leaves. Flowers 1-3, bracteate. Calyx campanulate, sepals 2 mm long, oblong, obtuse, adnate below, glandular pubescent. Petals white, 5 mm long, oblong to obovate, base cuneate. Stamens longer or shorter than the sepals. Styles long, divergent.

Saxifraga androsacea Linn.

Flower colour: White

Specimens examined : Bhellum 11093

Locality : Srinagar

Nativity : Europe and Asia

Flrs. and Frts. : April – November

Distribution : India, Europe and Asia.

S. brunonis Wall. ex Seringe

Herb, 5-10 cm high, with red, slender; leafless runners, terminating in a bud; leaves basally crowded, sessile, 7-11 mm long, elliptic-lanceolate, setose-ciliate, apex aristate, surfaces glabrous, flowers yellow, 2-4, in corymbs, pedicels 1-3 cm long, glandular. Sepals 3 mm long, ovate, obtuse, glabrous, basally united. Petals 7 mm long, ovate, capsule ca. 4 mm long. Seeds ellipsoid, very minutely papillose.

Flower colour: Pinkish tinged purple

Specimens examined : Bhellum 10293

Locality : Srinagar

Nativity : Nepal

Flrs. and Frts. : April – October

Distribution : India, Nepal and temperate Himalaya.

Saxifraga filicaulis Wall. ex Ser.

Branched annual with tufted growth, 7-10 cm high, stems glandular-pilose to glabrous, slender and wiry, leaves numerous, 5-6 mm long, alternate, sessile, linear-lanceolate, sparsely ciliate, surfaces usually glabrous, apex spinescent, bulbils present in leaf axils, flowers bright yellow, solitary, terminal, sepals c. 3 mm long, ovate, petals 7 mm long, ovate, base unguiculate, styles slender, 3 mm long, divergent; stigma capitate.

Flower colour: Bright yellow

Specimens examined : Bhellum 12213

Locality : Srinagar

Nativity : Nepal

Flrs. and Frts. : April – October

Distribution : India, and other parts of alpine Western Himalaya.

S. hirculus L.

Plants erect, 10-40 cm tall, with tufted growth; runners prostrate, hairy or not, basal leaves 8-15 mm long, glabrous, lanceolate, petiole sheathing. Cauline leaves sessile, oblong to lanceolate, brown-villous at the base, stem and pedicels brown villous, flowers 1-4, yellow, spotted reddish orange, sepals free, 3-4 mm long, oblong, margin brown-villous, petals 8-10 (-12) mm long, broadly elliptic, obtuse, stamens as long as or longer than the sepals, styles c. 1 mm long, capsule c. 1 cm long.

Distributed in the arctic and sub-arctic regions of Europe, Caucasus and C. Asia.

Saxifraga hirculus L.

Flower colour: Bright yellow

Specimens examined : Bhellum 1291

Locality : Srinagar

Nativity : Europe

Flrs. and Frts. : April – November

Distribution : India, Afghanistan and distributed in the arctic and sub-arctic regions of Europe, Caucasus and C. Asia and Schonbeck-Temesy.

S. sibirica L.

Flower colour: White

Specimens examined : Bhellum 11263

Locality : Srinagar

Nativity : Siberia

Flrs. and Frts. : April – October

Distribution : India and Sieberia

Saxifraga sibirica L.

Parnassiaceae

Parnassia palustris L,

Parnassia palustris Linn.

Plants 11-40 cm tall, radical leaves broadly cordate, 1-2 cm long, 0.6-l.8 cm broad, somewhat glaucous, cauline leaf situated below the middle of the scape. Scape angular, flowers 1.5-2 cm in across, calyx tube c.1 mm long, lobes 4-5 mm long, c.2-2.5 mm broad, elliptic, acute, brown spotted, petals 0.7-1 cm long, 5-7 mm broad, oblong-ovate, obtuse, usually 9 nerved, nerves mostly parallel and convergent at the top; staminodes spathulate, ending in 9-17 lobes tipped with pseudo-nectaries, capsule globose, c.1 cm long; seeds minute, somewhat cylindrical, testa loose, reticulate.

Flower colour: White

Specimens examined : Bhellum 10621

Locality : Jammu

Nativity : Europe

Flrs. and Frts. : May – August

Distribution : India, N. Asia, N. America and Europe.

Parnassia palustris L,

P. nubicola Wall. ex Royle

A glabrous herb; rootstock perennial; leaves radicle, long stalked, ovate or oblong-ovate; cordate entire actue; scape erect slender; flowers greenish yellow; calyx-tube adnate to the base of the ovary; sepals 5; petals 5, white; stamens 5, with 3 flattened fleshy staminodes; ovary ovoid, style short; capsule obovoid.

Flower colour: White

Specimens examined : Bhellum 10621

Locality : Jammu

Nativity : Afghanistan and Pakistan

Flrs. and Frts. : May – August

Distribution : India, Afghanisstan and Pakistan

Philadelphaceae

Deutzia scabra Thunb.

Erect shrubs; leaves opposite; flowers white, arranged in numerous panicles; calyx tube adnate to the ovary; stamens ca 8; ovary 1-celled, styles 2. fruits capsule.

Flower colour: White or Pink

Specimens examined : Bhellum 13512

Locality : Srinagar

Nativity : Japan

Flrs. and Frts. : May – October

Distribution : India, Pakistan, Afghanistan and Japan

D. staminea R. Br. ex Wall.

Erect shrubs, more or less stellately hairy; branches opposite; leaves simple, ovate, lancelate, long pointed, margin serrate; flowers in numerous panicles; flowers whit; ovary inferior, capsule globose, opening by 3-5 vlaves.

Deutzia staminea R. Br.ex Wall.

Flower colour: White

Specimens examined : Bhellum 12618

Locality : Srinagar

Nativity : America

Flrs. and Frts. : May – October

Distribution : India, Pakistan Afghanistan and America

Philadelphus confusus Pipe

Deciduous shrubs with 3-8 cm long leaves; flowers in 5-9 flowered cymes.

Specimens examined : Bhellum 11612

Locality : Srinagar

Nativity : America

Flrs. and Frts. : May – October

Distribution : India, Pakistan and America

P. confucius Piper var. *intectus* (Beadle) Moore

Deciduous shrubs; leaves opposite, serrate; flowers white

Flower colour: White

Flower colour:

Specimens examined : Bhellum 10698

Locality : Srinagar

Nativity : America

Flrs. and Frts. : April – November

Distribution : India and America

P. incanus Koehne.

Shrubs upto 4 m tall; branchlets brownish-purple turning grey-brown with age; leaves broadly ovate, densely white villous, margin serrate, apex abruptly acuminate; flowers in racemes; corolla white; capsule obovoid.

Flower colour: white

Specimens examined : Bhellum 12786

Locality : Srinagar

Nativity : China

Flrs. and Frts. : April – July

Distribution : India

Philadelphus incanus Koehne.

Crassulaceae

Kalanchoe verticillata Elliot

Perennial, glabrous herbs; stem succulent, upto 1.2 m in height; leaves alternate, simple, greenish ro dull green spotted dark green or red; inflorescence in cymes; corolla reddish or pale-yellow or red; stamens inserted on the base of corolla tube; seeds obovoid.

Flower colour: Yellow

Specimens examined : Bhellum 10675

Locality : Jammu

Nativity : South africa

Flrs. and Frts. : March – August

Distribution : India

Kalanchoe verticillata Elliot

Sedum japonicum Sieb.

Tufted, perennial herbs upto 16 cm tall; leaves brighter green; flowers yellow; grown as an ornamental plant, grows occasionally on rocky situations.

Flower colour: Yellow

Specimens examined : Bhellum 12567

Locality : Jammu

Nativity : Japan

Flrs. and Frts. : March – August

Distribution : India, Pakistan, Japan and China

Sedum japonicum Sieb.

Combretaceae

Quisqualis indica L.

Climbing tall subscandant, woody shrubs, leaves opposite, elliptic, obovate acuminate rusty pubescent beneath and on nerves above; flowers white-red, first white and turning pink with age arranged in terminal spikes; calyx-tube slender, limb 5-toothed; petals obovate oblong; stamens 10, shortly exserted 5, opposite the petals, 5-included or subincluded.

Flower colour: White- red

Specimens examined : Bhellum 11478

Locality : Jammu

Nativity : Burma, Malaya, New Guinea and Philipines

Flrs. and Frts. : May – September

Distribution : India, Burma, Malaya, New Guinea and Philipines

Quisqualis indica L.

Myrtaceae

Callistemon citrinus (Curt.) Stapf

An ornamental shrub or small tree; leaves linear, lanceolate,; stamens exserted; spikes resembles a brush; cultivated in the gardens for flowers.

Flower colour: Red

Specimens examined : Bhellum 11671

Locality : Jammu

Nativity Australia

Flrs. and Frts. : May – September

Distribution : India

Callistemon citrinus (Curt.) Stapf

Eucalyptus citriodora Hook.

Evergreen trees, often reaching a gigantic size; leaves usually alternate, penninerved, more or less falcate, usullly secreting aromatic resinous gums; flowers eracteate, white arranged in simple or paniculate umbels; calyx-tube adnate to the ovary; stamens many in various rows; fruits capsules opening by valves at the top.

Flower colour: White

Specimens examined : Bhellum 11972

Locality : Jammu

Nativity : Australia and Queenland.

Flrs. and Frts. : May – August

Distribution : India

Eucalyptus citriodora Hook.

Psidium guayava L.

Shrub, or small evergreen tree, generally 3-10 m high, many branches; stems crooked, bark light to reddish brown, thin, smooth, continuously flaking; root system generally superficial and very extensive, frequently extending well beyond the canopy, there are some deep roots but no distinct taproot. Leaves opposite, simple; stipules absent, petiole short,

3-10 mm long; blade oblong to elliptic, 5-15 x 4-6 cm, apex obtuse to bluntly acuminate, base rounded to subcuneate, margins entire, somewhat thick and leathery, dull grey to yellow-green above, slightly downy below, veins prominent, gland dotted. Inflorescence, axillary, 1- to 3-flowered, pedicles about 2 cm long, bracts 2, linear. Calyx splitting irregularly into 2-4 lobes, whitish and sparsely hairy within; petals 4-5, white, linear-ovate c. 2 cm long, delicate; stamens numerous, filaments pale white, about 12 mm long, erect or spreading, anther straw coloured; ovary inferior, ovules numerous, style about 10 cm long, stigma green, capitate. Fruit an ovoid or pear-shaped berry, 4-12 cm long.

Flower colour: White

Specimens examined : Bhellum 14216

Locality : Jammu

Nativity : Mexico

Flrs. and Frts. : April – August

Distribution : India

Psidium guayava L.

Lythraceae

Ammannia auriculata Willd.

Erect, glabrous herbs; stem quadrangular, usually branched; leaves opposite, oblong, linear –lanceolate, 1 – 5 cm long, auricled at base; inflorescence cymes; flowers pink; calyx campanulate, with 4 – 8 green ribs; petals cuneate or absent; stamens 6 or 8; capsule globose, longer than calyx tube, operculate or irregularly dehiscent; seeds discoid, brown.

Flower colour: Pink

Specimens examined : Bhellum 10621

Locality : R. S. Pura

Nativity : China

Flrs. and Frts. : May – August

Distribution : India, Pakistan and China

Lagerstroemia indica L.

Trees or shrubs; leaves opposite or nearly so; leaves 3-5 cm long or more elliptic oblong, sessile; flowers in axillary or terminal clusters, 2.5 – 3.5 cm across, white to rose pink; calyx tube about 6 mm long, angled, but not clearly ribbed; petals with 7 – 10 mm calw; fruits capsule, subglobose, coriaceous.

Flower colour: White to rose pink

Specimens examined : Bhellum 10621

Locality : R. S. Pura

Nativity : China

Flrs. and Frts. : May – August

Distribution : India,

Lathyrum salicaria L.

Herbs, usually 1-1.5 m tall, forming numerous erect stems growing from a single woody root, stems are reddish-purple or red to purple and square in cross-section, leaves are lanceolate, 3–10 cm long and 5–15 mm broad, downy and sessile, and arranged opposite or in whorls of three.Flowers are reddish purple, 10–20 mm diameter, with six petals (occasionally five) and 12 stamens, capsule small 3–4 mm, containing numerous minute seeds.

Flower colour: reddish purple

Specimens examined : Bhellum 15121

Locality : R.S. Pura

Nativity : Europe

Flrs. and Frts. : May – August

Distribution : India

Lawsonia inermis L.

A glabrous shrub, twigs quadrangular, often ending in thorn; leaves opposite, elliptic, rhomboid, broadly lanceolate, acute or obtuse, flowers of variable colour white creamy or rosy, fragrant, in terminal or pyramidal panicles; sepals 2 – 3 mm long, ovate, acute, persistent; petals 3 mm across; stamens 8 ; capsule 6 – 9 mm across; Very widely cultivated in the plains of the Punjab. Used as a hedge plant and pruned for dense branching, as a rare case, the plant has been seen a small tree where it was growing without pruning.

Flower colour: White, creamy or rose-coloured

Specimens examined : Bhellum 11216

Locality : Jammu

Nativity : Probably Persia

Flrs. and Frts. : April – July

Distribution : India

Woodfordia fruticosa (L.) S. Kurz

An evergreen shrub, bark peeling off in thin fibrous stripes; leaves opposite or in whorls of three, lanceolate, oblong-lanceolate or ovate-lanceolate, base cordate, apex acuminate, glabrous above with black dots scattered on surface; flowers red in dense axillary clusters; fruits capsule, splitting irregularly in the lower portion.

Flower colour: Red

Specimens examined : Bhellum 13236

Locality : Jammu

Nativity : Egypt

Flrs. and Frts. : April – June

Distribution : India, Pakistan tropical Africa Madagascar, China, Japan, Sumatra, Java and Ceylon.

Punicaceae

Punica granatum L.

A large deciduous shrub, often armed with axillary or terminal thorns; leaves opposite, oblong-lanceolate, glabrous, entire minutely pellucid-punctate, shining above, deep-green beneath; flowers 3-5 cm long and as much across; fruits globose, tipped with calyx limb; seeds with a watery outer coat, juice pink and inner coat horny.

Flower colour: Red

Specimens examined : Bhellum 10584

Locality : Jammu

Nativity : Afghanistan, Baluchistan and Persia

Flrs. and Frts. : March – August

Distribution : India, Baluchistan, Persia, Afghanistan, and subtropical regions.

Punica granatum L.

Onagraceae

Oenothera biennis L.

Perennial, herbs; stem usually many from the base; leaves alternate, basal leaves lyrately lobed, petiolate, cauline ovate, lanceolate, pubescent on both surfaces, margin entire, minutely dentate or undulate; flowers solitary axillary, pink, red or yellow; fruit a capsule, pubescent, 4-angular, opening by 4-valves; seeds many per capsule.

Flower colour: Yellow

Specimens examined : Bhellum 10582

Locality : Jammu

Nativity : N. America

Flrs. and Frts. : May – August

Distribution : India and N America

Oenothera biennis L.

Passifloraceae

Passiflora edulis L.

Evergreen, Climbing vine that clings by tendrils to almost any support, leaves are alternate, deeply 3-lobed when mature and finely toothed,, 3 to 8 inches long, deep green and glossy above, paler and dull beneath and, like the young stems and tendrils, tinged with red or purple, specially in the yellow form, single, fragrant flower, the bloom, clasped by 3 large, green, lifelike bracts, consists of 5 greenish-white sepals, 5 white petals and a fringelike corona of straight, white-tipped rays, rich purple at the base. ovary and triple-branched style forming a prominent central structure.

The passion fruit is a vigorous The fruit can be grown to eat or for its juice, which is often added to other fruit juices to enhance aroma. The unique flavor is appealing, musky, guava-like and sweet. Passion fruit is cultivated commercially for its fruit.

Passiflora edulis L.

Flower colour: White, purple

Specimens examined : Bhellum 13585

Locality : Jammu

Nativity : Tropical America

Flrs. and Frts. : May – August

Distribution : India, Tropical America, Northwestern South America, the Caribbean, Brazil, southern Florida, Hawaii, Australia, East Africa, Israel and South Africa.

Caricaceae

Carica papaya L.

An unbranched dioecious, shrub; juice milky; stem with large leaf scars; leaves palmately lobed, 22 – 75 cm wide, glabrous, petioled; male flowers in axillary panicles, rarely mixed with bisexuals, female solitary or in axillary cymes; bisexual with coroalla 3 – 3.5 cm long; staminal filament 6 – 9 mm long; ovary 1-celled, 2 – 3 cm long, glabrous, stigma spreading, many lobed yellow; berries yellow when ripe, pulp orange; seeds black.

Carica papaya L.

Flower colour: Pale yellow

Specimens examined : Bhellum 11852

Locality : Jammu

Nativity Central America and West Indies

Flrs. and Frts. : May – November

Distribution : India

Cactaceae

Cereus peruvianus Mill.

Erect glabrous; branches erect, parallel dull-bluish green; prickles at first about 8 in each tuft;

Flower colour: White

Specimens examined : Bhellum 11623

Locality : Jammu

Nativity : Tropical America

Flrs. and Frts. : May – August

Distribution : India, Pakistan and Tropical America

Cereus peruvianus Mill.

C. triangularis Haw.

A succulent climber, climbing by adventitious roots; branches 3-angled; prickles tufted; flowers large 10 – 15 cm across, very fragrant nocturnal; fruits ovoid edible.

Flower colour: White

Specimens examined : Bhellum 10097

Locality : Jammu

Nativity : Mexico

Flrs. and Frts. : May – August

Distribution : India, Pakistan and Mexico

Cereus triangularis Haw.

Opuntia coccinellifera Mill.

Flower colour: Shrubs ca 3 – 4 m tall; leaves thick, oblong, oblanceolate, blunt; oreoles usually without prickles; flowers red; perianth campanulate, the outer segments short, green; stamens much exceeding the perianth; filaments pinkish-red, anthers yellow; style exceeding the stamens; berry ellipsoid, red.

Specimens examined : Bhellum 10871

Locality : Jammu

Nativity : Mexico

Flrs. and Frts. : May – August

Distribution : India, Pakistan and China

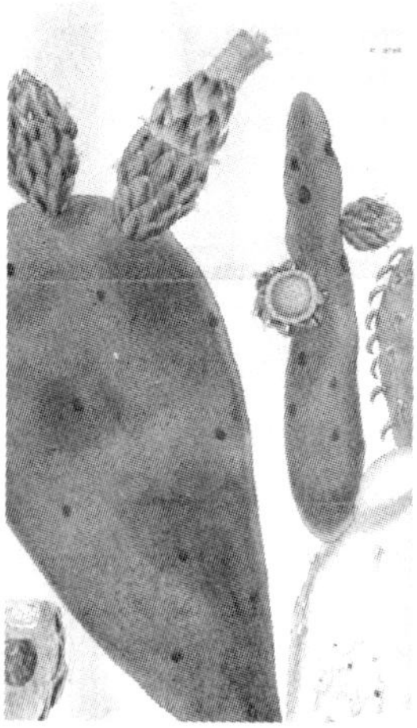

Opuntia coccinellifera Mill.

O. dillenii (Ker. Gawl.) Haw.

Shrubs branched from the base, leaves small, pale-green, conical at the base; flowers 6 – 10 cm across, yellow tinged with orange; perianth rotate, outer segments ovate, acute; stamens many, filaments unequal in lenth; style stout; berry pyriform, depressed at the apex.

Opuntia dillenii (Ker. Gawl.) Haw.

Flower colour: Yellow

Specimens examined : Bhellum 11287

Locality : Jammu

Nativity : South America

Flrs. and Frts. : May – August

Distribution : India Pakistan and S. America

O. monocantha Haw.

Branched shrubs; leaves dark-brown, slightly recurved, joints usually variable in size; areoles at least with 1-prickle or a few of which one is larger; flowers yellow; perianth rotate; stamens half as long as the inner perianth segmensts; style exceeding the stamens; berry pyriform, truncate and depressed at the apex.

Flower colour: Yellow

Specimens examined : Bhellum 10341

Locality : Jammu

Nativity : Brazil and Argentina

Flrs. and Frts. : May – August

Distribution : India, Pakistan, Brazil and Argentina

Opuntia monocantha Haw.

O. nigricans Haw.

Shrubs more than 3 m tall; leaves subulate, recurved, reddish at the tips; joints variable in size; areoles bearing slender straight prickle; flowers yellow, tinged with pink and later becoming rosy-crimson; berry pyriform, angular or more or less worty, reddish-purple when ripe.

Flower colour: Yellow tinged with pink

Specimens examined : Bhellum 13451

Locality : R. S. Pura

Nativity : China

Flrs. and Frts. : May – August

Distribution : India, Pakistan and China

Opuntia nigricans Haw.

O. vulgaris Mill.

Shrubs, usually 1 – 2.5 m tall; joins ovate to obovate; areoles with deciduous bristles and with solitary 2 – 3 cm long spines; leaves soon falling off; flowers solitary on upper part of the joints, flowers-bud red, turning when open yellowwithin and deep red on out side ; outer few tepals sepaloid, inner petaloid, spreading; stamens much shorter than the inner tepals; style stout, stigma shortly lobed.

Flower colour: Yellow

Specimens examined : Bhellum 11022

Locality : Jammu

Nativity : North America

Flrs. and Frts. : March – April

Distribution : India, Pakistan and N. America

O. vulgaris Mill.

Apiaceae

Angelica archangelica L.

Perennial herbs; leaves 2 – 3 pinnate, pinnae large, toothed; calyx teeth absent; petals subentire white; fruits ellipsoids, subquadrate or oblong, with three distinct midribs; commissure broad, lateral ones winged.

Flower colour: Cream-coloured

Specimens examined : Bhellum 13434

Locality : Srinagar, Gulmarg

Nativity : Europe and Asia

Flrs. and Frts. : June – August

Distribution : India, Nepal, north Europe, America and temperate Himalaya

Angelica archangelica L.

Bupleurum candollii Wall. ex DC.

Perennial, erect, tufted herbs upto 1 m tall; lower leaves linear to lanceolate, apex mucronate, base narrowed; upper leaves lanceolate, oblong or ovate, shorter subsessile; involucral bracts 1 – 4, lanceolate, oval, foliaceous; rays 5 – 10 involucel of lanceolate to oval bracteoles; flowers yellow; fruits 1 cm long, elliptic.

Flower colour: Yellow

Specimens examined : Bhellum 12237

Locality : Jammu

Nativity : Nepal

Flrs. and Frts. : March – April

Distribution : India, Nepal and temperate Himalaya

Coriandrum sativum L.

Annual erect, about 60 cm tall, glabrous herbs; stem terete, striate; lower leaves 1- pinnate, the leaflets opposite, deeply pinnate, segments cuneate, erregularly toothed, thin, upper leaves finely divided, segment narrow linear, flowers white or pink, in umbels with linear bracts at the base; middle flowers sterile, outer flowers longer fertile; fruits globular with prominent ribs.

Coriandrum sativum L.

Flower colour: White or Pink

Specimens examined : Bhellum 12497

Locality : Jammu

Nativity : South Europe

Flrs. and Frts. : March – April

Distribution : India and S. Europe

Centella asiatica (L.) Urban

Stoloniferous herbs with slender stems; leaves simple, palmatinerved, 1.5 – 2 cm across, orbicular, margin crenate; petiole 5 – 15 cm long, glabrous or sparsely puberulous; umbels solitary or 2 – 4 in the axil; bracts ovate, about 3 mm across; flowers 3 or 4 in each umbel, central one sessile, outer shortly pedicellate; petals minute, pink; anthers red; fruits 3 – 4 mm long, thinly pilose.

Flower colour: Pale green

Specimens examined : Bhellum 11612

Locality : Jammu

Nativity : Perhaps India

Flrs. and Frts. : May – October

Distribution : India, Pakistan, Nepal, Formosa, Tropical Asia, thc Pacific Islands, Africa and Worm or even tropical North and South America.

Centella asiatica (L.) Urban

Hydrocotyle sibthorpioides Lam.

Stem filiform, glabrous herbs; leaves orbicular or suborbicular, 0.5 – 2 cm across, shallowly 5 or 7-lobed; lobes crenate; petiole filiform, 0.5 to 3 cm long; umbel 3 – 10 flowered; pedicel very short or obsolete; flowers pale green; fruits suborbiculr, 0.5 – 1.5 mm across, broader than long.

Flower colour: Pale green

Specimens examined : Bhellum 12652

Locality : Srinagar

Nativity : France

Flrs. and Frts. : May – October

Distribution : India, Pakistan, Nepal, Corea. Wide spread in tropical Asia and introduced into the new world.

Hydrocotyle sibthorpioides Lam.

Torilis japonica (Houtt) DC.

Annual herbs; stem hispid or scabrid, generally rough; leaves 2 – 4 pinnate, bracts absent; bracteoles 3 – 4 narrow, filiform; rays 5 – 7 in an umbel; flowers purplish or white

Torilis japonica (Houtt) DC.

Flower colour: Pale yellow

Specimens examined : Bhellum 11359

Locality : Srinagar and Jammu

Nativity : Japan

Flrs. and Frts. : May – October

Distribution : India, Japan and China Burma, Formosa, Corea and Sumatra

T. stocksiana (Bioss.) Drude

Annual hispid, herbs; hairs appressed; stem 20-80 cm in height, sulcate, branched hispid or roughly hairy; leaves compound, 1-2 pinnate, segments lanceolate, hispidly appressed hairy on both srufaces; involucrres long, linear, hispid; rays 4-12; flowers white; stamens 5; fruits oval, laterally compressed, clothed with spine bearing straight or pointed tubercles.

Annual herbs; stems grooved.

Flower colour: White

Specimens examined : Bhellum 11429

Locality : Srinagar

Nativity : China and Japan

Flrs. and Frts. : April – May

Distribution : India and Iran

Caprifoliaceae

Lonicera japonica Thunb.

Evergreen twining shrub; leaves opposite, ovate, 4 – 8 cm long, obtuse, hairy on nerves; flowers white tinged with red or purple, yellow, fragrant; bract and bracteoles foliaceous; calyx tube ovoid, 5-toothed, teeth short; corolla 3 – 5 cm long distinctly 2-lipped; stamens 5, exserted; berries dintinct or united.

Lonicera japonica Thunb.

Flower colour: Whit tinged with red or purple.

Specimens examined : Bhellum 12589

Locality : Batote

Nativity : Japan and China

Flrs. and Frts. : May – November

Distribution : India, Japan and China

Viburnum opulus L.

A deciduous shrub; leaves opposite, rounded, in outline but divided int 3 – 5, coarsely toothed, pointed lobes; leaf-stalk with a pair of sessile glands at the top; flowersflowers white, scented; sepals 5, minute; corolla 5-lobed; anthers introse; ovary 1-locular; fruit a small, 1-seeded berry.

Commonly planted in the gardens.

Flower colour: White

Specimens examined : Bhellum 12677

Locality : Srinagar

Nativity : Europe and N. Africa

Flrs. and Frts. : April – May

Distribution : India, Pakistan, Europe and N. Africa

Viburnum opulus L.

V. tinus L.

An evergreen shrub; leaves elliptic or ovate oblong, dark above, paler beneath, more or less hairy on nerves; flowers white, fragrant.

Flower colour: White

Specimens examined : Bhellum 10299

Locality : Kashmir

Nativity : Mediterranean regions

Flrs. and Frts. : May – August

Distribution : India, Pakistan and Mediterranean regions

Viburnum tinus L.

Weigela florida DC.

Deciduous shrubs, branches arching; leaves opposite, oblong, margin toothed; inflorescence in corymbs; flowers pale-pink, funnel shaped, about 3 cm long.

Cultivated in the parks and gardens. The flowers are pretty beautiful.

Flower colour: Rose coloured.

Specimens examined : Bhellum 14559

Locality : Srinagar

Nativity : N. China

Flrs. and Frts. : April – June

Distribution : India and N. China

Weigela florida DC.

Sambucaceae

Sambucus nigra L.

A deciduous shrub; or small tree; stem with spreading, soft, branches; leaves 16cm long, opposite, pinnate with an odd terminal leaflets, elliptic, shortly acuminate, serrate; flowers white, or yellowish-white; stamens 5, alternating with corolla lobes, anthers extrose; fruits black.

Flower colour: White

Specimens examined : Bhellum 13310

Locality : Srinagar

Nativity : S. Europe and Asia Minor

Flrs. and Frts. : May-August

Distribution : India, Europe and Asia Minor

Sambucus nigra L.

Rubiaceae

Anthocephalus cadamba Miq.

A large tree; leaves opposite, elliptic-oblong, shortly acuminate, glabrous and shining above and more or less pubescent beneath; flowers orange in globular heads; fruits of many coriaceous pyrenes packed in fleshy globose mass, yellow when ripe, edible.

Flower colour: Orange Coloured

Specimens examined : Bhellum 14516

Locality : Jammu

Nativity : Nepal and Assam in India.

Flrs. and Frts. : April – November

Distribution : India

Anthocephalus cadamba Miq.

Gardenia jasminoides Ellis

An evergreen shrub; leaves opposite, elliptic or elliptic-oblong, 3.5 – 6 cm long, coriaceous, glabrous shining above, acute, base cuneate; stipule combined into an intrapetiolar membranous sheath, deeply split on one side; flowers solitary, terminal, 5 – 6 cm across, white, very fragrant; calyx tube campanulate, ribbed or winged, forming linear segment.

Flower colour: White

Specimens examined : Bhellum 14116

Locality : Srinagar

Nativity : China

Flrs. and Frts. : April – July

Distribution : India

Gardenia jasminoides Ellis

Hamelia patens Jacq.

An evergreen shrub; leaves in whorls, elliptic-oblong, apex acuminate, puberulous on both the surfaces; flowers scarlet in terminal panicles.

Flower colour: Scarlet

Specimens examined : Bhellum 14546

Locality : Jammu

Nativity : Tropical America

Flrs. and Frts. : April – July

Distribution : India

Hamelia patens Jacq.

Valerianaceae

Valeriana jatamansi Jones

Annual herbs, tomentose to pilose, 15 – 60 cm tall; rhizome with fibrous roots; radical leaves cordeate or ovate, 2 – 10 cm long; margin sinuate or crenate, cauline leaves, sessile, smaller, flowers in lax corymbose cymes; achenes tomentose.

Flower colour: White

Specimens examined : Bhellum 147646

Locality : Jammu

Nativity : Bhutan

Flrs. and Frts. : April – July

Distribution : India, Bhutan, Afghanistan and Himalayas.

Valeriana jatamansi Jones

Valerianella dentata (L.) Poll.

Annual or perennial herbs, stem dichotomous, 10 – 15 cm tall; leaves onlong or lanceolate, ciliate at the base; bracts 1.5 3 mm long; calyx obliquely truncate, shorter than the fruit; achenes narrowly ovoid, pubescent; style locule reduced; fruits 1-seeded.

Flower colour: White

Specimens examined : Bhellum 14546

Locality : Jammu

Nativity : S. Europe

Flrs. and Frts. : April – July

Distribution : India, Europe, USSR., N. Asia, Iran, Turkey, Pakistan and Afghanistan.

Valerianella dentata (L.) Poll.

V. muricata (Stev.) Baxt.

Annual or perennial herbs, 4 – 16 cm tall; leaves lanceolate, oblong-lanceolate, 2 – 4 cm long, base often toothed; bracts ovate to lanceolate, 2 – 4 mm long; calyx obliquely truncate, as long as or longe than fruits; achenes about 1.5 mm long, ovoid, pubescent.

Flower colour: White

Specimens examined : Bhellum 14846

Locality : Jammu

Nativity : USSR.

Flrs. and Frts. : April – July

Distribution : India,Pakistan and USSR.

V. muricata (Stev.) Baxt.

V. szovitsiana Fisch. & C. A. Mey.

Annual herbs, 10 – 25 cm tall; leaves 2 – 4 cm long, linear to lanceolate, often toothed at the base; bracts about 2.5 mm long, ovate to lanceolate, pubescent; calyx shorter than achene; achenes about 7 mm long, glandular pubescent, hispid, sterile locule pair longer than fertile.

Flower colour: white

Specimens examined : Bhellum 10846

Locality : Jammu

Nativity : Persia

Flrs. and Frts. : April – July

Distribution : India, C. Asia, USSR.,Syria Turkey Arabia Iran Afghanistan and Pakistan.

V. szovitsiana Fisch. & C. A. Mey.

Dipsacaeaeae

Dipsacus sativus (L.) Honck.

Herbs, 1-1.5 cm tall; leaves broadly lanceolate to oblong, margin entire or sinuately lobed, midrib spiny beneath; capitula ovoid to cylindrical 4-5 cm across; involucral bracts unequal, linear; florets pale-lilac.

Flower colour: purple

Specimens examined : Bhellum 13846

Locality : Patnitop

Nativity : France

Flrs. and Frts. : April – July

Distribution : India, Pakistan and France.

Asteraceae

Achillea millefolium L.

A perennial herb; leaves finely dissected, segments filiform; inflorescence in corymbose heads, flowers white. The plants are employed as a carmintive tonic and aromatic stimulant, oil is obtained by the decoction of the leaves and flowers.

Flower colour: white

Specimens examined : Bhellum 16491

Locality : Srinagar, and in Jammu regions,Banihal, Padder and Bhaderwah

Nativity : North Asia, Europe and America

Flrs. and Frts. : May-September

Distribution : India and all tropical countries of the world, Europe, America, Afghanistan, Persia, Baluchinstan and Pakistan.

Achillea millefolium L.

Ageratum conyzoides L.

Erect herbs; leaves opposite, or the upper alternate, 2 – 6 cm long, gland dotted and puberulous beneath, ovate, apex acute, margin crenate; flowers in heads, disc florets bisexual; pappus of 5 aristate bristles, dialated at the base; achenes 5-angled.

Flower colour: Purple.

Specimens examined : Bhellum 10895

Locality : R.S.Pura

Nativity : South America

Flrs. and Frts. : January-May

Distribution : India and all tropical countries of the world.

Ageratum conyzoides L.

A. houstanianum Mill

Annual or perennial herbs, stem slender, hairy; leaves opposite or the upper ones alternate, heads purple; disc florets bisexual; pappus of 5-aristate bristles; achenes 5-angled.

Ageratum houstanianum Mill

Flower colour: Purple

Specimens examined : Bhellum 10826

Locality : Udhampur

Nativity : Mexico

Flrs. and Frts. : Feb. – April

Distribution : India and tropical and subtropical countries of the world.

Artemisia abrotanum L.

Aromatic, undershrubs, 50-150 cm tall with woody base; stems numerous from base, branches brown, glabrous or sparsely hairy; leaves dark green, 2-3pinnatifid; heads nodding at maturity; florets yellow; *cypselae ellipsoid, glabrous.*

Flower colour: Yellow

Specimens examined : Bhellum 12690

Locality : Srinagar

Nativity : Asia

Flrs. and Frts. : April – May

Distribution : India, Iran, Afghanistan,Pakiatan and Asia

Artemisia abrotanum L.

A. absinthium L.

Perennial, tufted, herbs; stem erect, more than 1 m tall, brached, leaves ovate to obovate, 2 to 3 pinnatifid, segments linear lanceolate, white hairy or downy on both the surfaces, upper cauline leaves more or less divided or entire, sometimes pinnatifid; heads hemispherical arranged in paniculately branched racemes; involucral bracts 1 – 2 seriate, outer oblong, hoary, scarious; inner white or grey tomentose with membranous margins, persistent; achenes elliptic, oblong, slightly brownish, glabrous. The plants contains the essential oil and has a tonic which has a stimulating effect on the digestive organs. The plants contain the bitter glucoside absinthin, and a crystalline compound.

Flower colour: Yellow

Specimens examined : Bhellum 15649

Locality : Srinagar and Jammu,Batote

Nativity : British Iseles

Flrs. and Frts. : April – May

Distribution : India, Iran, Afghanistan,Pakiatan and, Europe, Minor Asia, Siberia, Armenia, Iran, Caucasus and British Iseles

Artesisia absinthium L.

A. dracunculus L.

Perennial, erect, herbs; stem branched, ribbed; leaves linear to linear-oblong, acute,upper entire, lower toothed or 3-fid; heads solitary or clustered, subglobose in paniculate racemes; involucral bracts broadly oblong, margin scarious; achenes subglobose, smooth. The essential oil obtained is used for flavouring vinegar and spices. The plants are cultivated in France for its essential oils known as 'Oil of Taragon'.

Artemisia dracunculus L.

Flower colour: Yellow

Specimens examined : Bhellum 14587

Locality : Jammu

Nativity : Europe

Flrs. and Frts. : May – July

Distribution : India, Nepal, Afghanistan, South and central Asia, Europe and temperate Himalaya

A. japonica Thunb.

Erect, perennial herbs; stem villous, hoary or glabrous, up to 100 cm tall; branches grooved; leaves 2 -5 cm long, stipulate, cauline leaves linear, variable, acute; heads greenish-white, secund in spreading panicles;

Flower colour: Greenish yellow

Specimens examined : Bhellum 12526

Locality : Srinagar

Nativity : Japan

Flrs. and Frts. : May – August

Distribution : India Afghanistn, China, Iran, Japan and Burma

Artemisia japonica Thunb.

A. vulgaris L.

Perennial, erect or ascending, aromatic woody, undershrubs; stem many, from the base branched, grooved, glabrous; leaves pinnatipartite to 2- pinnate, segments lanceolate, oblong, margin entire, glabrate above, densely tomentose beneath; heads in panicles, main axis white tomentose, 5 – 11 florets in each head; involucral bracts ovate, oblong, obtuse; achenes glabrous. The species is highly variable in height, leaves and number of flowers per head. In Indian medicine, the leaves and flower tops are administered in the form of an infusion in cases of nervous and spasmodic infections. It is also said to be antiseptic, expectorant and anthelmintic.

Flower colour: Yellow

Specimens examined : Bhellum 14989

Locality : Jammu and Banihal

Nativity : British Iseles

Flrs. and Frts. : March – April

Distribution : India, Nepal and temperate Himalaya

Artemisia vulgaris L.

Aster falconeri Clarke subsp. *nepalensis* Grierson

Perennial, erect, sparsely pubescent herbs; leaves broadly oblong-ovate, radical spathulate, narrow to a short petiole, upper sessile; heads solitary.

Specimens examined : Bhellum 10826

Locality : Srinagar

Nativity : Nepal

Flrs. and Frts. : May – August

Distribution : India and Nepal

Aster falconeri Clarke subsp. *nepalensis* Grierson

A. tibeticus Hook. f.

Perennial herbs, 10-25 cm long; stem pubescent; leaves small, radical 2-3 cm, oblong; heads 2-3 cm across; ligules 2-3 mm bright blue; achenes small, flat; pappus double, white.

Flower colour:

Specimens examined : Bhellum 10826

Locality : Udhampur

Nativity : Mexico

Flrs. and Frts. : Feb. – April

Distribution : India, Mexico and Tibet

Bellis perennis L.

Perennial herbs; leaves radical, spoon –shaped, obovate more or less toothed, pubescent; heads on peduncles, variable in size, 2 cm across or more; involucral bracts green, narrowly oblong, ray florets white tips tinged with pink; disc florets cream-yellow, slightly hairy above the middle; achenes slightly hairy.

Flower colour: Rays white; disc yellow

Specimens examined : Bhellum 10928

Locality : Patnitop, Jammu and Srinagar

Nativity : South Europe

Flrs. and Frts. : April-July

Distribution : India cultivated in gardens and often found as an escape.

Bellis perennis L.

Bidens comosa (Gray) Wiegand

Perennial herb, usually at moist places; disc florets pale-yellow or green; ray florets yellow; outer phyllaries large, foliaceous, usually much exceeding the disc; achenes narrow towards the base and broader towards the apex.

Flower colour: Yellow

Specimens examined : Bhellum 12896

Locality : Srinagar

Nativity : North America

Flrs. and Frts. : May – September

Distribution : India and North America

Bidens comosa (Gray) Wiegand

Centaurea calycitrapa L.

Annual herbs; stem erect or spreading, brached from the base; leaves pinnate or pinnatifid, lobes linear acute; heads terminal, sessile or peduncled; involucral bracts ovate, margins scarious; florets pale-purple; achenes white; pappus absent.

Flower colour: Purple

Specimens examined : Bhellum 12312

Locality : Srinagar

Nativity : Europe

Flrs. and Frts. : May – October

Distribution : India, Pakistan, Nepal, Europe, N Africa, Atlantic Islands and W. Asia

Centaurea calycitrapa L.

Centaurea cyanus L.

Annual or biennial erect herbs; lower leaves oblong, upper linear-lanceolate; heads ovoid; involucral bracts with scarious margins; outer florets dark-blue; achenes shining with puberulous hairs. Pappus present.

Flower colour: Purple

Specimens examined : Bhellum 12587

Locality : Srinagar

Nativity : Mediterrnean region and Europe

Flrs. and Frts. : May – August

Distribution : India and Mediterranean region, Europe and China

Centaurea cyanus L.

Chrysanthemum cinerarifolium Vis.

Perennial herbs, 50-150 cm tall; leaves deeply lobed; heads white, yellow or pink. Used as insecticide.

Flower colour: Rays white, disc yellow

Specimens examined : Bhellum 13521

Locality : Srinagar

Nativity : Yugoslavia and Italy; some authors are of the opinion that it is native of Dalmatia

Flrs. and Frts. : June – August

Distribution : India, Yugoslavia, Italy and Dalmatia

Chrysanthemum cinerarifolium Vis.

Conyza bonariensis L.

Annual erect, herbs, stem 20 – 75 cm tall or more; leaves linear, crowded, 5 – 10 cm long; entire or remotely serrate, frequently crispate; heads 5 – 6 mm across, arranged in loose panicles; outer involucral bracts with purplish tip, inner with scarious margin; achenes pale-brown, margin compressed.

Flower colour: White

Specimens examined : Bhellum 12326

Locality : Udhampur

Nativity : Argentina

Flrs. and Frts. : April – August

Distribution : India and Tropical America

Conyza bonariensis L

C. canadensis L.

Annual herbs, thinly clothed with rather stiff hairs, 30 – 60 cm tall; stem prominently ribbed; leaves linear oblanceolate, acute, slightly toothed or entire, fringed with rather stiff hairs; heads arranged in leafy panicles; ray florets white, tinged with purple, female disc florets bisexual, yellow; pappus white, minutely barbellate; achenes cylcendric, slightly hairy, hairs spreading.

Flower colour: White or white tinged with purple

Specimens examined : Bhellum 12650

Locality : Udhampur, Kishtwar

Nativity : North America, Canada

Flrs. and Frts. : April – August

Distribution : India and North America and now widely distributed all over the world.

Conyza canadensis L.

C. japonica (Thunb.) Less.

Erect softly hairy herbs; 20 – 50 cm tall; stem tufted simple or branched; leaves sessile, often crowded, obovate, spathulate, oblong or lanceolate, 2.6 – 7.5 cm long, coarsely toothed, base of the upper leaves sometimes dialated; heads globose arranged in terminal corymbos; involucral bracts acute.

Conyza japonica (Thunb.) Less.

Flower colour: White

Specimens examined : Bhellum 12124

Locality : Udhampur

Nativity : Japan

Flrs. and Frts. : April – August

Distribution : India, Afghanistan, Pakistan, Nepal, Burma, Japan, Indo-China and Thailand.

Dahlia imperialis Roezl. ex Ortgies

Perennial herbs, stem upto 4 m tall; leaves 3-pinnate, leaflet ovate, upto 5 cm long, incurved, serrate; heads white tinged with red.

Flower colour: White tinged with red

Specimens examined : Bhellum13169

Locality : Jammu

Nativity : Mexico

Flrs. and Frts. : May – September

Distribution : India, Mexico

D. pinnata Cav.

Tuberous herbs; leaves opposite, usually bipinnate, pinnae ovate, crenate, dentate; ray floret rose coloured; disc floret yellow.

Dahlia pinnata Cav.

Flower colour: Ray floret rose coloured, disc floret yellow

Specimens examined : Bhellum12569

Locality : Baggar

Nativity : Mexico

Flrs. and Frts. : May – September

Distribution : India, Mexico

Eclipta prostrata (L.) L.

Prostrate or erect, strigose herbs; stem 20 – 50 cm tall; leaves opposite, subsessile, or shortly petioled; heads one or two at a node, 7-10 cm across; ray florets longer than bread outer; bracts longer, inner shorter, narrow, spreading; disc florets tubular, 4- toothed; achenes about 2 mm long, compressed, pappus 0 or a few minute teeth.

Flower colour: White

Specimens examined : Bhellum 10239

Locality : Banihal

Nativity : South America

Flrs. and Frts. : July-September

Distribution : India and found as a cosmopolitan weed.

Eclipta prostrata (L.) L.

Eupatorium coelestunum L.

Perennial herbs; stem 30 cm tall or more; leaves triangular or ovate, margin coarsely toothed; inflorescence in heads, florets blue-violet.

Flower colour: Blue-violet

Specimens examined : Bhellum 12375

Locality : Srinagar

Nativity : Tropical America

Flrs. and Frts. : April – August

Distribution : India and Tropical America

Eupatorium coelestunum L.

Galinsoga parviflora Cav.

Erect herbs; stem weak, 20 – 45 cm tall or more; usually smooth towards base, hairy upwards; leaves opposite, ovate, lanceolate, more or less toothed; heads radiate on slender stalk; involucral bracts broad, green, smooth; pappus of about 15 spathulate, fringed scales; ligules few white; disc florets yellow, 5-toothed; achenes angled, roughly pubescent, crowned with the pappus scales.

Flower colour: White

Specimens examined : Bhellum 10387

Locality : Srinagar

Nativity : Tropical America

Flrs. and Frts. : March-June

Distribution : India, Tropical America and found as a cosmopolitan weed.

Galinsoga parviflora Cav.

G. quadriradiata Ruiz et Pavon

Annual herb, 10-50 cm tall; leaves 2-6 x 1.5-4.5 cm; involucres hemispheric, 3-6 mm across; phyllaries deciduous, broadly elliptic to ovate, innner ones linear lanceolate, entire or 2-3 lobed; rays white or pink, disc yellow; pappus of fimbriate scales; achenes of disc 1.3-1.8 mm and of rays 1.2- 2 mm long.

Galinsoga quadriradiata Ruiz et Pavon

Flower colour: White

Specimens examined : Bhellum 14526

Locality : Udhampur

Nativity : Mexico

Flrs. and Frts. : May – August

Distribution : India, Mexico and found as cosmopolitan weed.

Gnaphalium purpureum L.

Herbs, 20 – 60 cm tall more or less white wooly or cottony; stems usually many from the base; leaves alternate, spathulate, 3 – 13.5 cm long, entire; bracts many seriate, scarious; heads about 5 mm long in short leafy spikes; outer florets female, disc florets bisexual; stamens syngenesious; achenes oblong or ovoid, minute, papillulate.

Flower colour: Yellow

Specimens examined : Bhellum 10588

Locality : Jammu

Nativity : Tropical America

Flrs. and Frts. : May-July

Distribution : India, Pakiatan, Japan, and N. & S. America

Gnaphalium purpureum L.

Guizotia abyssinica (L. f.) Cass.

Annual herbs; stem upto 2 m tall, divaricately branched; leaves opposite, oblong, lanceolate, base amplexicaule; heads radiate, solitary axillary, subterminal, 2.5 – 4.5 cm across; involucral bracts in 2 rows, outer herbaceous, inner ones scarious; corolla yellow, style arms short, curved, disc florets many, campanulate, 5-lobed; achenes shining brown.

Flower colour: Yellow

Specimens examined : Bhellum 12386

Locality : Udhampur

Nativity : Tropical Africa

Flrs. and Frts. : April – August

Distribution : India and Tropical Africa

Helianthus annuus L.

Annual cultivated herbs, leaves ovate, In *Helianthus annuus*, the flower is actually a capitulum (also known as a *composite flower*) of numerous florets (small flowers). The outer petal-bearing florets are the sterile *ray florets* and can be yellow, red, orange, or other colors. The florets inside the circular head are called *disc florets*, which mature into acheve.

Helianthus annuus L.

Flower colour: Yellow

Specimens examined : Bhellum 11561

Locality : Jammu

Nativity : North and Central America

Flrs. and Frts. : July – September

Distribution : India and found as a cosmopolitan weed.

H. cucumerifolius Torr. and Grey

Annual or Perennial herbs; stem Ilaborous; leaves dettate; flowers pale yellow.

Cultivated and also found as an escape on wasteland.

Flower colour: yellow

Specimens examined : Bhellum13760

Locality : Baggar

Nativity : North America

Flrs. and Frts. : May – September

Distribution : India and Europe,

H. debilis Nutt.

Perennial herbs; stem decumbent or procumbent, glabrous; leaves 3-10 cm long, margin serrate; peduncles 10-20 cm long; florets of different colours; disc florets 10-14 mm long.

Flower colour: Yellow

Specimens examined : Bhellum11090

Locality : Baggar

Nativity : America

Flrs. and Frts. : May – September

Distribution : India and Europe,

Helianthus debilis Nutt.

H. tuberosus L.

Perennial rhizomatous herbs, 0.5-2.0 m tall; stem erect, hispid to hirsute, somewhat glacous; leaves opposite or alternate, ovate-lanceolate, margin entire or serrate; heads 3-15; phyllaries dark green; disc florets and rays yellow; cypselae glabrous at the base, hairy towards apex.

Flower colour: Yellow

Specimens examined : Bhellum12498

Locality : Baggar

Nativity :

Flrs. and Frts. : May – September

Distribution : India and Europe

H. tuberosus L.

Inula britanica L.

Perennial herbs, 10-75 cm tall; stem erect, villous; leaves lanceolate to linear lanceolate, base auriculate, margin entire or serrulate; peduncle 1-4 cm long; phyllaries linear, lanceolate on outer side, inner ones similar but smaller, scarious; corolla 5-lobed; achenes cylindric; pappus white.

Flower colour: yellow

Specimens examined : Bhellum 11312

Locality : Srinagar

Nativity : Europe

Flrs. and Frts. : July. – August

Distribution : India and Britain

Inula britanica L.

Parthenium hysterophorus L.

Annual herbs upto 1 m tall or more; stem furrowed, puberulous to strigose; leaves pinnately dissected, pinnules oblong, lanceolate, entire to deeply lobed, puberulous acute; inflorescence in panicles; heads radiate, white; ray florets biseriate; corolla white to light yellow; disc florets many; achenes flat; puberulous; pappus with reflexed awn.

Flower colour: White

Specimens examined : Bhellum 10616

Locality : Ramban

Nativity : Central and North America and West Indies

Flrs. and Frts. : June – October

Distribution : India, West Indies and America

Parthenium hysterophorus L.

Sclerocarpus africanus Jacq.

Erect, pubescent, hoary herbs, 30 – 60 cm tall; lower leaves opposite, upper alternate, ovate, acute, narrow into a short stalk; heads radiate at the end of forked branches; involucral bracts few, foliaceous; florets yellow, pappus none; ligules broad, spreading; disc florets 3 – 5 toothed; achenes curved, ribbed, enclosed in hard pointed scales.

Sclerocarpus africanus Jacq.

Flower colour: yellow

Specimens examined : Bhellum 10287

Locality : Jammu

Nativity : Tropical Africa

Flrs. and Frts. : March – October

Distribution : India, Tropical E. and W. Africa, Nepal and Pakistan.

Silybum marianum (L.) Gaertn.

Erect, stout, 50 – 100 cm tall or more, glabrous; stem usually simple; leaves sinuately lobed, 10 – 60 cm long, 5 – 25 cm broad, with white dusted on upper surface, margin strongly spinous; heads rose-purple, 2.5 – 5 cm across; excluding the coriaceous spreading, spinous involucral bracts; achenes ovoid-oblong, dark brown.

Flower colour: Purple or Crimson

Specimens examined : Bhellum 12652

Locality : Srinagar and Jammu

Nativity : S. Europe

Flrs. and Frts. : May – October

Distribution : India, Pakistan, Nepal, Europe and introduced in Britain

Silybum marianum (L.) Gaertn.

Solidago candida L.

Perennial, glabrous herbs; leaves alternate, linear, obovate, oblong or lanceolate; inflorescence in racemes forming panicles; heads yellow 2 – 4 mm across; involucral bracts 2-seriate, lanceolate; achenes 2 mm long, hairy; pappus almost equaling the corolla.

An ornamental shrub, cultivated throughout India and found as an escape.

Flower colour: Bright orange yellow

Specimens examined : Bhellum 12872

Locality : Srinagar and Jammu

Nativity : America

Flrs. and Frts. : May – October

Distribution : India, Pakistan, America

S. virga-aurea L.

Erect herbs, stem 30 – 70 cm tall; lower leaves oblong, lanceolate toothed, acute, narrowed towards the base; upto 12 cm long; head yellow in axillary or terminal spikes; ray florets upto 12mm long; disc florets 8 mm long or more; achenes pubescent; pappus hairs slender

Flower colour: Bright yellow

Specimens examined : Bhellum 13218

Locality : Srinagar

Nativity : N. America

Flrs. and Frts. : May – October

Distribution : India, Pakistan, Nepal, introduced in Asia and Europ

Soligago virga-aurea L.

Sonchus oleraceous L.

Erect annual herbs; stem angled, upto 1.5 m tall, hollow fleshy, sometimes winged, green or fleshed with purple; leaves thin commonly runcinate, pinnatifid, 10 – 40 cm long or more, auricles sometimes lobed; involucral bracts many serriate glandular hairy; heads yellow, 1.5 – 2 cm across; achenes muriculate between the ribs, not winged; pappus white, 8 – 10 mm long, copious, bristly.

Flower colour: Yellow

Specimens examined : Bhellum 10618

Locality : Throughout the state.

Nativity : Probably Europe and Eurasia

Flrs. and Frts. : April – August

Distribution : India, Europe, Asia, Africa and Australia

Stevia ovata Willd.

Perennial herbs; stem often purplish; leaves ovate to elliptic, margin entire, glandular punctuate on both the surfaces; heads 5- 8 mm across; involucral bracts narrowly oblong; achenes ribbed, hispid, pappus a crown of scales.

Flower colour:white

Specimens examined : Bhellum 10619

Locality : Jammu

Nativity : Brazil and Paraguay

Flrs. and Frts. : July – September

Distribution : Central America, South America, Venezuela and Ecudor, Brazil and Paraguay

Tagetes erecta L.

Erect, strongly aromatic herbs, sprangly branched; branches angular, ribbed; leaves opposite, decussate or upper ones alternate, pinnate, leaflets lanceolate, oblong, acute, base cuneate, remotely dentate; heads solitary, on terminal peduncles; ray florets ligulate, 1.5 – 2.5 cm long; disc florets bisexual, tubular, 5-toothed; stamens 5, included; anthers linear, flat, shortly tailed; stigma hairy; achenes black, about 10 mm long.

Flower colour: Yellow

Specimens examined : Bhellum 10619

Locality : Throughout the state.

Nativity : Africa or Mexico

Flrs. and Frts. : April – August

Distribution : India, Africa and Mexico

Tagetes erecta L.

T. minuta L.

Annual herbs, strongly aromatic; stem 1 – 2 m tall or more; leave opposite or alternate, often both the types on the same plant, od pinnate, 5 – 15 cm long, leaflets linear –lanceolate, sharply serrate margin dotted with yellow glands; heads many crowded, at the end o the branches, yellow; achenes linear lanceolate, black, 6 – 10 mm long scales unequal.

Specimens examined : Bhellum 11769

Locality : Batote, Kishtwar, and Srinagar

Nativity : South America

Flrs. and Frts. : April – August

Distribution : India, South America, Mexico

T. patula L.

Erect, strongly aromatic herbs; stem much branched; leaves opposite, upper ones sometimes alternate, pinnate or pinnatifid, leaflets lanceolate, oblong, sharply serrate with awned teeth; heads solitary or in cymes; ligules of the marginal florets yellow or orange; achenes angular, somewhat compressed.Cultivated or found as an escape.

Flower colour: Yellow

Specimens examined : Bhellum 11340

Locality : Throughout the state.

Nativity : Mexico

Flrs. and Frts. : April – August

Distribution : India, and S. America

Tridex procumbens L.

Annual, procumbent herbs, hirsute or slightly wooly; leaves opposite, 2-4 cm long, ovate, ovate-lanceolate, irregularly dentate; heads terminal, solitary; ray florets female, disc florets yellow bisexual; stamens syngenenesious, anthers sagittate; achenes turbinate or oblong.

Tridex procumbens L.

Flower colour: Rays white discs yellow

Specimens examined : Bhellum 10612

Locality Jammu

Nativity : South America

Flrs. and Frts. April – December

Distribution : India, S. America and fairly common in warm countries of the world.

Xanthium spinosum Wallroth

Annual herbs, stem much branched, 50 – 100 cm tall with 1 – 2 stout 3-fid, yellow spines in the axil of the leaf, sometimes spines replaced by leaf fascicles; leaves entire, white grey tomentose on the underneath, dark green above, sessile or shortly petioled; male heads in terminal inflorescence, female solitary, sessile in the leaf axis; spines yellow, hooked, slender, beak acicular.

Flower colour: Rays white, discs yellow

Specimens examined : Bhellum 10130

Locality :Srinagar

Nativity : South America

Flrs. and Frts. April – December

Distribution : Weed, cosmopolitan

Xanthium spinosum Wallroth

X. strumarium L.

Annual, unarmed, rough herbs upto 1 m tall or more; stem dark violet; leaves alternate, 5 – 10 cm long, toothed or broadly 5 – 7, lobed, base cordate or subcordate, strongly 3-nerved; heads solitary or clustered, unisexual; male heads in upper axils, globose, many flowered; involucral bracts 1 – 2 seriate, short, free, narrow; disc florets tubular 5-toothed, staminal filaments monadelphous, anthers free with inflexed mucronate tip; utricles ovoid or oblong, 1 – 2 cm long, beak incurved, spines glabrous.

Flower colour: Pale yellow

Specimens examined : Bhellum 10625

Locality : Jammu

Nativity : Europe

Flrs. and Frts. : June. – October

Distribution : India, Western Himalaya and Java.

X. strumarium L.

Youngia japonica (L.) DC.

Annual herbs; stem slender, hollow, 25 – 50 m tall; leaves alternate, rosulate, 5 – 15 cm long, margin sinuately lobed, lobes toothed, petiole upto 8 cm long, cauline leaves smaller, few; heads in corymbs; involucral bracts biseriate, outer 5 ovate, acute, inner 6- 8, oblong or lanceolate, green, acute; receptacle flat; ligules long, spreading, yellow; achenes fusiform, angular or subterete, small, finely ribbed.

Flower colour: Orange yellow

Specimens examined : Bhellum13135

Locality : Baggar and Kishtwar

Nativity : Japan

Flrs. and Frts. : May – September

Distribution : India and Japan

Youngia japonica (L.) DC.

Zennia elegans Jacq.

Annual herb, about 1 m tall; leaves cordate, ovate to elliptic, sessile; florets variously coloured.

Planted for showy flowers.

Flower colour: Pink, red orYellow

Specimens examined : Bhellum 12600

Locality : Srinagar and Jammu

Nativity : Mexico

Flrs. and Frts. : May – October

Distribution : India, Pakistan and Mexico

Z. haageana Regel

An ornamental flowering herb, planted for showy flowers.

Flower colour: Orange yellow

.*Specimens examined* : Bhellum 12600

Locality : Srinagar and Jammu

Nativity : Mexico

Flrs. and Frts. : May – October

Distribution : India, Pakistan and Mexico

Z. linearis Benth.

Annual herb, 20 – 35 cm in height; leaves linear-lanceolate, entire; heads upto 5 cm across, rays orange.

Flower colour: Orange

Specimens examined : Bhellum13712

Locality : Srinagar

Nativity : Mexico

Flrs. and Frts. : May – September

Distribution : India and Mexico

Campanulaceae

Codonopsis clematidea (Schrenk) C.B. Clarke

Strongly scented herbs; leaves shortly stalked, grey hairy, 2 cm long; flowers nodding; corolla 2.5 cm with rrecurved lobes, blue.

Flower colour: Blue

Specimens examined : Bhellum 13515

Locality : Srinagar

Nativity : USSR.

Flrs. and Frts. : March – April

Distribution : India, Afghanistan, USSR., C. Asia, Iran, and Pakistan.

Codonopsis clematidea (Schrenk) C. B. Clarke

Campanula latifolia L.

An annual or perennial, herb; stem 0.5 – 1 m tall; stem furrowed; leaves broadly ovate, lanceolate, 6 – 12 cm long; pubescent beneath, glabrous and gland dotted above, margin cremate or coarsely toothed; flowers axillary, usually one sometimes more, 2.5 – 5 cm long; dark-purple; calyx 5-toothed, teeth linear; margin ciliate; fruits a capsule, apex blunt.

Grows wild.

Flower colour: Purple

Specimens examined : Bhellum 13515

Locality : Jammu

Nativity : Mediterranean region and Europe

Flrs. and Frts. : May – September

Distribution : India, Europe Caucasus, Turkey and Mediterranean region of the world.

Campanula latifolia L.

C. leucantha Gilli

Annual herb, 8-20 cm tall, suffruticose, hirsute; root thick, elongated, woody. Stems light-brown, branched, leaves hirsute, oval to ovate, 10-20 x 3-10 mm, shortly petiolate to sessile, margin wavy to denticulate, apex ± acute, flowers at the tips of branches. Calyx segments lanceolate; appendage ± as long as the segments. Corolla 10-15 mm long, tubular, pubescent outside, style included, reaching the base of corolla lobes. common on the margins of fields.

Flower colour: Blue

Nativity : Afghanistan

Flrs. and Frts. : April - May.

Distribution: Afghanistan and Chitral.

C. obtusa (Chipp) Nannf.

Annual herb, on open situations.

Specimens examined : Bhellum 12615

Locality : Padder

Nativity : Afghanistan

Flrs. and Frts. : March – April

Distribution : India, Pakistan and Afghanistan

C. pallida Wall.

Annual herbs; stem 20 – 50 cm tall; leaves alternate, lanceolate, acute, hirsute on both surfaces; flowers in panicles; calyx 5-toothed, or entire, hairy without; corolla campanulate, 5-toothed or lobed, lilac; stamens free; capsule elongated, ovoid or rounded.

Flower colour: Lilac

Specimens examined : Bhellum 11614

Locality : Jammu

Nativity : Nepal

Flrs. and Frts. : April – June

Distribution : India, Pakistan, Afghanistan and Nepal.

C. sylvatica Wall.

Annual herb, ca. 25 cm tall; branches few, pilose; leaves linear, sessile, pilose; inflorescence 2-5 flowered; corolla campanulate, purple; grows wild.

Flower colour:

Specimens examined : Bhellum 12315

Locality : Kashmir

Nativity : Afghanistan

Flrs. and Frts. : March – April

Distribution : India, Afghanistan and Pakistan

Lobeliaceae

Lobelia erinus L.

Annual or perennial herbs; leaves simple, alternate, ovate or linear; flowers blue, purple or red; grown in the gardens for showy flowers.

Flower colour: Blue, Purple or Pink-red

Specimens examined : Bhellum 12380

Locality : Kashmir

Nativity : Afghanistan

Flrs. and Frts. : March – April

Distribution : India, Afghanistan and Pakistan

Lobelia erinus L.

Plumbaginaceae

Plumbago zeylanicum L.

Perennial, scandent, undershrubs; stem erect, branched, branches angular,striated; leaves altenate, ovate, oblong, glabrous, 3 – 10 cm long, base, auricled; flowers white in spikes, about 1.5 cm across; calyx 5-toothed, teeth short, covered with stalked, red tipped glands.

Cultivated in gardens and parks and also found as an escape.

Flower colour: White

Specimens examined : Bhellum 10667

Locality : Chanderkote

Nativity : Africa

Flrs. and Frts. : May – August

Distribution : India, Africa

Plumbago zeylanicum L.

Primulaceae

Anagallis arvensis L.

Annual, erect, decumbent glabrous herbs; stem quadrangular, narrowly winged; leaves sessile, opposite, ovate, or lanceolate, oblong, glabrous on both surfaces, often punctuate on upper surface, apex obtuse margin entire; flowers solitary axillary; sepals 5, green, margin scarious; petals 5, blue, spotted purple-pink at base, fringed with glands; capsule globose, splitting transversely, many seeded.

Common weed in cultivated wheat fields.

Flower colour: Red or Blue

Specimens examined : Bhellum 10615

Locality : Jammu

Nativity : Mediterranean region and Europe

Flrs. and Frts. : Feb. – March

Distribution : India, Europe, Africa, Australia Tropical America, W. Asia and other Mediterranean regions of the world.

Androsace staintonii Y. Nasir

Plants ± lax caespitose, leaves rosulate 7-8 mm latae, subglobose. Folia exteriora 4.6-5 x 1.5-1.8 mm, late lanceolata, siccitate brunnea vel subgrisea, carinata, obtusa, basi lata; folia interiora 3-4.2 x 1 mm, lanceolata, pilis albis vix 1 mm longis, marginem folii versus patentibus apicem versus adpressis. Scapus (5-) 14 mm longus, 3-5 (-6)-florus, pilis usque 1.1 mm longis, vestitus. Inflorescence dense villosa, compacta. Bractea 4-5 mm longa, lanceolata. Pedicellus bractea brevior vel sublongior vel ei aequilongus. Flores albi, oculo flavo. Calyx c. 3 mm longus, in lobos obtusos usque dimidium divisus, dense villosus. Corolla annulata, limbo 6 mm lato, lobis obtusis vel leviter lobatis. Annual herb, grows wild.

Flower colour: White with yellow spot

Specimens examined : Bhellum 12611

Locality : Jammu

Nativity : Pakistan

Flrs. and Frts. : Feb. – March

Distribution : India, Pakistan and Afghanistan

Lysmachia. japonica Thunb.

Annual decumbent ascending herbs; stem rooting from the base; leaves opposite, basal leaves long stalked, ovate, lanceolate, oblong, 2.5 – 3.5 cm long, gland-punctate on both surfaces, sparsely hairy or glabrescent; flowers in solitary or axillary pairs, yellow, 5 – 10 mm across; capsule shorter than calyx.

Lysmachia. japonica Thunb.

A beautiful herb, grows wild.

Flower colour: Yellow

Specimens examined : Bhellum 12415

Locality : Batote

Nativity : Japan

Flrs. and Frts. : March – April

Distribution : India, Yaman, China, Formosa, Ryukya Islands, Japan, Sumatra, Java and N. S. Wales

L. lobeloides Wall.

Annual up to 50 cm or more tall, erect, glabrous, stem branched, the branches ascending spreading, more or less angular, leaves elliptic-ovate or oblong-orbiculate, 25-40 x 9-18 mm long (including petiole), subacute, decurrent, alternate, glandular streaked on the margin only. racemes (5-) 7-20 cm long, lax, flowers white to pale pink, lowermost bracts 5-8 mm long, up to 12.5 mm in fruit and deflexed, longer than the bract, calyx campanulate, 3-5 mm long, lobes ovate-lanceolate, apiculate, margin glandular streaked, crisp, sparse glandulose, papillose towards the apex, corolla exceeding the calyx, 4.5 mm long, campanulate; lobes obovate-oblong, obtuse, crenulate to wavy, stamens exserted; filaments 3-4 (-4.5) mm long, sparse glandulose, barely adnate at the base; anther ovate-obtuse, 1 mm long, glandulose, ovary globose, 1.2-1.5 (-2) mm broad; style 4-4.5 mm long, persistent; stigma subcapitate, capsule ± 3.6 mm broad, globose, seeds as in the preceding species but weighing less.

Specimens examined : Bhellum 10128

Locality : Srinagar

Nativity : Nepal

Flrs. and Frts. : March – May

Distribution : India, Bhutan, Yaman, and Nepal

L. vulgaris L.

Perennial herbs , 60 – 120 cm tall, with creeping rhizomes, stems erect, terete or obtusely quadrangular, simple or paniculately branched, pubescent, leaves opposite or whorled; petiole 2 – 10 mm; leaf blade oblong-lanceolate to ovate-lanceolate, 6 – 17 X 1 – 5 cm, abaxially glabrescent, sparsely red or black glandular punctate, abaxially pubescent, base obtuse to subrounded, margin entire or obscurely repand, apex acuminate; panicles terminal and axillary; peduncle 1.5 – 4.5 cm; bracts linear-subulate, 2 – 8 mm. Pedicel 3 – 12 mm, calyx lobes lanceolate, corolla bright yellow, 8-11 mm, 1.5 – 2 cm in diam., deeply parted; lobes elliptic, adaxially densely glandular, filaments connate, anthers linear, dorsifixed, opening by lateral slits, ca. 3 mm, ovary ovoid, style 4 – 5 mm, capsule subglobose, 3 – 4 mm in diam.

Flower colour: Yellow

Specimens examined : Bhellum 12512

Locality : Jammu

Nativity : W. Europe

Flrs. and Frts. : July – August

Distribution : India, N. America, Europe, Turkey, Africa, Iran, Iraq, Aral-Caspian, Caucasus, Sieberia, Japan and Korea

Primula macrophylla D. Don

A stout perennial with a short rootstock, leaves, lanceolate to elliptic-lanceolate or oblanceolate, ± firm, entire, denticulate to finely crenulate, farinose or efarinose; the farina white, rarely yellow, apex acute to obtuse, midrib impressed on the upper surface, petiole broad sheathed, scape up to 32 cm long, fairly stout, bracts 7-20 mm long, acute to obtusish, puberulous (especially on the margin), blackish; pedicel 1.5-4 cm long, exceeding the bracts, puberulous or glabrous; flowers heteromorphic, purple, pink-purple, violet or lilac; calyx up to 12 mm long, subcylindric, often tinged black (in the dried state), lobes lanceolate, longer than or equalling the tube, puberulous; corolla tube 9-12 mm long, exceeding the calyx; limb 1.5-1.8 cm broad, lobes obtuse or bibbed, 6-10 mm broad, entire; ovary globose to slightly depressed, 2.5-3 mm broad, style 8-9 mm long; capsule 12-17 mm long, broad cylindric, usually much exceeding the calyx; seeds 1 mm long, angular, papillose. Grows wild.

Flower colour: Purple or Pink purple

Specimens examined : Bhellum 11515

Locality : Padder

Nativity : Nepal

Flrs. and Frts. : March – August

Distribution : India, Afghanistan, Bhutan and Nepal

Samolus valerandi L.

Perennial herbs; stem erect, basal leaves rosette; leaves oblong, margin entire, apex obtuse, pedicels longer than flowers.

Flower colour: White

Specimens examined : Bhellum 12455

Locality : Kashmir

Nativity : West Europe

Flrs. and Frts. : March – April

Distribution : India, W. Europe

Samolus valerandi L.

Ebenaceae

Diospyros kaki L. f.

Deciduous tree, stem single or many, 25 ft. high and at least as wide. The branches are somewhat brittle and can be damaged in high winds, leaves are alternate, simple, ovate and up to 7 inches long and 4 inches wide, often pale, slightly yellowish green in youth, turning a dark, glossy green as they age. Under mild autumn conditions the leaves often turn dramatic shades of yellow, orange and red. Tea can also be made from fresh or dried leaves. Flowers surrounded by a green calyx tube and female flowers are single and cream-colored while the pink-tinged male flowers are typically borne in threes, persimmon trees are usually either male or female, but some trees have both male and female flowers. On male plants, especially, occasional perfect (bisexual) flowers occur, producing an atypical fruit. A tree's sexual expression can vary from one year to the other. Many cultivars are parthenocarpic.

Diospyros kaki L. f.

Grown in the gardens and also found in wild state.

Flower colour: Pink

Specimens examined : Bhellum 10389

Locality : Ramban

Nativity : China

Flrs. and Frts. : May – November

Distribution : India,

Jasminaceae

Jasminum officinale L.

A woody climber or twining shrub; stem branched, sparsely hairy; leaves opposite, imparipinnately compound, leaflets 5 – 7, ovate, lanceolate, terminal leaflet largest, puberulous, above glabrous beneath, margin entire; flowers white, fragrant; berry subglobose, black when ripe.

Flower colour: White

Specimens examined : Bhellum 10419

Locality : Ramban

Nativity : Persia

Flrs. and Frts. : May – November

Distribution : India and Persia

Jasminum officinale L.

Oleaceae

Forsythia viridissima Lindl.

A deciduous shrub, flowers cover the branches before the appearance of leaves, leaves opposite, usually simple but sometimes trifoliate with a basal pair of small leaflets, margin serrated is or entire, flowers bright yellow with a deeply four-lobed corolla, the petals joined only at the base, these become pendant in rainy weather thus shielding the reproductive parts. The Forsythia's flowers are impressive with the fact that they are able to produce lactose (lactose the milk sugar), the dry capsule, contain several winged seeds.

Flower colour: Pretty Yellow

Specimens examined : Bhellum 10619

Locality : Amar Singh College, Srinagar

Nativity : China

Flrs. and Frts. : April – November

Distribution : India and China

Forsythia viridissima Lindl.

Fraxinus oxycarpa Willd.

Deciduous tree, young branches somewhat upright; leaves lustrous, opposite or subopposite, dark green, turning red to purple in autumn; leaflets lanceolate, margin serrate; flowers inconspicuous.

Flower colour: white

Specimens examined : Bhellum 13879

Locality : Ladakh and Srinagar

Nativity : Caucasus

Flrs. and Frts. : May – November

Distribution : India

Ligustrum lucidum Ait. f.

Shrubs or small trees; leaves opposite, simple, margin entire; flowers bisexual, raised to terminal panicles; flowers strongly scented; corolla funnel shaped; fruits 2-locular berry. It is the largest species in the genus, growing as a tree up to 25 m tall, leaves opposite, glossy dark green, 6-17 cm long and 3-8 cm broad, the plant is often used as an ornamental tree, sometimes as a cultivar.

Flower colour: White

Specimens examined : Bhellum 10231

Locality : Srinagar

Nativity : China

Flrs. and Frts. : May – November

Distribution : India

Ligustrum lucidum Ait. f.

Syringa vulgaris L.

Deciduous shrubs or small trees, ranging in size from 2–10 m tall, with stems up to 20–30 cm diameter. Leaves opposite (occasionally in whorls of three) simple and heart-shaped to broad lanceolate in most of the species.

Syringa vulgaris L.

Flower colour: Purple

Specimens examined : Bhellum 13419

Locality : Ladakh and Srinagar

Nativity : Persia

Flrs. and Frts. : May – July

Distribution : India, Pakistan, Persia

Apocynaceae

Nerium indicum Mill.

Unarmed, shrubs, evergreen, stout; latex milky; leaves whorled, usually 3 per whorl, linear lanceolate, thickly coriaceous, 14 – 35 cm long, acuminate, midribs very stout, nerves numerous, fast green, margin entire; inflorescence dichasial cymes or panicles; flowers red, pink or white, fragrant; follicles 15 – 25 cm long, seeds numerous, crowned with a tuft of short hairs.

Grown for fragrant and showy flowers.

Flower colour: Rose coloured

Specimens examined : Bhellum 10689

Locality : Ramban, Jammu and Srinagar

Nativity : Mediterranean and China

Distribution : India, Pakistan, China and Mediterranean region.

Nerium indicum Mill.

Plumeria alba L.

A deciduous, small tree; leaves spirally arranged, oblanceolate, obtuse, aggregated to terminal extremities; flowers white tinged with pale yellow, fragrant; stamens inserted near the base of the corolla tube; ovary inferior.

Flower colour: White tinged with pale yellow

Specimens examined : Bhellum 12341

Locality : Kashmir

Nativity : West Indies

Flrs. and Frts. : March – May

Distribution : India, Afghanistan, West Indies and Pakistan

Plumeria alba L.

Plumeria rubra L.

A small tree, leaves spirally arranged; flowers arranged in terminal panicles; stamens inserted on the base of the corolla tube; ovary inferior.

Grown for sweet, fragrant flowers.

Flower colour: White tinged yellow rose

Specimens examined : Bhellum 10265

Locality : Jammu

Nativity : America

Flrs. and Frts. : March – October

Distribution : India and America

Plumeria rubra L.

Vinca major L.

Evergreen trailing shrub, leaves opposite, broadly ovate; flowers blue, solitary axillary; corolla salver-shaped; stamens included, inserted in the middle of the corolla tube; disc of two rounded glands alternating with the carpels.

Grows in shady places in the Parks and gardens.

Flower colour: Purple

Specimens examined : Bhellum 10882

Locality : Srinagar

Nativity : S. Europe

Flrs. and Frts. : April – July

Distribution : India and S. Europe

Vinca major L.

Vinca rosea L.

A small shrub; leaves opposite, obovate, glossy-green above; flowers rosy or white in axillary pairs; corolla salver-shaped; stamens included, inserted in the middle of the corolla tube; follicle single, seeds black, tubercled.

Grown for fragrant flowers.

Flower colour: White or Rose coloured.

Specimens examined : Bhellum 10675

Locality : Ramban

Nativity : West Indies and Madagascar

Flrs. and Frts. : April – November

Distribution : India, W. Indies and Madagascar

Vinca rosea L.

Buddlejaceae

Buddleja alternifolia Maxim.

A large shrub, stems long slender with weeping habit, with flowers are lilac-blue, sometimes pink, borne in early summer and are fragrant. Grown as an ornamental.

Flower colour: Lilac purple

Specimens examined : Bhellum 12341

Locality : Srinagar

Nativity : China

Flrs. and Frts. : June - August

Distribution : India,Pakistan Afghanistan and China

Hydrophyllaceae

Phacelia tanacetifolia Benth.

Annual herbs; stem upto 75 cm tall, somewhat woody towards base; branches somewhat greenish purple, grooved, silky-pubescent especially towards the apices; leaves 9 – 19.5 cm long, 2-pinnatisect, lobes up to 5 mm long, ovate, lanceolate; flowers purplish, in long scorpioid compact cymes; sepals 5, sparsely hairy; corolla broadly campanulate, lobes ovate, purplish, distinctly veined; stamens 5, filaments filiform, as long as the style of the ovary; seeds usually 2, greyish-brown.

Flower colour: Purple

Specimens examined : Kaul 26

Locality : Barzulla, Srinagar

Nativity : U.S.A.

Flrs. and Frts. : June-August

Distribution : India and U.S.A.

Ehretiaceae

Cordia dichotoma L.

Dioecious or polygamous trees; branches densely tomentose; leaves 5 – 8 cm long, elliptic-ovate, pubescent; flowers in dichotomous cymes; male flowers and bisexual flowers almost similar, but bisexual flowers larger than the male flowers; drupe 15 mm broad, yellowish-red.

Flower colour: White

Specimens examined : Bhellum 10293

Locality : Jammu

Nativity : New Caledonia

Flrs. and Frts. : April – November

Distribution : India and New Caledonia

Cordia myxa L.

Deciduous trees; young shoots and branches with rusty pubescence; leaves suborbicular to elliptic ovate, 3-nerved, acute, tomentose underneath; flowers white; drupe 20 mm long, ovoid, apiculate brownish yellow, base partly surrounded by enlarged cupular calyx.

Flower colour: White

Specimens examined : Bhellum 13673

Locality : Srinagar

Nativity : Egypt to - Malabaria

Flrs. and Frts. : April – July

Distribution : India, Pakistan, Sri Lanka, W. Tibet, Persia, Arabia.

Ehrtia laevis Roxb.

A medium sized tree; shoots and branches pubescent or glabrescent; leaves elliptic-ovate, oblong, acute or obtuse, minutely pubescent underneath, base rounded or oblique; inflorescence axillary or terminal cymes; flowers white; calyx 5-partite, corolla 5-lobed, lobes ovate, lanceolate; ovary ovoid, 2 mm long; drupe black and wrinkled when ripe.

Flower colour: White

Specimens examined : Bhellum 10290

Locality : Jammu

Nativity : Baluchistan and Pakistan

Flrs. and Frts. : April – August

Distribution : India, Pakistan, Ceylon, Persia, China and Australia.

E. obtusifolia Hichst. ex DC.

Shrubs about 3 m tall; young shoots glandular hairy with brownish hairs; leaves obovate, cuneate, spathulate, 2.5 – 8 cm long, margin entire or undulate coriaceous pubescent; calyx 2 mm long, 5-partite, shallow, copular, glandular; corolla white, tinged bluish, lobes obtuse; ovary ovoid, styles 2, spreading; drupe sub globose, 5 – 6 mm broad.

Flower colour: White tinged bluish

Specimens examined : Bhellum 12343

Locality : Srinagar

Nativity : Abyssinia

Flrs. and Frts. : April – August

Distribution : India, Abyssinia, Pakistan, Afghanistan and Burma.

Boraginaceae

Anchusa officinalis L.

Flower colour: Red, blue

Specimens examined : Bhellum 15403

Locality : Srinagar

Nativity : Warm regions of Europe

Flrs. and Frts. : April – July

Distribution : India, Iran, Afghanistan and Pakistan, and Warm parts of Europe

Arnebia euchroma (Royle ex Benth.) I. M. Johnston

An erect, hairy perennial; root-stock thick; stem several arising from the base; basal leaves lanceolate, upper ones shorter, strigosely hairy; flowers yellow to purple; calyx villous with brownish-white hairs; corolla 5-lobed, lobes suborbicular; nutlets about 3 mm long, rugose tuberculate, greyish, keeled.

Flower colour: Yellow tinged purple

Specimens examined : Bhellum 16293

Locality : Srinagar

Nativity : Kunawar

Flrs. and Frts. : April – May

Distribution : India, Iran, Afghanistan and Pakistan

A. griffthii Boiss.

Annual erect herbs 20 – 40 cm tall; leaves broadly lanceolate, bracts small, linear; flowers orange yellow, spotted near the throat; calyx 5-partite; corolla 5-lobed, lobes spreading; nutlets 2 mm long, tubercled.

Flower colour: PurpleYellow spotted near throat

Specimens examined : Bhellum 14670

Locality : Srinagar

Nativity : Afghanistan

Flrs. and Frts. : April – May

Distribution : India, Afghanistan and Pakistan

A. speciosa Aitch.

Perennial herbs upto 70 cm tall; stem simple; leaves hallow, hairy inflorescence interrupted, shorter bracts smaller than calyx; corolla bluish to bluish purple, glabrous on outside; nutlets ovoid, rugose, tuberculate.

Flower colour: Bluish purple

Specimens examined : Bhellum 12296

Locality : Srinagar

Nativity : Afghanistan

Flrs. and Frts. : April – May

Distribution : India, Afghanistan and Pakistan

Asperugo procumbens L.

Annual herbs upto 60 cm tall; stem branched, branches fistular, striate, scabrid with setose or scabrid hairs; leaves oblanceolate, to broadly lanceolate, hairy on both surfaces with appressed hairs arising from the swollen base; calyx 5-lobed, hairy; corolla blue, 2 – 4 mm long, slightly exceeding the calyx; nutlets about 3 mm long, laterally compressed, minutely tubercled.

Flower colour : Blue

Specimens examined : Bhellum 12357

Locality : Srinagar

Nativity : Europe

Flrs. and Frts. : May-August

Distribution : India, N. Africa, Asia and Europe

Buglossoides arvensis (L.) Johnston

Annual herbs upto 50 cm tall; stem branched from the base; basal leaves oblanceolate or lanceolate, longer than the upper ones; upper leaves about 1 – 3 cm long; flowers in terminal racemes; calyx lobes linear, about 5 mm long; corolla pale blue to white, hairy on outside; nutlets pear-shaped, grey to brown.

Flower colour : White streaked blue

Specimens examined : Bhellum 12947

Locality : Srinagar

Nativity : Europe

Flrs. and Frts. : April-May

Distribution : India, S. Europe Iraq, Iran, Afghanistan Pakistan and Japan.

B. tenuiflora (L f.) Jhonston

Annual, decumbent, robust herbs; stem branched from the base; leaves oblanceolate, hairy on both the surfaces, 3 – 6 cm long; flowers in terminal racemes; calyx 5-lobed, lobes linear, clothed with yellow hairs; corolla blue to white; nutlets bigibbous.

Flower colour : White streaked purple

Specimens examined : Bhellum 12587

Locality : Srinagar

Nativity : Aegypt

Flrs. and Frts. : May-August

Distribution : India, N. Africa, N.E. Europe, C. Asia, Afghanistan and Pakistan.

Cynoglossum lanceolatum Forssk.

Biennial or perennial herbs; stem much branched, clothed with rigid white hairs arising from tuberculate base; basal leaves lanceolate, petiolate, 10 – 20 cm long, upper surface clothed with appressed hairs, lower surface densely hairy; flowers pale blue in axillary cymes; calyx lobes 5, hairy on outside, glabrous inside; corolla 5-lobed, lobes ovate, obtuse, throat scales broader than long; nutlets nearly 2 mm long, style stout, persistent.

Flower colour : White streaked purple

Specimens examined : Bhellum 12987

Locality : Banihal

Nativity : Yemen

Flrs. and Frts. : May-August

Distribution : India, Africa, Pakistan, Sri Lanka, Burma, Nepal, China and Malaysia

C. glochidiatum Wall. ex Benth.

Annual or biennial herbs; stem branched, hispid in lower parts; basal leaves petiolate to obovate, cauline leaves generally longer and with shorter petioles, upper ones smaller in size; flowers bluish to white, in scorpioid cymes; calyx lobes oblong, slightly enlarged in fruits; corolla lobes-5, throat scales bifid, puberulous; nutlets round to ovate, dorsal area with sparse to dense erect appendages.

Flower colour : White streaked purple

Specimens examined : Bhellum 13917

Locality : Banihal

Nativity : Nepal

Flrs. and Frts. : May-August

Distribution : India, Afghanistan, Nepal and Bhutan

Heliotropium curassavicum L.

A glabrous perennial herb, upto 50 cm tall; stem and branches decumbent; leaves oblanceolate or linear lanceolate, obtuse, glabrous; flowers white, in cymes; calyx 5-partite, persistent; corolla white, tube short, lobes obtuse; nutlets about 2 mm long, brown or black, rugose.

Flower colour: White

Specimens examined : Bhellum 12213

Locality : Srinagar

Nativity : America

Flrs. and Frts. : April – May

Distribution : India, America, Europe, Australia and Africa

H. strigosum Willd.

Perennial decumbent or prostrate herbs; stem branched, upto 30 cm tall; leaves linear lanceolate, acute, appressed strigosely hairy on both the surfaces; calyx 5-partite, lobes lanceolate, hairy on outside; corolla 5-lobed, lobes obtuse; nutlets 4, densely pilose, dark beown.

Flower colour: Pinkish tinged purple

Specimens examined : Bhellum 10293

Locality : Srinagar

Nativity : Guinea

Flrs. and Frts. : April – November

Distribution : India, Afghanistan, Pakistan, Nepal, Burma and Malaya.

Lithospermum officinale L.

Perennial hispidly hairy herbs; stem upto 70 cm tall, usually branched from the base, hairy, hairs with tuberculate base; leaves alternate, lanceolate, 3 – 6 cm long, hairy on both surfaces, margin entire; inflorescence in axillary or terminal racemes; flowers white; calyx 5-

lobed, lobes linear, hairy, accrescent; corolla white tubular, tube cylindric, 5-lobed, lobes spreading; stamens 5, anthers oblong, bithecous; ovary 4-lobed, style slender, stigma apiculate; nutlets 3 – 4 mm long.

Flower colour : White

Specimens examined : Bhellum 12907

Locality : Srinagar

Nativity : Europe

Flrs. and Frts. : May-August

Distribution : India, Europe and C. Asia

Mattiastrum bungei (Boiss.) Rech. f.

Annual herbs; stem weak, branches few, appressed hairy; leaves lanceolate cauline sessile, clothed with hairs on both the surfaces arising from tuberculate bases; calyx lobes lanceolate, hairy; corolla 5-lobed, blue; nutlets ovoid, about 4 mm long, margin winged.

Flower colour : White streaked Blue

Specimens examined : Bhellum 12481

Locality : Banihal

Nativity : Persia

Flrs. and Frts. : May-August

Distribution : India, Iran, Afghanistan, Pakistan, Soviet C. Asia

Myosotis arvensis (L.) Hill.

Perennial herbs, upto 30 cm tall or more; stem thinly branched, villous; basal leaves elliptic-oblong, to oblanceolate, cauline leaves smaller, sessile; flowers about 3 mm across; calyx lobes 5, lanceolate, clothed with spreading hairs, incurved in fruiting; corolla blue or bluish-purple; nutlets oblong, black-brown, smooth, shining.

Flower colour : White streaked purple

Specimens examined : Bhellum 12987

Locality : Srinagar

Nativity : Europe

Flrs. and Frts. : May-August

Distribution : India, Europe, N. E. Africa and Pakistan

Onosma dichroanthum Boiss.

Annual or perennial, hispid, herbs; root-stock thick; stem 20 – 45 cm tall, hairy, hairs setose, soft, long and short hairs intermixed, arising from a tubercled base; basal leaves spathulate, linear to linear lanceolate, densely clothed with spreading hairs, margin recurved, cauline leaves similar, alternate, smaller, sessile, hairy; inflorescence in forked cymes; flowers yellow; nutlets smooth, shining.

Flower colour : Cream coloured

Specimens examined : Bhellum 12317

Locality : Srinagar

Nativity : Trans caucasia

Flrs. and Frts. : May-August

Distribution : India, Turkestan, Afghanistan and Pakistan.

O. yamagytae L

Perennial, hispid, herbs; stem 20 – 30 cm tall, hairy, hairs setose, base tuberculate; basal leaves spathulate, linear to lanceolate, 15 – 30 cm long, densely clothed with intermixed hairs, margin recurved; cauline leaves similar, but smaller, densely hispid; inflorescence in congested, capitate cymes; flowers pedicellate, bisexual; calyx segments linear lanceolate, acute; corolla campanulate, slightly lobed, lobes deflexed, obtuse; stamens 5, filaments inserted on the corolla lobes; nutlets smooth, shining.

Flower colour : Pale yellow

Specimens examined : Bhellum 13917

Locality : Padder

Nativity : Afghanistan

Flrs. and Frts. : May-August

Distribution : India and Afghanistan

Rochelia bungei Trautv.

Annual herbs 10 – 35 cm tall; stem branched, clothed with appressed hairs; basal leaves oblanceolate to obovate, hairy on both the surfaces; inflorescence second, lax in fruiting; calyx 5-lobed, lobes, pubescent; corolla white streaked purple ; nutlets tuberculate.

Flower colour : White streaked purple

Specimens examined : Bhellum 12997

Locality : Srinagar

Nativity : USSR.

Flrs. and Frts. : May-August

Distribution : India, Iran, Afghanistan, Pakistan, Soviet and C. Asia.

R. stylaris Boiss.

Annual or perennial erect herbs; stem branched from the base; leaves oblanceolate, clothed with appressed hairs; flowers in second; calyx lobes 5, lanceolate; corolla pale-blue, tube short; nutlets about 2 mm yellowish-brown, papillose.

Flower colour : White streaked purple or pale blue

Specimens examined : Bhellum 13797

Locality : Srinagar

Nativity Afghanistan

Flrs. and Frts. : May-August

Distribution : India, Afghanistan and Pakistan

R. cardiosepala Bunge

Annual herbs upto 30 cm tall or more; stem branched, from the base clothed with appressed hairs; leaves oblanceolate, clothed with hairs on both the surfaces; calyx lobes 5, lanceolate, 6 mm long; corolla 5-lobed; nutlets 4, grayish papillose.

Flower colour : White streaked purple

Locality : Srinagar

Specimens examined : Bhellum 13579

Nativity : Turkestan

Flrs. and Frts. : May-August

Distribution : India, Iraq, Iran, Afghanistan, Pakistan, Caucasus and Soviet C. Asia.

Convolvulaceae

Calystegia hederacea Wall

Prostrate, twining, glabrous herbs; stem slender; leaves petiolate, entire or lobed, 1.5 – 7.5 cm long, triangular, obtuse, slightly emarginate, base sagittate or cordate, glabrous; flowers solitary axillary; pedicel upto 7 cm long or more; bracts 2, large, enclosing the calyx, persistent; sepals 5, ovate, oblong; corolla campanulate, limb 5-plaited, subentire, pinkish-purple; stamens 5, included; disc cup-shaped; ovary glabrous, style filiform, stigma elongate, oblong; capsule glabrous, about 8 mm long, beaked; seeds reddish or black, glabrous.

Flower colour : White streaked purple

Specimens examined : Bhellum 12987

Locality : Srinagar

Nativity : Europe

Flrs. and Frts. : May-August

Distribution : India, Pakistan Afghanistan, Europe and Britain

Convolvulus arvensis L.

Prostrate, creeping or twining herbs; juice milky; stem weak, angular, glabrous; leaves alternate, ovate, lanceolate, oblong, upto 10 cm long, nearly glabrous on both surfaces; flowers white tinged pink, usually solitary, rarely 2 or 3 in cymes; sepals 5, united, green; corolla tube short, limb spreading, obscurely 5-lobed; stamend 5, unequal, epipetalous, attached at the base of the corolla tube, filaments glandular hairy, anthers bithecous, white, pollen wall smooth; ovary 2-celled, ovules 2 in each cell; capsule ovoid-globose, 4-seeded.

Flower colour:White tinged with pink

Specimens examined : Bhellum 10690

Locality : Throughout the state

Nativity : Mediterranean regions and Europe

Flrs. and Frts. : Feb. – March

Distribution : India, Pakistan, Afghanistan and Ceylon

Evolvulus numularius L.

Prostrate herbs; stem rooting from nodes, 8 – 45 cm long, clothed with scattered hairs on the older parts and young parts densely pubescent; leaves orbicular or suborbicular, broadly oblong, apex rounded or nearly notched, base truncate or subcordate, slightly oblique, nearly pubescent beneath; petiole 1 – 5 mm long, pilose; flowers solitary axillary or rarely in pairs; peduncle about 2.5 mm long, recurved in fruiting; sepals 5, ovate, oblong, 2.5 – 3.8 mm long, equal, sparsely pubescent on outside or glabrous, apex obtuse, or subacute, mucronate, margin ciliate; corolla salver-shaped, about 6 mm long, white, tube very short, limb about 7 mm across, distinctly lobed into 5 bands, sparsely pubescent; stamens 5, staminal filaments inserted at the base of the corolla tube; ovary glabular, glabrous, capsule equaling or longer than sepals; capsule 2-celled, 4-valved; seeds 4 or less.

Flower colour: pale yellow

Specimens examined : Bhellum 10615

Locality : Jammu

Nativity : Tropical America

Flrs. and Frts. : May – October

Distribution : India, Pakistan and nearly all the tropical and subtropical regions of the world.

Ipomoea alba L.

A large climber, stout, glabrescent, with milky juice; stem often muricate; leaves broadly ovate, acuminate, base deeply cordate, margin entire; petiole stout, as long as the leaves; flowers white, fragrant, arranged solitary or axillary cymes; corolla salver-shaped, tube 8 – 10 cm long, white with greenish plaits; stamens 5, unequal, filaments often hairy at the base; capsule 3 – 4 valved, ovoid-globose, glabrous.

Flower colour: White

Specimens examined : Bhellum 10253

Locality : Jammu

Nativity : Tropical America

Flrs. and Frts. : March – October

Distribution : India, Pakistan and Tropical America

I. batatas Lamk.

A prostrate herb, juice milky; roots tuberous; leaves triangular, usually irregularly lobed, base more or less cordate; flowers in axillary peduncles, purple with short pedicel; corolla campanulate, limb spreading; stamens 5, unequal; capsule globose.

Flower colour: Purple

Specimens examined : Bhellum 12204

Locality : Jammu and Srinagar

Nativity : Tropical America

Flrs. and Frts. : July – October

Distribution : India, Pakistan and tropical America

I. fistulosa Mart. ex Choisy

Erect or ascending, suffruticose, perennial undershrubs; stem fistular, usually glabrous except puberulous young parts; leaves alternate, ovate, cordate, 12 – 26 cm long, 5 – 15 cm broad, margin entire; flowers in cymes; sepals ovate, rounded, green; corolla bell-shaped, limb obscurely 5-lobed, purplish-pink; stamens 5, unequal, attached at the corolla tube, filaments dilated at base, anthers bithecous, white, pollen wall spinulose; ovary bicelled, globose, glabrous, stigma capitate; seeds brown, villous, 7 – 8 mm long.

Flower colour: White tinged purple

Specimens examined : Bhellum 10222

Locality : Jammu, Chanderkote

Nativity : America

Flrs. and Frts. : March – October

Distribution : India, Pakistan, Afghanistan and S. America

Ipomoea fistulosa Mart. ex Choisy

I. hederifolia L.

A slender, glabrous, twiner; leaves ovate, entire or lobed, acuminate; inflorescence a few flowered pedunculate cymes, peduncle 8 – 11 cm long; bracts inconspicous; sepals upto 4 cm distinctly awned on back; corolla salver-shaped, 3.5 cm long, limb short, subentire; stamens 5, exserted; ovary 4-locular.capsule globose.

Cultivated in America but now wild and commonly found in Ramgarh, Vijaypur of Jammu region

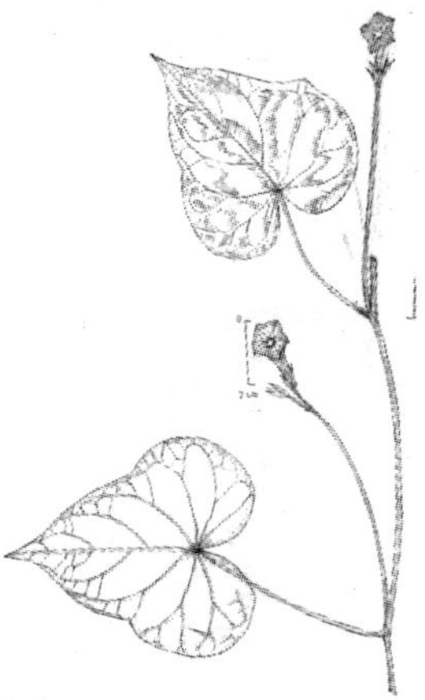

Ipomoea hederifolia L.

Flower colour: White tinged purple

Specimens examined : Bhellum 10223

Locality : Jammu

Nativity : Tropical America

Flrs. and Frts. : March – October

Distribution : India, Pakistan and tropical America

I. nil (L) Roth

Annual, hairy twiner; stem slender, villous; leaves ovate, cordate, usully palmately 3-lobed, lateral lobes acute, central one acuminate, hairy on both surfaces; flowers pink or blue in 1 or few cymes; sepals 5, linear, densely villous at base; corolla funnel-shaped, upto 8 cm long, limb spreading; stamens 5, unequal, anthers bithecous; ovary 3-celled, stigma capitate; capsule subglobose, nearly 8 mm across.

Flower colour: White tinged purple, pink or blue

Specimens examined : Bhellum 12322

Locality : Jammu

Nativity : Tropical America

Flrs. and Frts. : March – October

Distribution : India, Pakistan, Tropical America and all other tropical and subtropical regions of the world.

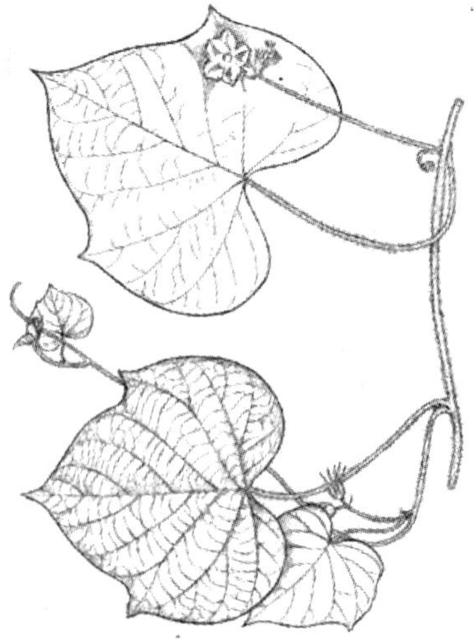

Ipomoea nil (L) Roth

I. palmata Forssk.

A perennial, glabrous climber; stem somewhat rough when old; leaves as long as broad, palmately cut into oblanceolate lobes, lobes 3 – 7, obtuse, mucronate, glabrous; flowers in axillary peduncles, pale blue or purple; corolla campanulate, 3 – 5 cm long, stamens 5, unequal; ovary usually 2, rarely 3 or 4 celled; disc annular; fruits dry indehiscent, 2 – 4 seeded.

Often cultivated in the Gardens; sometimes found as an escape.

Flower colour: Purple or pale blue

Specimens examined : Bhellum 14516

Locality : Throughout the state

Nativity : Tropical countries

Flrs. and Frts. : April – November

I. pes-tigridis L.

Annual hispid, climber or twiner; leaves ovate or elliptic, upto 15 cm across, hairy, deeply cut into ovate or elliptic lobes; flowers 2.5 – 3 cm across, crowded in capitate cymes; peduncles upto 18 cm long; stamens 5; sepals, hairy on outside; corolla funnel-shaped, limb spreading, white tinged purplish pink; seeds black.

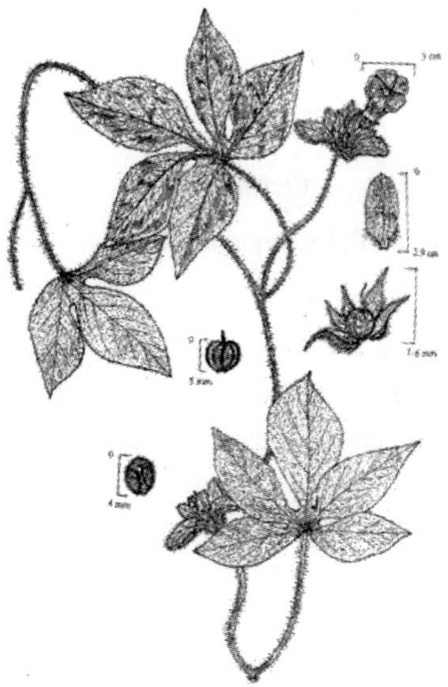

Ipomoea pes-tigridis L.

Flower colour: White tinged purple

Specimens examined : Bhellum 12831

Locality : Jammu

Nativity : Ceylon

Flrs. and Frts. : July – October

Distribution : India, Pakistan, Ceylon and all other tropical and subtropical regions of the world.

I. purpurea Roth

Annual, twining herbs; stem slender, weak, retrosely hairy; leaves alternate, ovate, cordate, 4 – 7 cm long, pubescent on both the surfaces, apex abruptly acute, margin entire; inflorescence solitary axillary or few flowered cymes; flowers rosy-pink; sepals 5, free, about 1 cm long; corolla funnel-shaped, 3 – 4.5 cm long, tube short, limb spreading, obscurely 5-lobed; stamens 5, unequal, anthers bithecous, white, filaments glabrous except at the base; pollen spinulose; ovary 2 or 3-celled, ovules 2 in each locule; capsule about 5.5 mm across; seeds glabrous.

Cultivated extensively for showy flowers in all the tropical countries of the world and now wild in various parts of the state.

Flower colour: White or pale blue

Specimens examined : Bhellum 12545

Locality : Jammu and Srinagar

Nativity : Tropical America

Flrs. and Frts. : July – October

Distribution : India, Pakistan and tropical America

I. pomoea quamoclit L.

A perennial, glabrous climber; stem somewhat rough when old; leaves pinnately dissected, into fine pinnatisect segments, opposite rarely alternate, glabrous; flowers solitary or in axillary peduncles, red; sepals elliptic oblong, 5 – 7 mm long, glabrous; corolla salver-shaped, 3 – 5 cm long, deep red; stamens 5, unequal; ovary usually 2, rarely 3 or 4 celled; disc annular; capsule ovoid, dry indehiscent, 6 – 8 mm long, dark brown to black, with patches of trichomes, scattered irregularly, 2 – 4 seeded.

Cultivated in the gardens and parks for pretty, showy flowers.

Flower colour: Red

Specimens examined : Bhellum 10345

Locality : Jammu and Srinagar

Nativity : Tropical America

Flrs. and Frts. : July – October

Distribution : India, Pakistan and tropical America

Merremia dissecta (Jacq.) Hallier f.

Herbaceous twining herbs, clothed with spreading brownish-yellow hairs; leaves upto 15 cm across in outline, lobed, lobes palmatisect, lanceolate; peduncles 1 to 2 flowered; sepals ovate, margin scarious; corolla white with rose-purple throat, 3.5 – 4 cm long and across; capsule about 1.5 cm across, glabrous, usually 4-seeded.

Flower colour: Rose-purple

Specimens examined : Bhellum 12048

Locality : Jammu and Srinagar

Nativity : Tropical America

Flrs. and Frts. : July – October

Distribution : India, Pakistan and tropical America

Merremia dissecta (Jacq.) Hallier f.

Solanaceae

Capsicum annuum L.

Annual, glabrous, herbs 30 – 50 cm tall; leaves ovate, lanceolate, acute, flowers white, calyx 5-toothed ; corolla rotate, 5-lobed; stamens 5; fruits elongate, green first turning red when ripe.

Flower colour: White

Specimens examined : Bhellum 10822

Locality : Jammu

Nativity : Tropical America

Flrs. and Frts. : March – October

Distribution : India, Pakistan Bangladesh and Ceylon

Cestrum nocturnum L.

An evergreen, subscandent shrub; stem about 3.5 m tall; leaves lanceolate, acuminate, 5 – 8 cm long, inflorescence in panicles; flowers yellowish green, fragrant.

Much cultivated in the gardens and parks throughout the state.

Flower colour: White or pale-yellow

Specimens examined : Bhellum 11253

Locality : Jammu

Nativity : America

Flrs. and Frts. : March – October

Distribution : India, Pakistan and America

Datura innoxia L

Annual, somewhat shrubby, strongly foetid; stem upto 1.2 m tall, softly tomentose; leaves deep-bluish green, broadly ovate to ovate-lanceolate, 10 – 25 cm long, entire or repand-toothed; flowers white, 10 – 15 cm long with spreading 10 toothed corolla-limb; fruiting calyx enlarged and reflexed; capsule globose, 4 – 5 cm across, nodding, covered with long spines; seeds brown.

Flower colour: White

Specimens examined : Bhellum 10789

Locality : Jammu

Nativity : Tropical America

Flrs. and Frts. : March - September

Distribution : India, Pakistan and tropical America

D. metel L.

Annual looking like shrubby perennial; stem upto 1.5 m tall, green, shining,dark-purple; leaves ovate, about 10 – 15 cm long, sinuate or repand-toothed; flowers white, or dirty-white, purplish on outside; 12 – 15 cm long or more; fruiting calyx cup or saucer-like; capsule globose, included or nodding upto 5 cm across.

Flower colour: White and Purple or violet on outside

Specimens examined : Bhellum 10615

Locality : Udhampur

Nativity Tropical America

Flrs. and Frts. March – September

Distribution : India, Pakistan, and tropical America.

D. strumarium L.

Annual herbs, stem upto 1 m tall, glabrous at base, pubescent above; leaves ovate, 10 – 18 cm long, sinuately lobed or toothed; flowers white, 4 – 7 cm long; calyx 5-lobed, angular, angles 5, corolla lobes 5, erect, thrown into elongated points; capsule ovoid, sharply spinous; seeds black.

Flower colour:White

Specimens examined : Bhellum 11612

Locality : Srinagar

Nativity : Tropical America

Flrs. and Frts. : May – October

Distribution : India, Pakistan, Nepal, Tropical America and Britain

Physalia minima L.

Annual or diffuse puberulous, herbs, 30 – 50 cm tall; leaves ovate, entire or irregularly toothed or sinuate, 3 – 8 cm long; flowers solitary, deflexed, yellow, rarely spotted with brown at the base within; calyx 5-toothed or lobed, corolla 5-lobed; stamens 5; berries greenish-yellow, 8 – 12 mm across.

Flower colour: Pale yellow

Specimens examined : Bhellum 12261

Locality : Gajanshu

Nativity : South America

Flrs. and Frts. : May – September

Distribution : India, Ceylon, Afghanistan, tropical Africa, Pakistan, and S. America

Solanum pseudo-capsicum L.

An erect, undershrub, upto 1m tall; stem branched, branches spreading; leaves oblanceolate, or oblong, entire or repand, bright green and shining; attenuate at the base into a short petiole; flowers in extra-axillary or few flowered umbellate, cymes; coroalla rotate, 5-lobed; white or purple; berries globose, bright red when ripe, 12 mm across.

Flower colour: White

Specimens examined : Bhellum 12451

Locality : Batote

Nativity : South Africa & China

Flrs. and Frts. : Mayl – October

Distribution : India, Naturalised in Australia, S. Africa and China

S. seaforthianum Andr.

A glabrous climber somewhat woody; basal leaves thin, pinnately divided, upper ones entire; inflorescence peduncled axillary compound cymes; flowers 2 cm across, bluish purple; calyx 5-toothed; corolla rotate; berries globose, 8 mm across, red when ripe.

Flower colour: Bluish purple

Specimens examined : Bhellum 12101

Locality : Jammu

Nativity : Tropical America

Flrs. and Frts. : July – October

Distribution : India, Tropical America, Italy

S. torvum Sw.

A tomentose shrub, branches herbaceous with few prickles; leaves ovte, sinuately or coarsely lobed, acute one or two prickles on the midrib on undersurface, stellate tomentose above densely so beneath; flowers in extra-axillary dichotomous cymes much shorter than the leaves; calyx 5-lobed, pubescent; corolla rotate, white; lobes triangular, stellate pubescent on outside; berries 10 – 12 mm across, yellow.

Flower colour: White

Specimens examined : Bhellum 10272

Locality : Jammu

Nativity : America

Flrs. and Frts. : March – October

Distribution : India, Pakistan, America

Scrophulariaceae

Antirrhinum majus L.

Perennial herbs, 0.5-1 m tall; leaves spirally arranged, broadly lanceolate, 1-7 cm long; inflorescence spikes, flowers upto 5 cm long, pink or purple, often with yellow lips; fruit an ovoid capsule; seeds many.

Flower colour:

Specimens examined : Bhellum 10567

Locality : Ramban

Nativity : Mediterranean region and Europe

Flrs. and Frts. : May – August

Distribution : India, Pakistan, Europe and Mediterranean region of the world.

Mazus japonica (Thunb.) Kuntze

Annual herbs; stem erect, forming dense hairy tuft; leaves mainly radical, obovate, or obovate-spathulate, margin crenate or dentate; flowers white with pale shades, mixed with yellow.

Flower colour: White with pale-blue shades mixed with yellow

Specimens examined : Bhellum 10528

Locality : Ramban and Jammu

Nativity : Japan

Flrs. and Frts. : November – May

Distribution : India, Bhutan, Pakistan, Afghanistan, Java, china, Japan, Philippine Islands

Veronica anagallis-aquatica L.

Annual or decumbent ascending herbs; stem simple or branched, glabrous towards base and glandular hairy towards apex; leaves sessile, lanceolate, oblong, base semi-amplexicaule, margin crenate to serrate; flowers in axillary lax, 7 – 15 cm long, racemes, bisexual, pink or purplish; calyx 4-lobed, lobes spreading, patently gland-hairy; corolla white; capsule oval, stongly flattened, emarginate, glandular ciliate.

Flower colour: Pink or purple

Specimens examined : Bhellum 10890

Locality Jammu

Nativity : Temperate regions

Flrs. and Frts. : Feb. – May

Distribution : India, Pakistan and temperate regions of the world.

Bignoniaceae

Bignonia venusta Ker-Gawl.

An evergreen climbing shrub; leaves pinnately compound, 2-foliate, lower leaves often 3-foliate, ovate, acuminate, gland-dotted, about as long as broad; flowers orange-red, showy, in drooping corymbose racemes; corolla 5 – 7.6 cm long, slightly curved upwards; stamens 4, didynamous; fruit an elongated capsule.

Flower colour: Orange-red

Specimens examined : Bhellum 13418

Locality : Jammu

Nativity : Brazil

Flrs. and Frts. : March – April

Distribution : India, Pakistan and Brazil

Campsis grandiflora Loir

A climbing shrub; leaves imparipinnate, leaflets 7 – 11, broadly ovate, ovate-lanceolate, acuminate, margin serrate, glabrous; flowers arranged in loose panicles, orange-scarlet; corolla about 5 cm long, tube short; ovary 2-celled, supported by annular disc; fruit an elongated capsule.

Cultivated in gardens and parks for beautiful flowers.

Flower colour: Orange scarlet

Specimens examined : Bhellum 13096

Locality : Jammu

Nativity : United States

Flrs. and Frts. : April – November

Distribution : India, Pakistan and America

Catalpa bignonoides Walt.

A deciduous tree, medium sized; branches spreading; leaves occasionally larger, apex rounded or abruptly acute; flowers 5 – 7.5 cm across,yellow with orange blotches and purple spots; calyx 5-lobed, glabrous; capsule 15 – 50 cm long.

Flower colour: Orange yellow with purple spots

Specimens examined : Bhellum 14516

Locality : Srinagar

Nativity : South United States

Flrs. and Frts. : April – November

Distribution : India, Pakistan and America

Jacaranda mimosaefolia D. Don

A small tree; leaves opposite, bipinnate; inflorescence in terminal panicles; corolla tube curved, throat wide, limb 2-lipped; flowers about 5 cm long; stamens 4; capsule ovate, obtuse about 7.5 cm long; seeds winged

Flower colour: Light blue, Purple or mauve

Specimens examined : Bhellum 10312

Locality :. Jammu

Nativity : Brazil and probably North West Argentina.

Flrs. and Frts. : April – July

J.ovalifolia

Distribution : India, Pakistan, America, Brazil and Argentina

Kigelia pinnata DC.

A medium-sized spreading tree with alternate, imparipinnate leaves crowded at the end of the branches, leaflets 20 cm long or more, elliptic oblong, shortly acuminate bade unequal-sided, coriaceous, dark green, scabrid on both the surfaces; flowers dull liver-coloured in very lax racemes, hanging from rope like more than 1 m long peduncles; corolla broadly campanulate, tube short, limb nearly bilabiate, lobes 4 – 5, spreading; stamens 4 ; fruits elongate, woody, indehiscent gourd-like.

Flower colour: Yellow spotted purple

Specimens examined : Bhellum 10435

Locality : Jammu

Nativity : Tropical Africa

Flrs. and Frts. : May – December

Distribution : India, Pakistan and Tropical Africa

Tecoma australis R. Br.

Twining glabrous; leaves pinnately compound, leaflets ovate, oblong, usually entire; flowers red with purple spots, about 2 cm across.

Cultivated in gardens and park for showy flowers.

Flower colour: white with red or purple spots

Specimens examined : Bhellum 10582

Locality : Jammu

Nativity : Australia

Flrs. and Frts. : May – December

Distribution : India, Pakistan and Australia

T. capensis Lindl.

A shrub, about 2 m tall; leaves pinnately compound, 5 – 10 cm long; leaflets broadly elliptic, obtuse, terminal leaflet the largest; flowers orange-red or scarlet; calyx lobed, lobes deltoid; corolla curved; stamens and style exserted.

Flower colour: Orange red or scarlet

Specimens examined : Bhellum 10582

Locality : Jammu

Nativity : Tropical Africa

Flrs. and Frts. : May – December

Distribution : India, Pakistan and Tropical Africa

T. grandiflora Delaun

A deciduous climbing shrub; leaves glabrous; calyx about 3 cm long, cleft nearly half way down, lobes glandular; corolla less than twice as long as calyx.

Flower colour: Orange scarlet

Specimens examined : Bhellum 14678

Locality : Jammu

Nativity : China and Japan

Flrs. and Frts. : April – November

Distribution : India, Pakistan and America

T. jasminoides Lindl.

A deciduous climbing large shrub; leaves pinnately compound; flowers pale rose or deep red in throat; corolla tube 2.5 cm long, limb nearly 5 cm across.

Occasionally cultivated in gardens and parks for its flowers.

Flower colour: Pale rose, deep red in throat

Specimens examined : Bhellum 10189

Locality : Jammu

Nativity : Australia

Flrs. and Frts. : May – December

Distribution : India, Pakistan and Australia

T. stans Juss.

A medium sized shrub; leaves 15 – 25 cm long, pinnately compound, leaflets lanceolate, acuminate, margin serrate, glabrous or pubescent; flowers yellow, about 2.5 cm across arranged in terminal panicles; calyx 5-toothed, teeth smll; corolla campanulate, tube, short, slender; capsule upto 17 cm long, compressed.

Flower colour: Yellow

Specimens examined : Bhellum 14190

Locality : Jammu

Nativity : Tropical America

Flrs. and Frts. : April – November

Distribution : India, Pakistan and America

Verbenaceae

Clerodendrum philippinum Schauer

A shrub, 1 – 3 m tall; tender parts pubescent; leaves opposite, broadly ovate, cordate, base rounded, apex acute; pubescent beneath along nerves, margin dentate; inflorescence terminal dense corymbs; flowers white tinged with pink; calyx campanulate, 5-toothed, cleft half way down; corolla 5-lobed, lobes spreading; stamens 4, didynamous, protruded; ovary tetralocular, stigma shortly bifid; fruit obovate, 4-lobed.

Flower colour: White tinged pink

Specimens examined : Bhellum 10358

Locality : Jammu

Nativity : Eastern Asia

Flrs. and Frts. : March – October

Distribution : India, Pakistan and Eastern Asia

Duranta plumieri Jacq.

An evergreen, bushy, thorny shrub; leaves opposite, elliptic, lanceolate, or obovate, acuminate, margin serrate; flowers in terminal axillary racemes; corolla white or blue; fruit a berry, orange when ripe.

Cultivated as a hedge plant in Jammu region.

Flower colour: Purple

Specimens examined : Bhellum 10882

Locality : Jammu

Nativity : Tropical America from Mexico to Brazil

Flrs. and Frts. : May – October

Distribution : India, Pakistan, and Tropical America

Tectoma grandis L.f.

Deciduous, large, 40-50 m tall tree; leaves opposite, 30-60 cm or more, somewhat whorled; inflorescence terminal racemes; fruit a drupe, 4-celled.

Flower colour: White

Specimens examined : Bhellum 10762

Locality : Jammu

Nativity : Indo-Malaysia

Flrs. and Frts. : March – October

Distribution : India, Malaya

Lamiaceae

Mentha arvensis L.

Medium sized, strongly scented perennial herbs; leaves ovate, lanceolate, oblong, 2.5 – 7.5 cm long, sharply toothed, acute, nearly sessile, grey velvety above, white felted below; inflorescence axillary terminal, cylindric tapering spikes, 2.5 – 5 cm long; lower bracts foliaceous, upper ones smaller lanceolate; calyx 5-toothed, teeth sharp, hairy; corolla 4-lobed, lobes erect, nearly equal; stamens 4 equal, protruding; style arms short; nutlets 4, netted.

Flower colour:

Specimens examined : Bhellum 10765

Locality : Batote

Nativity : Japan

Flrs. and Frts. : May – September

Distribution : India, Pakistan, Japan

Mentha arvensis L.

M. piperita L.

Rhizomatous perennial herb growing to 30–90 cm tall, with smooth stems, square in cross section. Rhizome wide-spreading, fleshy, and bears fibrous roots, leaves are 4–9 cm long and 1.5–4 cm broad, dark green with reddish veins, and with an acute apex and coarsely toothed margins, leaves and stems are usually slightly hairy, flowers are purple, 6–8 mm long, with a four-lobed corolla about 5 mm in diameter; produced in whorls (verticillasters) around the stem, forming thick, blunt spikes. Flowering is from mid to late summer.

Flower colour: Purple

Specimens examined : Bhellum 10799

Locality : Jammu

Nativity : Europe and Temperate regions

Flrs. and Frts. : May – August

Distribution : India, Pakistan, Europe and temperate regions

M. piperita L.

M. pulegium L.

An aromatic perennial herb; stem prostrate and creeping, quadrangular, 10 – 50 cm tall; leaves subsessile, oval to suborbicular; flowers mauve-coloured, 5 – 6 mm long; calyx upto 3 mm long; corolla 4-lobed, hairy on outside; stamens as long as or slightly longer than the corolla; nutlets ovoid, pale-brown.

Cultivated in Jammu and Kashmir by Dr.Handa in 1956.

Flower colour: Bluish-lilac or Pale-purple

Specimens examined : Bhellum 11529

Locality : Batote

Nativity : Europe

Flrs. and Frts. : May – October

Distribution : India, South-West and Central Europe, northwards to Ireland and Central Poland and extending to Western and Southern Ukraine.

Prunella vulgaris L.

Erect, annual, thinly hairy herbs; stem quadrangular, 10 – 35 cm tall; leaves ovate, oblong, 3 – 6 cm long, bracts purple margined, hairy; flowers bisexual, purple; calyx bell-shaped; corolla 2-lipped, tube longer than calyx, upper lip erect, hood-like, notched, lower lip 3-lobed, middle lobe larger; stamens 4, didynamous, exserted, filament with minute tooth, below anthers, anther-cell diverging; style bilobed, lobes subulate; nutlets oblong, smooth.

Flower colour: Crimson

Specimens examined : Bhellum 13618

Locality : Srinagar

Nativity : Europe

Flrs. and Frts. : May – October

Distribution : India, Pakistan, Nepal, Europe and Britain and widely distributed in tropics and subtropics.

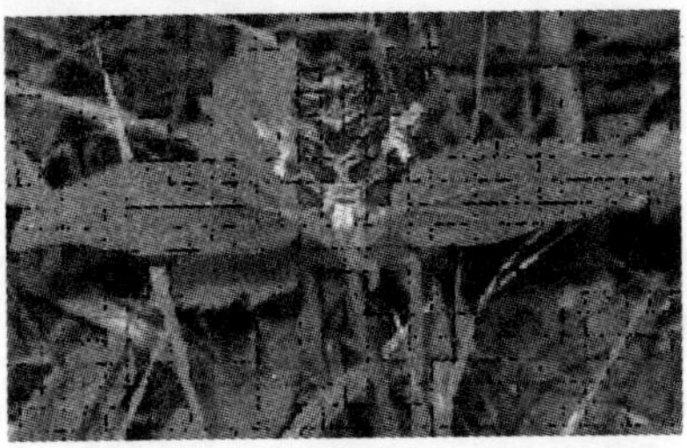

Prunella vulgaris L.

Sideritis montana L.

Annual herbs; stem upto 20 cm tall, branched from the base, angular, wooly all over jointed; leaves simple, opposite, 1.5 – 4.0 cm long, oblong, lanceolate, hairy all over, more on the margins; flowers bracteate, bracts leafy, longer than the flowers; calyx gamosepalous, copular with spine tipped lobes; corolla gamopetalous, bilipped, upper lip with three conspicuous lobes, lower lip with three lobes; stamens 4, included in the corolla tube, didynamous; style gynobasic, included in the corolla tube; nutlets 4, slightly brown.

Flower colour: Yellowish with brown dots turning brown at maturity

Specimens examined : Kaul 11 and 25

Locality : Burzulla and Rawalpora, Srinagar

Nativity : Europe

Flrs. and Frts. : May – October

Distribution : India and Europe

Sideritis montana L.

Plantaginaceae

Plantago aitchisonii Pilger

Perennial herb with a short or long rhizome; leaves 7-9 in rosettes, coriaceous, fragile, 5-9 cm long, 2-3 cm broad, lamina narrow elliptic-ovate, 5-7 nerved, glabrous, narrowed upwards, obtuse, at the base tapering into short to 8 cm long petioles, dilated at the base, irregularly dentate; spikes pedunculate; peduncles 10-20 cm long, erect, glabrous or with short white scattered hairs; spikes 10-16 cm long, with distantly set single or clusters of flowers; bracts shorter than the calyx, broad to round-ovate, carinate, apices membranous, acute, sepals glabrous, about 2.5 mm long, anterior and posterior sepals dissimilar, broad elliptic to rotundate, apices of the posterior sepals rotundate to ± obtuse, not or slightly membranous, minutely ciliate, lateral lamina rigid, carina prominent on the middle dorsal side, then disappearing in the lateral lamina, carina in the anterior sepal running throughout the length, lateral lamina equal, corolla lobes 1.25 mm long, rotundate ovate, narrowed shortly in the upper part, apex obtuse; anthers 2.25 mm long; capsule immature, depressed; seeds 4-5.

Flower colour: Dull white

Specimens examined : Bhellum 12479

Locality : Ladakh and Srinagar

Nativity : Afghanistan and Pakistan

Flrs. and Frts. : May – July

Distribution : India, Afghanistan and Pakistan

P. major L.

Perennial herbs; root-stock short, with numerous adventitious roots; acaulescent; leaves in rosettes, spirally arranged, ovate or ovate-elliptic, glabrous on both the surfaces, apex acute or obtuse, base attenuate10 – 20 cm long, margin serrate, subentire or sinuately dentate, 3 – 9 nerved; scapes many erect, glabrous or slightly pilose; spikes dense or lax, 4 – 15 cm long; bracts ovate, acuminate, margin scarious; corolla salver-shaped, 4-lobed, lobes ovate to narrowly triangular, greenish or yellowish white, glabrous, acute or apiculate, reflexed; stamens 4, inserted on corolla tube; ovary 3 – 5 ovuled; capsule globose or subconic, glabrous; seeds 6 – 10.

P. major L.

Flower colour: Greenish yellow

Specimens examined : Bhellum 13419

Locality : Ladakh and Srinagar

Nativity : Europe

Flrs. and Frts. : May – August

Distribution : India, Europe, Northern and Central Asia now introduced all over the world.

Nyctaginaceae

Bougainvillea glabra Choisy

Shrubs vinelike, stems thick, branches pendent, glabrous or sparsely pubescent; spines axillary, 5-15 mm., petiole 1 cm; leaf blade ovate or ovate-lanceolate, 5-13 × 3-6 cm.

Flower colour: Purple
Specimens examined : Bhellum
Locality : Jammu
Nativity : Brazil
Flrs. and Frts. : March – August
Distribution : Europe, S. America, Asia and India.

B. spectabilis Willdenow

Branches and leaves densely pubescent; spines recurved, leaves petiolate; leaf blade elliptic or ovate, base rotund, bracts dark red or light purple-red, elliptic-ovate, 2.5-6.5 × 1.5-4 cm, base rotund to cordate, perianth tube green, narrowly tubular, rounded, 1.6-2.4 cm, densely pubescent, apex 5-6-lobed, lobes spreading, yellow, 3.5-5 mm.

Flower colour: Purple, red
Specimens examined : Bhellum
Locality : Jammu
Nativity : Brazil
Flrs. and Frts. : March – September
Distribution : India, China and America.

Mirabilis jalapa L.

Perennial herbs, much branched; roots tuberous; leaves ovate, acuminate, upto 10 cm long or more, half as broad as long; flowers variously coloured, purple, but sometimes yellow, white, or variegated; seeds black.

Cultivated in the gardens and parks and often grown up from self sown seeds.

Flower colour: Purple, White or Yellow tinged red, variegated

Specimens examined : Bhellum 10120

Locality : Jammu

Nativity : Tropical America

Flrs. and Frts. : March – October

Distribution : India,

Illecebraceae

Herniaria hirsuta L.

Annual or perennial hairy herbs; stem prostrate, much branched, 5 – 15 cm tall, spreading from the base; leaves opposite, sessile or subsessile lanceolate or elliptic about 3 mm long and 2 mm broad; stipule scarious; flowers in dense axillary clusters; perianth, 5-parted, green, segments ovate, acute; stamens 5, antipetalous, tepals alternate with the staminodes, filamens short; ovary ovoid, subglobose, 1-celled, styles 2, short, diverging; seeds minute, ovoid, brown.

Flower colour: Green

Specimens examined : Bhellum 11717

Locality : Padder

Nativity : Europe

Flrs. and Frts. : July. – September

Distribution : India.

Amaranthaceae

Aerva javanica (Burm f.) Juss. ex. J. A. Schultes

A small wooly herb, upto 1 m tall; leaves sessile, linear, oblong, margin recurved; spikes wooly; sepals 4-5, wooly; stamens 4-5, jointed below, alternating with staminodes in a cup; style short; fruit dry 1-seeded; seeds annular, black.

Flower colour: Greenish white

Specimens examined : Bhellum 13893

Locality : Jammu

Nativity : Java

Flrs. and Frts. : April – July

Distribution : India, Burma, Ceylon, Asia, Africa, Morocco, Uganda, Tanzania, Australia and Madagascar.

Amaranthus caudatus L.

Erect, annual herbs; stem 1 m tall, much branced in upper parts, angular, angles obtuse, tinged purple; leaves ovate, elliptic, rhomboid or oblong, glabrous, 3 – 20 cm long, acute, acuminate, often tinged purple, margin entire or sinuate; inflorescence in drooping terminal or axillary panicles; flowers unisexual, male flowers bracteate, bracts ovate, slightly longer than tepals; tepals subequal, acute; female flowers with obovate tepals, base spathulate; ovary 1-celled, ovule 1, erect.

Flower colour: Pale green

Specimens examined : Bhellum 11625

Locality : Jammu

Nativity : Sweden

Flrs. and Frts. : Feb. – March

Distribution : India, Nepal and Pakistan.

Alternanthera pungens Kunth..

Perennial, creeping herbs; stem upto 70 cm tall, terete, striated, densely villous, often rooting at the lower joints; leaves opposite, usually in unequal pairs, broadly rhomboid, ovate-obovate, rounded to subacute, apex mucronate; inflorescence sessile, axillary, globose to cylindrical, prickly heads; bracts and bracteoles unequal, ovate, acuminate, spinescent, hairy on outside; perianth 5-parted, tepals unequal, outer tepal 2, spinescent, glochidiate hairy; stamens 2 – 5, filament united at the base, anther 1-celled; ovary compressed or nearly so, style short, stigma capitate.

Flower colour: Greenish white

Specimens examined : Bhellum 10605

Locality Rajgarh

Nativity : Tropical America

Flrs. and Frts. : June – October

Distribution : India, Pakistan and widely distributed in tropical and subtropical countries of old and new world.

Deeeringia amranthoides (Lam.) Merr.

Scandent shrubs; stem branched, branches often drooping, young parts glabrescent; leaves ovate, lanceolate, or oblong, 4 – 12 cm long, apex acute or acuminate; inflorescence in axillary or terminal racemes, usually combined into leafy panicles; bracts ovate, narrowly deltoid, lanceolate, acute; bracteoles ovate, acute or obtuse; flowers bisexual; perianth 5-parted, segments ovate, concave, spreading, reflexed with age, green, tinged red; stamens 5, united at the base; ovary ovoid, stigma 3, flexuous; berry globose, scarlet, 3 – 9 seeded.

Flower colour: Cream coloured

Specimens examined : Bhellum 11619

Locality : Chanderkote

Nativity : America

Flrs. and Frts. : April . – June

Distribution : India, Pakistan and America.

Digera muricata (L.) Mart.

Annual herb, simple or with ascending or very sparingly pilose, with pale ridges, leaf-blade narrowly linear to broadly ovate or rarely subrotund, glabrous or the petiole and principal veins of the lower surface of the leaf spreading-hairy, acute or acuminate at the apex, narrowed to the base; petiole slender, in the lower leaves up to 5 cm, shortening in the upper leaves, flowers glabrous, white tinged with pink to carmine or red, usually becoming greenish-white in fruit, in long and slender or shorter and denser axillary racemes, long-pedunculate, up to c. 30 cm long, laxer below; peduncles slender, inflorescence axis glabrous or sparingly spreading-hairy; bracts persistent, deltoid-lanceolate, acuminate; inflorescence of 3 flowers, central flower fertile, the 2 membranous, navicular outer perianth segments 3-4.5 mm long, oval or oblong, 7-12-nerved (in Asia), acute; the 2-3 inner segments slightly shorter, more delicate, blunt or erose, 1-3-nerved, hyaline, with a darker central vitta; stamens sub-equalling or shorter than the style; style 1.5-4 mm, the 2 stigmas finally recurved. Lateral flowers appressed; style persistent.

Flower colour: White tinged purple

Specimens examined : Bhellum 10674

Locality : Ramgarh

Nativity : Probably Notrth America

Flrs. and Frts. : May – August

Distribution : India, Asia, Arabia, Yemen, Afghanistan, Pakistan, Ceylon, Malaysia, Indonesia, Tropical Africa and Madagascar.

Gomphrena celosoides Mart.

Annual prostrate or decumbent herb, much branched from the base, white tomentose; stem hollow, cylindric, finely furrowed, swollen at the nodes; leaves opposite, elliptic, oblong or ovate-oblong, base spathulate, glabrescent above and densely wooly beneath; inflorescence in terminal or axillary spikes; flowers dirty white; bracts ovate, oblong; bracteoles narrowly lanceolate; perianth 5-parted, wooly without; stamens 5, monadelphous, tube long, anthers extruded; fruit utricles.

Flower colour: Shinning white

Specimens examined : Bhellum 10610

Locality : Rajgarh

Nativity : Tropical America

Flrs. and Frts. : May – September

Distribution : India, S. America, and Pakistan.

Chenopodiaceae

Chenopodium ambrosioides L.

Annual or perennial, strongly aromatic herbs; stem branched, angular, ribbed, minutely pubescent; leaves lanceolate, oblong or elliptic, 5 – 10 cm long, margin coarsely serrate, dentate, thinly pilose, gland-dotted beneath; inflorescence in axillary clusters or panicled spikes; flowers bisexual, green, pentamerous; tepals 5, gland-dotted and hairy without; stames 3 – 5; stigmas 3 – 5; seeds reddish –brown, smooth, enclosed in persistent, accrescent perianth.

Flower colour: Pale green

Specimens examined : Bhellum 12110

Locality : Rajgarh

Nativity : Tropical America

Flrs. and Frts. : May – September

Distribution : India, America,

Polygonaceae

Bistorta pacifica Kamarov

Perennial ascending herbs; stem branched, rootstock woody; leaves alternate, simple, coriaceous, hairy, basal leaves petiolate, oblong-lanceolate, ciliate, 20 – 30 cm long, 4 – 10 cm broad; cauline leaves amplexicaule, subsessile, lanceolate, acuminate, crenulate, ciliate; ocrea tubular, tip free, brown; flowers pinkish-green, in more or less curved dense spicate heads; perianth segments 5, in two whorls; stamens 8 in 2 whorls, filaments long, exserted; ovary 3-gonous, styles 3, long exserted; nutlets trigonous, brown, shining.

Flower colour: Pinkish-green

Specimens examined : A. H. Munshi 1690 Bobjan, Kashmir

Locality : Bobjan, Kashmir

Nativity : Russia

Flrs. and Frts. : June - August

Distribution : India, Russia

Emex australis Steinh.

Annual, glabrous herbs; stem rather thick,spreading or ascending, 30 – 60 cm tall; leaves ovate or oblong, base cordate or truncate, margin entire, petiole usually equaling the lamina, apex apiculate, stipule ochreate, scarious; flowers small, monoecious, in clusters; male flowers pedicellate, on terminal or axillary peduncles; female flowers axillary and sessile; fruiting perianth much accrescent, erect or erecto-patent, spinescent; nuts 4 mm long, trigonous.

Flower colour: Pale green

Specimens examined : Bhellum 12930

Locality : Ramban and Jammu

Nativity : Australia

Flrs. and Frts. : March– April

Distribution : India, Australia, Kenya, Hawaii, Rhodesia, Newzealand, Taiwan, America and South Africa

Note: The species is fast spreading as a weed in Jammu and Kashmir state.

Koenigia nepalensis D. Don

Annual decumbent, branched, herbs; stem tufted, sparingly strigose, more or less flaccid, 15 – 20 cm long; leaves distant, petiolate, ovate, lanceolate, acute, rarely obtuse, ciliate, much strigose beneath, 8 – 9 mm long; ocrea thick, 2 – 3 partite with appressed hairs; flowers in terminal clusters; perianth 5-partite, segments rounded, outer two smaller; stamens 3, alternate with 5 staminodes; ovary 3-gonous, styles 3, short, free, stigma rounded; nuts trigonous.

Flower colour: Pale green

Specimens examined : A. H. Munshi 820 Khilanmarg

Locality : Ramban and Jammu and Srinagar (Khilanmarg)

Nativity : Nepal

Flrs. and Frts. : July - September

Distribution : India, Nepal, Tibet, W. China and Taiwan

Persicaria nepalensis (Hamilt. ex D. Don) Nakai

Annual, erect, or ascending; hairy or glandular –hairy; stem simple or branched, grooved; leaves petiolate, ovate, oblong, acute, amplexicaule; ocrea tubular, slightly truncate; flowers in terminal corymbose heads; perianth segments 4 – 5 clefted; blue or slightly pink; stamens 5 – 6, filaments short, anthers dorsifixed; ovary biconvex, styles 2, unequal, connate at the base, stigma capitate or rounded; nutlets biconvesx or rounded, brown, shining.

Flower colour: Pale pink or green

Specimens examined : A. H. Munshi 261 Harwan

Locality : Srinagar (Harwan)

Nativity : Nepal

Flrs. and Frts. : July - September

Distribution : India, Nepal, Tibet, W. China, Japan, Malaya and Afghanistan

Polygonum aviculare L.

Annual, erect, ascending, glabrous, mostly branched herbs; internodes more grooved; leaves shortly petiolate, 10 – 20 mm long, and 3 – 10 mm broad, ovate- elliptic, acute, dotted, venation prominent; ochrea 2-partite, silvery hyaline, prominently many veined; flowers in axil mostly solitary; perianth segments 5, elliptic-ovate, acute or obtuse; stamens 4 – 5, filaments short, anthers dorsifixed; ovary 3-gonous, style very short; nuts trigonous.

Flower colour: Pale green

Specimens examined : A. H. Munshi 532 Ganderbal, Srinagar

Locality : Ganderbal, Srinagar

Nativity : Europe and N. Asia

Flrs. and Frts. : July - September

Distribution : India, Western Himalaya, Nepal, Tibet, W. China and Taiwan

Rumex nepalensis Spreng.

Perennial, ascending or erect, branched herbs; stem salcate, glabrous; basal leaves petiolate, cauline sessile, oblong-ovate or oblong to lanceolate, acute; cauline leaves lanceolate-oblong; ocrea minute, 1 – 2 mm long; flowers 1 mm across; nutlets brown shining.

Flower colour: Pale green

Specimens examined : A. H. Munshi 63

Locality : Srinagar (Khilanmarg and Gulmarg)

Nativity : Nepal

Flrs. and Frts. : July - September

Distribution : India, Nepal, Tibet, W. China, Bhutan, Java, Turkey and S. Africa

Proteaceae

Grevillea robusta A. Cunn.

A large tree with young shoots, ferrugineous, tomentose; leaves alternate, pinnate, deeply pinnatifid, segments usually lanceolate, margin recurved, nearly glabrous above silky beneath; flowers orange-coloured arranged in short racemes; perinnth segments 4, glabrous; stamens 4, antitepalous; fruits oblique follicle, tipped with a persistent style.

Flower colour: Orange coloured

Specimens examined : Bhellum 10684

Locality : Jammu

Nativity : Queenland and New South Wales and Eastern Australia

Flrs. and Frts. April – June

Distribution : India

Lauraceae

Laurus nobilis L.

Deciduous, evergreen shrub or small tree; bark blackish brown; brachlets terete; leaves alternate, oblong, lanceolate, upto 12 cm long, glabrous; inflorescence in umbels; perianth tube short; tepals 4, obovate; stamens 12 in 3 whorls; female flowers with 4 staminodes; ovary 1-celled, style short; fruit dark purple.

Flower colour: Greenish yellow

Specimens examined : Bhellum 16071

Locality : Srinagar

Nativity : Mediterranean region

Flrs. and Frts. : April – November

Distribution : India, Mediterranean region

Thymelaeaceae

Wikstroemia canescens Meisn.

Shrubs upto 1 m tall; stem much branched, solid, glabrous or pubescent ; leaves usually opposite, occasionally alternate, thinly hairy on both the surfaces, becoming glabrous with age, acute or obtuse, margin entire; inflorescence in axillary or terminal heads or spikes becoming panicles; flower bisexual, yellow; perianth tube 5 – 7 mm long; stamens 8, biseriate, epipetalous; filaments short, anthers oblong; ovary 1-celled, villous, style enclosed inside the perianth, stigma capitate, large, yellow; fruit ovoid, 4 – 4.5 mm long, ovoid.

Flower colour:Greenish yellow

Specimens examined : Bhellum 13719

Locality : Ladakh and Srinagar

Nativity : Nepal

Flrs. and Frts. : May – November

Distribution : India, Pakistan and Nepal, Ceylon, China and Afghanistan.

Loranthaceae

Arceuthobium oxycedri M. Bieb.

Plants 5-16 cm tall; branches opposite; inflorescence on terminal brachlets; male flowers 1-3, greenish yellow; female flowers solitary axillary or terminal; fruit a berry.

Flower colour: Greenish yellow

Specimens examined : Bhellum 14589

Locality : Ladakh and Srinagar

Nativity : France

Flrs. and Frts. : May – November

Distribution : India, Europe, France, W. Asia, Africa, Australia and Pakistan

Karthalsella opuntia (Thunb.) Merrill.

Perennial herbs upto 15 cm tall, internodes 5-14 mm long; flowers 4-12 per node in a cupular bract; perianth lobes 1 mm long, oblanceolate, acute or obtuse, berries obovoid.

Flower colour:

Specimens examined : Bhellum 12489

Locality : Ladakh and Srinagar

Nativity : Japan

Flrs. and Frts. : May – November

Distribution : India, Japan,

Loranthus vestitus Wall.

Parasitic robust shrubs; young parts of the stem and petioles clothed with soft tomentum ; leaves ovate, oblong, or ovate-lanceolate, 1 – 10 cm long, glabrous above, rusty below, margin entire, recurved; inflorescence in axillary pedunculate fascicles; calyx limb absent; corolla brown tomentose outside, glabrous and purple within, lobes 4, obtuse; ovary oblong, stigma capitate.

Flower colour: Brown on outside and purple within

Specimens examined : Bhellum 12489

Locality : Ladakh and Srinagar

Nativity : Europe and W. Asia

Flrs. and Frts. : May – November

Distribution : India, Pakistan, W. Himalaya and Subtropical regions.

L. pulverulentus Wall.

Stout, parasitic with dark-grey bark; leaves opposite, broadly ovate, oblong, coriaceous, mealy when young; racemes solitary or in fascicles; calyx limb absent; corolla slender, tubular, tube curved, segments 4, linear, green; fruit turbinate, grey-toment lose.

Flower colour:

Specimens examined : Bhellum 12719

Locality : Srinagar

Nativity : Nepal

Flrs. and Frts. : May – November

Distribution : India, Pakistan and Burma.

Viscum album L.

A large green dichotomously branched shrub; stem terete; leaves oblong or obovate, leathery, sessile, apex obtuse, base cuneate, margin entire; flowers in axillary fascicles, unisexual, upto 0.5 cm long, greenish; bracteoles usually 2, free or connate, ciliate; perianth lobes 3 or 4, free, 1 mm long, triangular, thick and deciduous; stamens 4; ovary obovoid, stigma conicle; berry succulent, globose.

Flower colour: White

Specimens examined : Bhellum 14589

Locality : Ladakh and Srinagar

Nativity : Europe

Flrs. and Frts. : May – November

Distribution : India, Europe, Africa, W. Asia, Japan, Afghanistan and Pakistan.

V. japonicum Thunb.

A much branched, tufted, parasitic shrub, stem dark-grey; leafless; flowers minute; perianth segments 3 or 4, persistent; anthers sessile, epiphyllous, opening by many pores; fruits globose, succulent, greenish-yellow.

Flower colour: Pale green

Specimens examined : Bhellum 14984

Locality : Ladakh and Srinagar

Nativity : Japan

Flrs. and Frts. : May – November

Distribution : India, Europe, Japan, Afghanistan and Pakistan.

Elaeagnaceae

Elaeagnus angustifolia L.

A tall spiny shrub; leaves lanceolate, 3-5 cm long, silvery beneath; flowers pale-yellow in axillary clusters, fragrant; fruits ovoid, fleshy, red.

Flower colour: pale-yellow

Specimens examined : Bhellum 14789

Locality : Ladakh and Srinagar

Nativity : Europe and W. Asia

Flrs. and Frts. : May – November

Distribution : India

Elaeagnus angustifolia L.

Euphorbiaceae

Croton bonplandianus Baill.

Monoecious, woody herb or shrub; stem upto 1.5 m tall; leaves altenate or subopposite, lanceolate, 3 – 5.5 cm long, apex acute, base cuneate, margin serrate-crenate, dark green; stipule subulate; inflorescence in terminal racemes; male flowers pedicellate, glabrous, calyx 5-lobed, lobes elliptic, ovate, greenish –yellow; corolla with 5 petals; female flowers subsessile, calyx 5-lobed, lobes triangular, subacute ; petals absent; fruit ellipsoid, trigonous.

Croton bonplandianus Baill.

Flower colour: Greenish yellow

Specimens examined : Bhellum 13282

Locality : Jammu

Nativity : Argentina

Flrs. and Frts. : May – August

Distribution : India, Pakistan, America, Bolivia, Paraguay, Brazil, Bangladesh and now widespread in the Pantropics.

Euphorbia geniculata Ort.

Annual, erect, glabrous herbs; stem 30 – 80 cm tall or more, fistular, ribbed, branched towards apex; leaves lanceolate, linear-lanceolate, elliptic-oblong, 3 – 10 cm long, sparsely hairy on both surfaces, puberulous on margin; petiole 1 – 5 cm long; flowers of both the sexes present within an involucre; fruits 3-lobed, smooth; seeds tuberculate.

Note: Closely allied to *E. heterophylla* L. often distinguished from *E. geniculata* Orteg. by longer petioles and red or red blotched floral leaves.

Flower colour: Pale green

Specimens examined : Bhellum 10582

Locality : Jammu

Nativity : Tropical and subtropical America

Flrs. and Frts. : May – August

Distribution : India, throughout tropical and subtropical America

Euphorbia geniculata Ort.

E. heliscopia L.

Erect, annual herbs pilose or glabrescent; stem upto 50 cm tall; leaves alternate, shortly petiolate, obovate, spathulate, upto 4.5 cm long, apex obtuse, rounded, or retuse, serrulate; ray leaves whorled or opposite; cythia pedunculate to subsessile; fruits triloate, deeply grooved; seeds ovoid.

Flower colour: Pale yellow

Specimens examined : Bhellum 10352

Locality : Jammu

Nativity : Mediterranean region

Flrs. and Frts. : May – August

Distribution : India, Pakistan, nearly throughout Europe N. Africa and Asia

Euphorbia heliscopia L.

E. heterophylla L.

Annual, biennial or perennial, erect, bright green, pubescent to subglabrous; stem simple or branched, woody below the branches, ascending or lower one spreading, leafy at the ends; leaves altenate, except at the topmost ones ovate, lanceolate, irregularly sinuate or dentate, margin entire or undulate, panduriform, blotched purple or red; stipules minute, reduced in small glands; inflorescence in corymbose or dense cymes which are subtended by the upper leaves; seeds oblong, ovoid, black.

Flower colour: Bracts red

Specimens examined : Bhellum 10582

Locality : Jammu

Nativity : Tropical America

Flrs. and Frts. : May – August

Distribution : India, Pakistan and throughout tropical America

Euphorbia heterophylla L.

E. heterophylla L. var. *genuina* Boiss.

An erect subglabrous or sparingly-pubescent annual up to 90 cm tall. Leaves mostly opposite, all petiolate, the petioles up to 4 cm long. Leaf-blades variable, elliptic-obovate to elliptic-oblanceolate or sometimes narrowly-lanceolate, 1-15 x 0.5-8 cm, the upper often narrower than the lower, acute, subacute or obtuse at the apex, cuneate or rounded-cuneate at the base, entire, denticulate or dentate, lateral nerves up to 20 pairs, subglabrous and dull green above, sparingly-puberulous and paler beneath, the upper leaves sometimes faintly purplish-blotched at the base, stipules sessile, glandular, Inflorescence a pseudo-dichasium or rarely a triradiate pseudopleiochasium, with the cyathia aggregated together in dense terminal clusters, glands 1-2 (-3), stipitate, circular, concave, fruits roundly trilobate, 4-4.5 x 5-5.5 mm, smooth, glabrous, Styles connate at the base, 1 mm long, bifid, seeds is quadrangular-ovoid, basally truncate, 2-2.5 x 1.5-2 mm, coarsely bluntly tuberculate, dark brown, ecarunculate.

Flower colour: Bracts red

Specimens examined : Bhellum 10582

Locality : Jammu

Nativity : Tropical America

Flrs. and Frts. : May – August

Distribution : India, Pakistan, and throughout tropical America

E. heterophylla L. var. *cyathophora* Griseb.

An erect subglabrous or sparingly-pubescent annual up to 125 cm tall, leaves mostly opposite, all petiolate, the petioles up to 4 cm long, leaf-blades variable, elliptic-obovate to elliptic-oblanceolate or sometimes narrowly-lanceolate, lower leaves pandurate, the upper leaves mostly querciformThis variety is widely cultivated in the tropics.

Flower colour: Bracts red

Specimens examined : Bhellum 10582

Locality : Jammu

Nativity : Tropical America

Flrs. and Frts. : May – August

Distribution : India

E. hirta L.

Erect, ascending, hispid, hairy herbs; stem herbaceous, branched, hairy, green, latex milky; leaves opposite,superposed, simple, subsessile, ovate, oblong or elliptic, base oblique or retuse, 1 – 3.5 cm long, margin serrate; cyathia aggregated into axillary clusters, each cyathium consists of 5 involucres, fused forming a cup, gland on inner side of a bract, raddish; flowers of both the sexes present within an involcure, single female flower in the centre surrounded by many male flowers; ovary 3-carpellary syncarpous, superior, trilocular, styles 3, each bifid; fruit a capsule, brown, transversely ribbed.

Flower colour: Pale green

Specimens examined : Bhellum 10615

Locality : Ramban.

Nativity : Tropical America

Flrs. and Frts. : May – August

Distribution : India

Euphorbia hirta L.

E. lathyris L.

Annual or biennial glabrous herbs; juice milky; stem erect, hollow, 70 – 90 cm tall, branched above the middle; leaves lanceolate, opposite or whorled; cythia pale-green, glands 2-horned; male flower each with 1 stamen, anther pale-yellow; female flower with stalked ovary, carried above the male flowers, styles three, each 2-lobed, erect or recurved, 3 mm long; fruit hexalobate, subglobose, 0.8 – 1.4 cm long, 1.3 – 1.6 cm broad, turning wrinkled with age.

Flower colour: Pale yellow

Specimens examined : Bhellum 12430

Locality : Jammu

Nativity : France and Italy

Flrs. and Frts. : May – August

Distribution : India, Pakistan, Europe, Africa, Caucasus, USSR, China, Japan, N. & S. America and Itlantic Islands.

E. milii Des Moul.

A small suberect spiny, semi succulent, shrub; stem upto 60 cm tall; stem leaves alternate, stipulate, obovate, to oblanceolate, apex obtuse, mucronate; cyathia in axillary pedunculate cymes; floral bracts scarlet, pinkish, red, showy ; spines arising from the expanded base, straight, about 2.5 cm long;

Flower colour: Bracts red, scarlet or pink

Specimens examined : Bhellum 12450

Locality : Jammu

Nativity : Madagascar

Flrs. and Frts. : March – October

Distribution : India, Pakistan and Madagascar.

E. peplus L.

An erect or somewhat ascending herb, upto 30 cm tall or more; stem branched from the base; leaves alternate, petiolate, elliptic, obovate, apex obtuse, base cuneate or attenuate, margin entire, membranous; ray leaves opposite, rhombic-ovate or ovate-deltoid; cythia yellow; glands semilunar, truncate on outer edge; fruit trilobite, smooth, pale green.

Flower colour: Pale green

Specimens examined : Bhellum 12960

Locality : Jammu

Nativity : Europe

Flrs. and Frts. : April – August

Distribution : India, Europe, N. Africa, C. Asia, Iran, Turkestan, Australia, and N. and C. America

E. prsotrata Ait.

Annual, prostrate herbs; stem weak, terete, puberulous or pubescent; leaves subsessile, ovate, oblong, apex rounded, base oblique, marigin serrulate in upper half; stipule linear, lanceolate, remotely fimbriate; cythia solitary, pedunculate; invloucre campanulate or elongate, turbinate, glabrous or solitary puberulous; glands 4, red or purple, suborbicular; flowers of both the sexes present within an involucre; capsule subglobose, long stalked, trigonous, hairy on angles; seeds reddish brown.

Flower colour: Pale green

Specimens examined : Bhellum 10460

Locality : Jammu

Nativity : Tropical and subtropical America

Flrs. and Frts. April – October

Distribution : India, West Indies and tropical and subtropical America.

Euphorbia prsotrata Ait.

E. pulcherrima Willd.

Perennial shrubs; stem upto 2 m tall, erect, branched; stem leaves alternate, long petiolate, petiole upto 5 cm long; elliptic-ovate, dentete-panduriform obtusely acuminate at the apex; flowers in cythia; floral leaves uniformally red or pink or occasionally white; fruits rounded trilobite, smooth, glabrous.

Now widely cultivated in tropical and subtropical countries of the world.

Euphorbia pulcherrima Willd.

Flower colour: Red, pink or white

Specimens examined : Bhellum 12410

Locality : Jammu

Nativity : C. America

Flrs. and Frts. : April – October

Distribution : India, Mexico, and in tropical and subtropical countries of the world.

E. serpens Kunth

Annual, glabrous or sparsely hairy herbs upto 30 cm tall, stem weak, many from the base, much branched, spreading, rooting from the nodes; leaves opposite, unequal, obliquely oblong, rounded or quadrate, base cordate, apex rounded, truncate or retuse; cythia subsolitary, axillary, glabrous; capsule 2 mm across, glabrous.

Flower colour: Pale green

Specimens examined : Bhellum 10680

Locality : Jammu

Nativity : Venezula, America

Flrs. and Frts. : May – October

Distribution : India, S. W. Asia, Africa, America and introduced in the Mediterranean region of the world.

E. tirucalli L.

A large shrub, about 6 m tall, succulent, unarmed, glabrous; bark brown, cracked; branches spreading, terete; leaves very small, oblong, linear, deciduous, arising only at the ends of the branches; the stem look like completely leafless; cythia small, densely crowded; fruits rounded, trilobite.

This is a very typical plant, often cultivated as hedge or wind-break. On account of its poisonous nature of the sap, this plant though unarmed, is considered very good hedge as it is not eaten by the browsing animals.

Flower colour: Pale yellow

Specimens examined : Bhellum 10167

Locality : Udhampur

Nativity : Africa

Flrs. and Frts. June – October

Distribution : India, Pakistan, Africa, Angola, and widely cultivated in tropics.

Euphorbia tirucalli L.

Jatropha curcas Miers.

A glabrous shrub or small tree; bark smooth, shining; juice milky; leaves palmately quinquelobat, upto 15 cm long or more; bracts linear; male flowers greenish-yellow; female flowers pale yellow; fruits ellipsoid, subtrilobate, greenish yellow.

Jatropha curcas Miers.

Flower colour:pale yellow

Specimens examined : Bhellum 10615

Locality : Kashmir

Nativity : Tropical America

Flrs. and Frts. : Throughout the year

Distribution : India, Brazil, Colombia, Africa and Indonesia.

Ricinus comminis L.

A large shrub like perennial herbs; stem erect, fistular,glabrous, 1 – 3 m tall or more; leaves alternate, peltate, orbicular in outline, palmatifid, lobes ovate, lanceolate, acuminate, coarsely serrate, 20 – 40 cm across, diffused with red; petiole glandular at the tip and base; stipule united to form caducous sheath; flowers unisexual, male flowers towards base with perianth 3 – 5 partite, stamens numerous in repeatedly branched filaments, anthers globose, anther-cell separate; female flowers towards apex, ovary 3-celled, ovule 1 in each cell, stigma red; regma extending with soft spines, seeds oblong, mottled.

Flower colour: male yellow and female reddish.

Specimens examined : Bhellum 10460

Locality : Jammu

Nativity : Africa

Flrs. and Frts. : Feb. – November

Distribution : India, W. Indies, Africa and Pakistan.

Ricinus comminis L.

Sapium sebiferum (L.) Roxb.

Deciduous tree or small shrubs; stem branched; leaves simple, aternate, somewhat triangular, or rhomboid-ovate, 5 – 8 cm long, glabrous on both surfaces, approximately deltoid, distantly acute, margin entire or toothed; flowers in terminal 4 – 10 cm long, catkins; male flowers pedicellate, perianth 2-clefted; stamens 2, short; female flowers few; tepals ovate, acute; ovary globose, 3-celled, glabrous, styles 3, short, recurved; seeds 3.

Flower colour: Pale green

Specimens examined : Bhellum 14160

Locality : Jammu

Nativity : China

Flrs. and Frts. : April – July

Distribution : India, Taiwan, Japan and cultivated in tropical countries of the world.

Sapium sebiferum (L.) Roxb.

Buxaceae

Buxus sempervirens L.

A shrub with many branches; leaves opposite, ovate, lanceolate, margin entire; flowers in axillary heads or spikes, unisexual, small, yellow-green, strongly scented; male flowers with 4 sepals; stamens 4, far prodruding; ovary rudimentry; female flowers with 6 sepals; ovary tricarpellary; capsule ovoid, 3-horned, 1-1.2 mm long.

Flower colour: Pale green

Specimens examined : Bhellum 10341

Locality : Patnitop and Srinagar

Nativity : N. Africa and W. Asia

Flrs. and Frts. : August-October

Distribution : India, North Africa and W. Asia.

Buxus sempervirens L.

Cannabaceae

Humulus lupulus L.

Dioecious, perennial, climbing, scabrid reflexed hairy herbs; stem 3 – 6 m tall; leaves opposite, broadly ovate, petiolate, base cordate, palmately 3-lobed, margin serrate, apex acuminate; stipule lateral, deciduous; male inflorescence much branched, cymose; female spicate in axillary fascicles; flowers yellow 10 mm across; style purple; etaerio of achenes 3 – 4 cm across.

Flower colour: yellow

Specimens examined : Bhellum 12621

Locality : Kashmir

Nativity : Europe

Flrs. and Frts. : April – August

Distribution : India, C. Asia, N. America, S. Europe. Pakistan and Afghanistn.

Moraceae

Ficus carica L.

A deciduous small tree or shrub; leaves variable, ovate, acute or acuminate glabrous above and pubescent underneath; stipule lanceolate; fls axillary, solitary.

Flower colour: Brown

Specimens examined : Bhellum 14623

Locality : Between Batote and Doda

Nativity : Mediterranean regions and Western Asia but Parker supposed it to be a native of Syria and Palestine.

Flrs. and Frts. : Feb. – March

Distribution : India

Morus alba L.

A medium sized deciduous tree; bark of the trunk fissured vertically; leaves petiolate, lamina ovate, cordate, or truncate, 5 – 7.5 cm long, apex acute, obtuse or shortly acuminate, margin crenate; flowers in spike, unisexual, male and female flowers often borne on different branches; fruit white.

Flower colour: Cream coloured

Specimens examined : Bhellum 10901

Locality : Miran Sahib

Nativity : China

Flrs. and Frts. : May-July

Distribution : India, China

Morus alba L.

M. nigra L.

Deciduous, 10-13 m tall shrubs or trees; leaves stalked, downy beneath, ovate, acute; catkin having male short spikes; fruits blackish or purple in compound clusters of several drupletrs, edible.

Flower colour: Cream coloured

Specimens examined : Bhellum 10619

Locality : Jammu

Nativity : Asia and probably Persia

Flrs. and Frts. : Feb. – March

Distribution : India and Persia

Morus nigra L.

Platanaceae

Platanus orientalis L.

A large deciduous tree; young shoots tomentose, covered with stellate hairs; bark peeling off in strips; leaves alternate, 5 – 7 palmately lobed, lobes coarsely toothed, about 8 – 30 cm across; stipule foliaceous connate below, usually 2 cm long; inflorescence globose capitulum 1 – 2 cm across pendent; flowers actinomorphic, unisexual, male capitulum subsessile, globose, 4 – 5 mm across, perianth lobes free; stamens 3 – 8, anthers oblong; female capitulum sessile, globose; perianth lobes spathulate; carpels 3 – 8, free, ovary linear, style hooked at the tip; achenes 7 – 9 mm long, obpyramidal, densely clothed with long, jointed hairs at the base, style persistent.

Flower colour: Yellow

Specimens examined : Bhellum 10219

Locality : Banihal

Nativity : Europe and W. Asia

Flrs. and Frts. : April – November

Distribution : India, Europe and Asia

Juglandaceae

Juglans regia L.

Large erect woody trees; bark smooth, olive-brown when young and silvery-grey on older branches, fissures scattered, broad with a rougher texture, leaves 30 – 60 cm long, imparipinnately compound, leaflets 7 – 9 odd pinna terminal, long stalked, opposite sessile, ovate, oblong, margin entire, nearly glandular pubescent beneath; flowers in dotted black catkins, 10 – 16 cm long, pale green; male and female flowers separate; fruit drupe, ovoid, 3 – 5.5 cm across, 2-valved, edible part corrugated The whole fruit, including the husk, falls in autumn; seeds with large, and a relatively thin shell, and edible, with a rich flavour.

Flower colour: Pale green

Specimens examined : Bhellum 10629

Locality : Ramban Banihal and Srinagar

Nativity : Central Asia

Flrs. and Frts. : April – November

Distribution : India and C. Asia

Juglans regia L.

J. nigra L.

Large woody trees; stem fissured, black; leaves odd-pinnate; flowers in dotted black catkins, 10 – 16 cm long, pale green; male and female flowers separate; fruit drupe, ovoid, 3 – 5.5 cm across, 2-valved, edible part corrugated. The whole fruit, including the husk, falls in autumn; seeds with large and a relatively thin shell, and edible, with a rich flavour.

J. nigra L.

Flower colour: Pale green

Specimens examined : Bhellum 10122

Locality : Srinagar

Nativity : America

Flrs. and Frts. : April – November

Distribution : India, America

Betulaceae

Betula utilis D. Don

Deciduous, trees or large shrubs; bark brownish or reddish-white, peeling off in papery layers, twigs dotted yellow; leaves ovate, acute, or acuminate, margin irregularly serrate, pilose to pubescent; male inflorescence pendulous in catkin; female flowerers in solitary or erect or pendulous dense spikes; nuts 3-lobed, winged or margined.

Flower colour: Pale green

Specimens examined : Bhellum 12761

Locality : Ladakh, Padder and Srinagar

Nativity : Nepal

Flrs. and Frts. : May – November

Distribution : India, Nepal, Pakistan, Afghanistan,

Fagaceae

Castanea sativa Mill.

A medium sized to large sized, deciduous tree; stem branched; leaves glabrous above nearly pubescent beneath, oblong, elliptic, acuminate, cuspidate, serrate; flowers in erect axillary spikes, 10 – 20 cm long; stamens numerous; female flowers usually 3 per invloucre; ovary 3-celled, styles 6; nuts pale yellow, nearly 7 cm across, surrounded by dense 2 – 4 lobed spinous involucres.

Flower colour: Pale yellow

Specimens examined : Bhellum 10341

Locality : Jammu

Nativity : West Asia Spain

Flrs. and Frts. : April-July

Distribution : India, W. Asia and Spain

Corylaceae

Corylus colurna L.

A large shrub or tree; leaves ovate, margin toothed, acuminate; catkin bearing small hairy bracts; male catkin drooping; perianth tubular, adnate to the ovary wall; stamens 8, fialments short; ovary 2-celled, styles 2, long, linear; fruits ovoid, nuts hard.

Flower colour: Pale yellow

Specimens examined : Bhellum 10621

Locality : Kishtwar

Nativity : Turkey

Flrs. and Frts. : May – August

Distribution : India and Turkey

Corylus colurna L.

Salicaceae

Populus capsica Bornm.

Medium sized tree; leaves 3-5 lobed, undersurface white wooly, lamina 4-8 cm, petiole upto 5 cm long or more; catkins pendulous upto 20 cm long.

Flower colour: Green

Specimens examined : Bhellum 10689

Locality : Srinagar

Nativity : W. Asia

Flrs. and Frts. : April – June

Distribution : India and W. Asia.

Populus capsica Bornm.

P. deltoids Marsh.

A large tree, 20-40 m tall; bark silvery white, smooth, slightly fissured; leaves deltoid, 4-10 x 7-13 cm, margin coarsely toothed, teeth curved and gland tipped; male catkin 8-10 cm long, purple; female catkin 7-13 cm long; capsule split in early summer to shed their seeds attached to cottny strands.

Flower colour: Pale green

Specimens examined : Bhellum 10681

Locality : Srinagar

Nativity : North America

Flrs. and Frts. : April – June

Distribution : India and N. America

P. canadensis Moench.

Deciduous trees; leaves triangular, bark smooth; flowers greenish – brown.

Flower colour: Pale Green

Specimens examined : Bhellum 11256

Locality : Srinagar

Nativity : France

Flrs. and Frts. : April – July

Distribution : India, France.

P. canadensis Moench.

P. nigra L.

A large tree with fastigiated branches forming a narrow crown; buds sticky; leaves ovate-rhomboid, nearly as long as broad glabrous, crenate, acuminate; male catkin 7.5 cm long; bracts purplish; stamens many, anthers purplish; female catkins longer than the male catkins; stigmas 2; capsule shortly pedicellate.

Populus nigra L.

Cultivated throughout the valley as an avenue tree.

Flower colour: Pale green

Specimens examined : Bhellum 10531

Locality : Ramban

Nativity : Europe

Flrs. and Frts. : April – July

Distribution : India, Pakistan and Europe

Salix aegyptica L.

A small deciduous tree; leaves 6 – 10 cm long, white below; stipules falcate; male catkins very fragrant

Flower colour: Yellow green

Specimens examined : Bhellum 13869

Locality : Srinagar

Nativity : Egypt

Flrs. and Frts. : March – April

Distribution : India, Egypt, Pakistan

S. alba L.

Trees or shrubs; leaves 5 – 10 cm long, narrowly lanceolate, white silky on both the surfaces, becoming glabrous with age, margin minutely toothed; stipule lanceolate, deciduous; male and female catkins separate; ovary 1-celled, stigma deeply notched; capsule nearly sessile, ovoid or conical, pubescent; seeds minute, many in silky hairs.

Flower colour: pale-yellow

Specimens examined : Bhellum 10132

Locality : Srinagar

Nativity : Asia, Europe and N. America

Flrs. and Frts. : March – April

Distribution : India, Asia, Europe, and N. America, Caucasus, West Siberia and Iran

S. babylonica L

A medium sized tree with pendulus branchlets; linear lanceolate,serrulate, acuminate, pubescent when young, glabrous later or slightly pubescent beneath; flowers and leaves appear almost together; male and male catkins appear on leafy peduncles; bracts minute, pale coloured; stamens 2, filaments free, villous at the base; capsule sessile, glabrous.

Cultivated as an ornamental; commonly grown on marshy places.

Flower colour: pale-yellow

Specimens examined : Bhellum 13133

Locality : Jammu and Srinagar

Nativity : China

Flrs. and Frts. : March – June

Distribution : India, Pakistan and China

S. babylonica L

S. caprea L.

A large shrub or small tree; leaves elliptic-obovate, glabrous above, more or less tomentose beneath, margin crenate or nearly entire; male catkin 4 cm long; female catkin little shorter than male; stamens 2, filaments free, glabrous; capsule stipitate, downy.

Flower colour: Green

Specimens examined : Bhellum 13587

Locality : Jammu and Srinagar

Nativity : Europe

Flrs. and Frts. : March – June

Distribution : India, Pakistan and Europe

Salix caprea L.

S. fragilis L.

Erect small trees or large shrubs; branchlets brittle at joints, olive-green; twigs fragile or flexible; leaves lanceolate, caudate-acuminate; flowers appear after the leaves; male catkins about 3 cm long; female catkins longer than the male; stamens 2, filaments free; capsule glabrous, stipitate.

Cultivated for its flexible twigs.

Flower colour: Pale green

Specimens examined : Bhellum 10449

Locality : Srinagar

Nativity : Europe and W. Asia

Flrs. and Frts. : March – April

Distribution : India, Europe and W. Asia

Salix fragilis L.

S. purpurea L.

A rather slender shrub with bitter bark yellow inside; branchlets purplish; twigs tough slender, glabrous, shining green; catkin appearing before leaves; stamens 2, connate throughout.

Flower colour: Green

Specimens examined : Bhellum 10247

Locality : Srinagar

Nativity : Europe and Central Asia

Flrs. and Frts. : March – April

Distribution : India, Europe and C. Asia.

Salix purpurea L.

Ceratophyllaceae

Ceratophyllum demersum L.

Submerged aquatic herbs; stem much branched, densely leafy, green; leaves dichotomously divided into thread-like toothed lobes, segments filiform, minutely toothed, spreading in water; flower solitary, axillary, unisexual; male and female flowers on the different nodes; perianth segments connate at the base; staminate flowers bear 10 – 30 stamens, without staminodes, anther subsessile; ovary minutely tuberculate, style persistent, stigma simple; fruit a warty nutlet, compressed, with or without 2 spines near the base.

Flower colour: Green

Specimens examined : Bhellum 12454

Locality : Srinagar

Nativity : Europe

Flrs. and Frts. : March – July

Distribution : India, Europe and now cosmopolitan

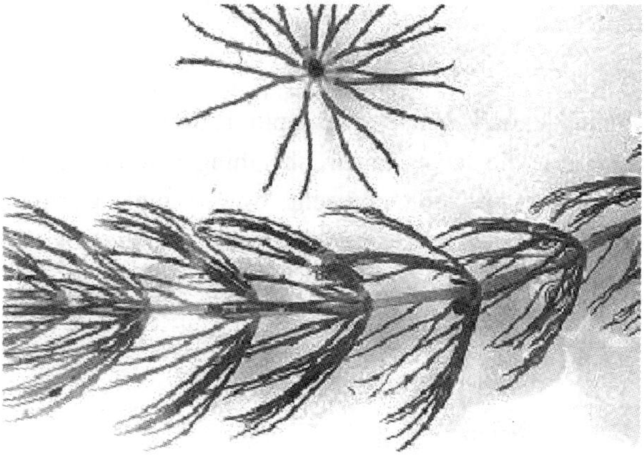

Lemnaceae

Wolffia columbiana Karsten

Annual aquatic, free floating herbs; stem solitary, fronds submerged, upper flat portion touching the surface, green; flowers unnoticed, reproduces vigorously, vegetatively by budding.

Flower colour: Green

Specimens examined :Srinagar

Locality : Gagribal near Dal gate, Srinagar

Nativity : USA

Flrs. and Frts. : March – July

Distribution : India and America

W. papulifera Thomps

Annual herbs, submerged, free floating; stem simple, green, broadly ovoid, up to 2 mm long and 1 – 1.3 mm broad; conspicuously punctuate on all the sides, dorsal surface bearing the papilla-like outgrowth in the middle of the thallus; vegetative growth is not vigorous.

Flower colour: Green

Specimens examined : AMK. 3240

Locality : Gagribal near Dal gate, Srinagar

Nativity : USA.

Flrs. and Frts. : March – July

Distribution : India

Butomaceae

Butomus umbellatus L.

Perennial aquatic herbs; scapes upto 150 cm tall, erect; leaves all radical, as long as the scape, linear, sheathing at the base; inflorescence cymose; bracts and bracteoles present; flowers pink; perianth segments 6, biseriate, obovate; stamens variable, many; anther bicelled; carpels many; follicle oblong; seeds minute, numerous, oblong.

Flower colour: White or pink

Specimens examined : Bhellum 12870

Locality : Srinagar

Nativity : Europe

Flrs. and Frts. : March – July

Distribution : India, Pakistan, Europe and now temperate and subtropical Eurasia

Agavaceae

Agave americana L.

Large rhizomatous herb with stolons, leaves borne in a spirally crowded mass, ensiform, usually with marginal spines, apex spinescent, scape thick bearing erect flowers in large panicles, perianth segments ± equalling the hypanthial tube, stamens exserted; stigma 3-lobed; ovary inferior; seeds black, flattened; used for yielding fibres for domestic and small scale commercial purposes.

Flower colour: Yellow

Specimens examined : Bhellum 10655

Locality : Jammu and Rajouri

Nativity : Mexico

Flrs. and Frts. : April – July

Distribution : India , Pakistan, Mexico and tropical S. America

Yucca aloifolia L.

Shrubby plants, usually with a trunk, leaves in rosettes at the base, stiff, often toothed with pungent apices, flowers nodding, pedicellate, in erect panicles, perianth campanulate, segments free, filaments fleshy, included; anthers small, hardly distinguished from the filaments, ovary superior; style usually short, stigma 3-lobed, fruit a capsule or fleshy and berry-like.

Flower colour: Cream coloured

Specimens examined : Bhellum 10141

Locality : Srinagar

Nativity : West Indies

Flrs. and Frts. : May - October

Distribution : India and W. Indies

Liliaceae

Asparagus officinalis L.

Herbs, erect, 1–2.5 m; rhizomes fibrous. Stems annual, densely branched distally; branches finely dissected, ascending to perpendicular, unarmed; cladophylls in clusters of 2-25 per node, filiform, straight or curved, 1–3 cm; leaves scalelike, 3–4 mm; blade lanceolate, base hardened, inflorescences in axillary racemes, 1–3-flowered, flowers unisexual; perianth campanulate, yellow or yellowish green; tepals connate 1–2 mm, greenish white, 3–8 × 1–2 mm; pedicel 8–12 mm, jointed at or above middle, berries red, 6–10 mm, seeds 2–4.

Flower colour: yellowish-green or yellow

Specimens examined : Bhellum 10615

Locality : Jammu

Nativity : America and North Europe

Flrs. and Frts. : April – August

Distribution : India, America and N. Europe.

Asparagus officinalis L.

Dioscoriaceae

Dioscorea bellophylla Voigt ex Haines

Rhizomatous climbers; stem twining to right; leaves opposite or alternate, variable ovate, lanceolate, acuminate, base deeply cordate, sagittate, glaucous beneath; male spikes in the axil of the leaf or leafless panicles; stamens 6; female spikes often solitary; capsule 2.5 cm long, obovate or obcordate.

Flower colour: Pale green

Specimens examined : Bhellum 12514

Locality : Jammu

Nativity : India and Pakistan

Flrs. and Frts. : April – August

Distribution : India and Pakistan

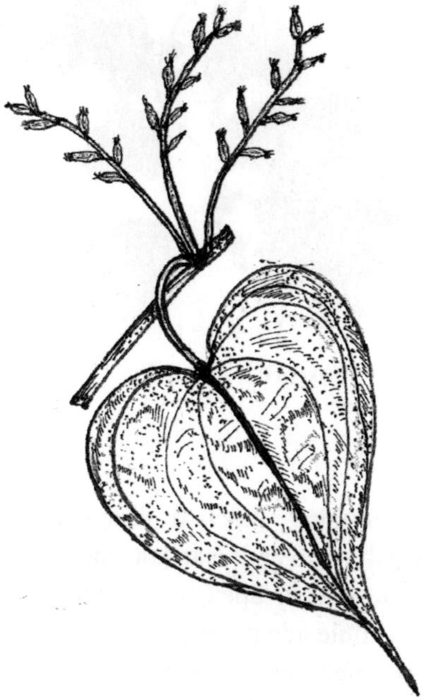

Dioscorea bellophylla Voigt ex Haines

D. deltoidea L.

Slender, twiner, creeping with rhizomes; stem sulcate; leaves alternate, ovate, or cordate, narrowing abruptly, glabrous above, hispid beneath, 5 – 8 cm long, margin rarely sinuate, apex acuminate; petiole 5 – 10 cm long or more; inflorescence in solitary spikes; bulbils rare; male spikes 5 – 10 cm long or more; bract ovate; flowers actinomorphic unisexual, borne in distant clusters on the spikes; tepals 6, oblong, margins scarious; stamens 5, included, all anther bearing, anthers bithecous; female flowers having the spikes about 15 cm long; capsule reflexed, broadly rounded, 2.2 cm across, winged, green streaked purple, stripes 2 - 4 mm long.

Specimens examined : Bhellum 13411

Locality : Jammu

Nativity : Nepal

Flrs. and Frts. : April – August

Distribution : India, Pakistan and Nepal

Dioscprea deltoidea L.

Smilacaceae

Smilax aspera L.

Armed, slender, climbing; brached shrubs; branches sulcate, zig-zag, more or less prickly; leaves linear lanceolate, cordate, orbicular, 5 – 15 cm long, 5 – 9 nerved, apex acuminate, coriaceous, glabrous, often white blotched; stipule adnate, modified into tendril; flowers white, unisexual; perianth 6-parted, tepals oblong, obtuse; stamens 6, included; female flowers with 6 staminodes; fruits globose-ovoid, red, turning bluish-black when ripe.

Specimens examined : Bhellum 12631

Locality : Jammu

Nativity : Spain

Flrs. and Frts. :April – August

Distribution : India, Pakistan and Spain.

Smilax aspera L.

S. vaginata Decne.

Climbing shrubs; branches smooth, often mottled; leaves ovate, or nearly orbicular, without tendrils, inflorescence axillary or solitary stalked umbels; flowers minute, purple; male flowers having stamens much shorter than the sepals; females flowers having 6 staminodes; berries 12 mm across, blue-black.

Smilax vaginata Decne.

Flowers : Purple

Specimens examined : Bhellum 12765

Locality : Jammu

Nativity : Pakistan

Flrs. and Frts. : April – August

Distribution : India and Pakistan.

Pontederiaceae

Eichhornia crassipes (Mart.) Solms.

Floating on stagnant or slow running water; leaves thick, glossy, rosulate, broadly ovate to obovate or orbicular 5 -12 cm across, spongy with bladder-like petioles; flowers sessile, violet-blue, in large peduncled spicate inflorescence.

Grows gregarious as weed mostly in stagnant water but also found on the slow running shallow streams.

Flower colour: Bluish violet

Specimens examined : Bhellum 13217

Locality : Jammu

Nativity : Brazil and Tropical and subtropical America

Flrs. and Frts. : August. – October

Distribution : India, Brazil and tropical and subtropical America

Eichhornia crassipes (Mart.) Solms.

Arecaceae

Roystonea regia Cook.

Tall palm with trunk swollen in middle or at base; leaves arranged in tuft at the top, 3-5 m long, pinnate, leaflets arranged in several ranks; flowers white, cup-shaped, borne in panicles.

Flower colour: White stamens pinkish

Specimens examined : Bhellum14567

Locality : Jammu

Nativity : West Indies

Flrs. and Frts. : May – September

Distribution : India, West Indies and now it is spread to the Tropics of the whole world.

Araceae

Acorus calamus L.

Perennial, erect, aromatic herbs; root-stock thick, creeping roots fibrous; stem 30 – 60 cm tall; leaves radical, tufted, linear, 30 – 80 cm long; spathe leaf-like, long, narrow; spadix 3 – 6 cm long, not enclosed within the spathe; flowers greenish yellow; perianth segments 6, free, oblong-obovate, persistent; stamens 6; ovary 3-celled, ovules many; berries yellowish-green, angular, 1 – 3 seeded.

Flower colour: Greenish yellow

Specimens examined : Bhellum13760

Locality : Baggar

Nativity : Europe

Flrs. and Frts. : May – September

Distribution : India, Europe, N. & C. America

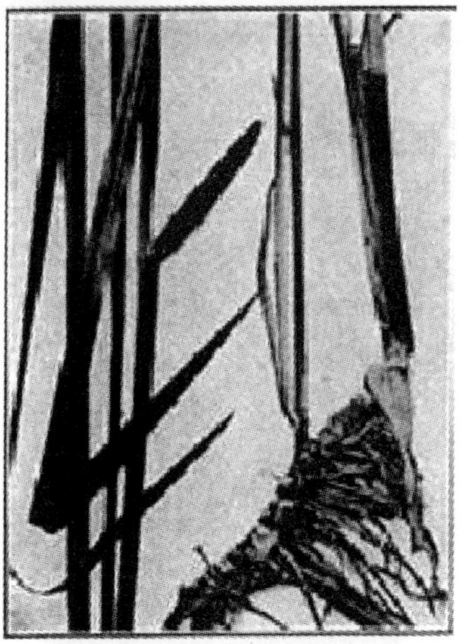

Acorus calamus L.

Alocasia indica Schott.

Stem caulescent; petiole 1 m long, sheathy in the lower parts, posterior lobes rounded, margin entire or subundulate; peduncle ca. 30 cm, spathe ca. 25 cm long; spadix ca. 20 cm long.

Flower colour:pale-green

Specimens examined : Bhellum10312

Locality : Rajouri

Nativity : Malaya

Flrs. and Frts. : May – September

Distribution : India and Malaya

Alocasia indica Schott.

Arisaema tortuoum (Wall.) Schott.

Monoecious or dioecious; tuber depressed, 2 – 3 cm across; leaves 2 or rarely 3 pedate compound, leaflets oblong, elliptic, shortly acuminate, very variable in shape; spathe lanceolate, 3 – 5 cm long; spadix variable, usually 16 30 cm long; male florets long, stipitate; ovaries ovoid; seeds obovoid, subglobose.

Arisaema tortuoum (Wall.) Schott.

Flower colour: pale green

Specimens examined : Bhellum10342

Locality : Rajouri

Nativity : Nepal

Flrs. and Frts. : May – September

Distribution : India, Nepal, China, Burma and tropical and subtropical regions of the world.

A. flavum (Forsk.) Schott.

Perennial, erect, herbs; roots tuberous; tuber globose; stem 15 – 40 cm tall; leaves compound, leaflets 5 – 11, sessile or nearly so, lanceolate, long-pointed, base cuneate, margin entire; spathe very short, 2 – 4 cm long, thick, yellow, appendage included within spathe; lower flowers female, upper male; anthers 2 per flower; ovary obovoid, stigma discoid; fruit globose, 4 – 6 mm across.

Flower colour: Greenish yellow

Specimens examined : Bhellum13312

Locality : Padder

Nativity :Yeman

Flrs. and Frts. : May – September

Distribution : India, China, Afghanistan, Yemem, Pakistan and Temperate Himalaya

Arisaema flavum (Forsk.) Schott.

Pothos aureus Lindl.

A climbing shrub or perennial herbs; stem weak, glabrous; leaves ovate, cordate, acute, green or variegated, glabrous, shining.

Flower colour: Pale-yellow

Specimens examined : Bhellum 10733

Locality : Jammu

Nativity : Solomons Islands

Flrs. & Frts. : February – March

Distribution : India, Solomons Islands

Pothos aureus Lindl.

Alismataceae

Alisma lanceolata With.

Perennial herbs; leaves lance shaped, 12- 20 x 4- 5 cm, petiole remain submerged in water; inflorescence erect; flowers pink; fruits small achenes, 2 – 3 mm long.

Flower colour: Purplish pink

Specimens examined : Bhellum 13421

Locality : Jammu

Nativity : Britain

Flrs. & Frts. : June . – September

Distribution : India and Britain

A. plantago – aquatica L.

Submerged glabrous herbs, stems many from the base; leaves broadly ovate –lanceolate; inflorescence a panicle with many flowers, white or pale purple; sepals 3, petals 3; stamens 6, anthers yellow; achenes oblong, 1-2 grooved, black or pale brown.

Flower colour: White or pale pink

Specimens examined : Bhellum 12421

Locality : Jammu

Nativity : Europe

Flrs. & Frts. : March – April

Distribution : India and Europe

A. plantago – aquatica L.

A. gramineum Lej.

A small aquatic herb; leaves above the water, leaf blade 7.0 x 2.0 cm; flowers white to pinkish; sepals 3, broadly ovate; petals 3, suborbicular, white, and larger than sepals; achenes obovoid, brown.

Flower colour: Purplish pink

Specimens examined : Bhellum 13128

Locality : Jammu

Nativity : Belgium

Flrs. & Frts. : June – August

Distribution : India

Alisma lanceolata With.

Caldesia oligococca (F. Fuell.) Buchen

Glabrous herbs; leaves ovate, 6- 15 x 4- 7 cm, base cordate; inflorescence scapose; flowers white, 1 cm across; sepals ovate, petals longer than sepals; achenes reniform.

Flower colour: White

Specimens examined : Bhellum 12061

Locality : Jammu

Nativity : Australia

Flrs. & Frts. : March – April

Distribution : India and Australia

Caldesia oligococca (F. Fuell.) Buchen

A. reniformis (D. Don) Makino

Glabrous herbs; leaves broadly ovate, orbicular, reniform, 2.5- 10 x 3- 10 cm, deeply cordate; inflorescence scapose panicle; flowers white, 1 cm across; sepals broadly ovate, achenes obovate, 2- 3 mm long, rigid.

Flower colour: White

Specimens examined : Bhellum 12821

Locality : Jammu *Nativity* : Nepal

Flrs. & Frts. : June – September

Distribution : India and Nepal

Sagittaria trifolia L.

Aquatic glabrous herbs; leaves mostly emergent, sagittate, somewhat hastate, basal lobes triangular; inflorescence an unbranched scapose raceme, 30- 50 cm long; flowers unisexual, white; petals broadly elliptic-suborbicular; stamens about 20; achenes subglobose, 1 cm across.

Flower colour: White

Specimens examined : Bhellum 13981

Locality : Srinagar

Nativity : China

Flrs. & Frts. : June – August

Distribution : India, Pakistan, Europe, Asia and N. America.

Potamogetonaceae

Potamogeton alpinus Balbis

Perennial rhizomatous herbs; stem branched, leaves sessile, oblanceolate to elliptic 7 – 10 cm long, cuneate or semiamplexicaule at base, apex rounded or obtuse; flowers in whorls, tetramerous, sessile, small; perianth segments small, obtuse, entire; stamens 4, sessile or subsessile; fruitlets about 3 mm long.

Flower colour: Green

Specimens examined : Bhellum 13211

Locality : Srinagar

Nativity : Italy

Flrs. & Frts. : July – September

Potamogeton alpinus Balbis

Distribution : India and Italy

Potamogeton alpinus Balbis

P. crispus L.

Perennial aquatic herbs; leaves submerged, sessile, broadly linear to oblong, undulate, translucent, serrate, 3 – 5 veined, acute or obtuse; stipule free; spike ovoid, oblong; fruitlets 4 – 5 mm long.

Flower colour: Pale-green

Specimens examined : Bhellum 11641

Locality : Srinagar

Nativity : Europe

Flrs. & Frts. : July – September

Distribution : India, Pakistan and throughout tropical and subtropical regions of the world.

P. gramineus L.

Perennial rhizomatous herbs; stem branched, leaves submerged, sessile, oblanceolate to elliptic, cuneate or rounded at base, apex acute or acuminate, margin minutely denticulate ; stipule present, conspicuous; flowers in whorls, tetramerous, sessile , small; perianth segments small, obtuse, entire; stamens 4, sessile or subsessile; fruitlets about 3 mm long.

Flower colour: Green

Specimens examined : Bhellum 12671

Locality : Srinagar

Nativity : Europe

Flrs. & Frts. : July – September

Distribution : India, Europe

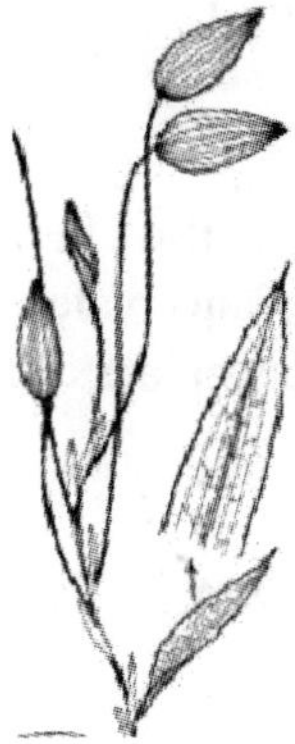

P. gramineus L.

P. filiformis Pers.

Perennial herbs, submerged; rhizome extensively creeping with horizontal stolons, tubers white; stem simple or branched, cylindrical, 25 – 35 cm tall; leaves obtuse, 1 – 3 nerved, yellowish green; stipule adnate to the leaf and sheathing the stem, scarious; spikes cylindrical up to 15 cm long; flowers 4 – 5 mm across; perianth reddish - green or olive - green; carpels 4, style inconspicuous, stigma broad and sessile; achenes obovoid, slightly compressed, 2 – 3 mm long, shortly beaked, reticulately veined.

Flower colour: Reddish - green or Olive - green.

P. filiformis Pers.

Specimens examined : Bhellum 11657

Locality : Srinagar

Nativity : British Isles

Flrs. & Frts. : July – August

Distribution : India

P. lucens L.

Perennial rhizomatous, aquatic, herbs; stem branched; leaves subsessile, lanceolate to elliptic lanceolate, translucent veins 7 or more, margin dentate; stipule free, lanceolate; inflorescence in dense spikes; fruitlets 3 – 4 mm long.

Flower colour: Green

Specimens examined : Bhellum 12411

Locality : Srinagar

Nativity : Europe

Flrs. & Frts. : July – September

Distribution : India and Europe

P. natans L.

Perennial, submerged, glabrous herbs; root - stock creeping; stem cylindric; leaves alternate, upper ones opposite, stalked, oblong, leathery, 5 – 10 cm long, glabrous on both surfaces; stipule free, linear, persistent; flowers in spike; tepals 4, free, green; stamens 4, free, sessile; pistil 4, superior, stigma sessile on short style; fruit 4 - drupelets, each with a single reniform, smooth seed.

Flower colour: Green

Specimens examined : Bhellum 11611

Locality : Jammu

Nativity : Europe

Flrs. & Frts. : July – September

Distribution : India and Europe

P. natans L.

P. nodosus L.

Perennial rhizomatous herbs; stem branched, terete; leaves petiolate, lanceolate, oblanceolate to elliptic 7 – 10 cm long, cuneate at base, apex rounded or obtuse ; spikes cylindric; stipules free; flowers tetramerous, sessile , small; perianth segments small, obtuse, entire; stamens 4, sessile or subsessile; fruitlets about 3 mm long, obovoid, spongy.

Flower colour: Green

Specimens examined : Bhellum 13671

Locality : Jammu

Nativity : Caranary Islands

Flrs. & Frts. : July – September

Distribution : India, Pakistan, Burma, Malaya and Sandwich Island.

P. nodosus L.

P. pucillus L.

Perennial, aquatic herbs; stem filiform, branched; leaves submerged, sessile, linear; stipules free upto 8 mm long, acute; spikes a few flowerd; perianth segmented, broadly obtuse; nutlets 2 mm long, obovoid.

Flower colour: Green

Specimens examined : Bhellum 12511

Locality : Srinagar

Nativity Sweden

Flrs. & Frts. : July – September

Distribution : India and Sweden

Poaceae

Aristida adscensionis L.

Perennial, tufted, slender upto 75 cm tall; culm erect , ascending; leaves linear, filiform upto 27 cm tall or more; panicle lax, linear, interrupted; braches drooping usually filiform; spikelets green or purplish, about 8 mm long, 1 - flowered; glumes unequal, linear lanceolate; lemma linear, awned, awn 3 - partite, lateral branches shorter than the central one.

Flower colour: Pale green

Specimens examined : Bhellum 10676

Locality : Jammu

Nativity : North Africa

Flrs. & Frts. : May – September

Distribution : India, N. Africa and widely distributed in old and new world.

Aristida adscensionis L.

Avena sativa L. var. *sericea* Hook f.

Annual herbs; culms 40 – 150 cm tall; erect or geniculately ascending, stout; blade 10 – 45 cm long, 3 – 15 cm wide, glabrous, scabrid; panicles drooping, narrowly to broadly pyramidal, 10 - 35 cm long, upto 20 cm wide, loose with rough spreading branches; spikelets pendulous, 2 – 3 flowered.

Flower colour: Pale green

Specimens examined : Bhellum 10321

Locality : Jammu

Nativity : Estern Europe *Choloris barbata* Sw.

Choloris barbata Sw.

Annual or perennial herbs; culm upto 1m tall; leaf - blade 5 - 35 cm long, apex acuminate, base with few long hairs; ligule in the mouth, memberanous; inflorescence of 1.5 – 10 cm long spikes; spikelets on one side of an angled scabrid rachis; lower glume about 1.6 mm long, lanceolate, acute; upper glume about 2 mm long, acuminate or shortly awned; lemma broadly ovate, margin of the upper half densely bearded, awn scabrid; palea oblanceolate, awned; caryopsis 1.5 mm long.

Choloris barbata Sw.

Flower colour: Pale green

Specimens examined : Bhellum 10631

Locality : Jammu

Nativity : Tropical Africa

Flrs. & Frts. : May – September

Distribution : India.

Cymbopogon citratus (DC) Stapf

Perennial tufted herbs; leaves lanceolate, acuminate, glaucous beneath, margin scabrid; panicles decompound, brick red at maturity; glume awned grooved on the lower half.

Flower colour: Dark rusty

Specimens examined : Bhellum 10589

Locality : Gajanshu.

Nativity : Malesia or Ceylon

Flrs. & Frts. : July – October

Distribution : India, Malesia and Ceylon

Pennisetum glacum (L.)

Annual, erect, tufted herbs upto 1 m tall; culms smooth, only rough below inflorescens leaves linear lanceolate, upto 25 cm long, acuminate, hairy below; inflorescence dense, erect,yellowish at maturity, upto 12 cm long; lower floret male or baren; upper hermaphrodite.

Flower colour: Pale green

Specimens examined : Bhellum 10863

Locality : Jammu

Nativity : Tropical Africa

Flrs. & Frts. : July – September

Distribution : India, Pakistan, America and Australia.

Sorghum halepense Pers.

Perennial upto 2.5 m tall; leaf - blade 15 – 50 cm long or more, margin scabrid, serrulate, midrib stout, sheath glabrous; ligule short, membranous; flowers in decompound panicle; lower glume ovate or elliptic; upper glume lanceolate, shining, apex acuminate; caryopsis dorsally compressed.

Flower colour: Pale green

Specimens examined : Bhellum 10127

Locality : Jammu

Nativity : Tropical America and Mediterranean region

Flrs. & Frts. : July – September

Distribution : India, nearly in all the tropical and subtropical countries of the world.

Sorghum halepense Pers.

4

Summary and Conclusion

Plant taxonomy – the mother of all the branches of botany has grown as a major discipline in India since independence. Considerable literature has accumulated on this subject but remaind largely confined to the indigenous flora. Concomitant with rest of the country, almost similar situations prevails in Jammu and Kashmir state as well. Various researchers and explorers botanised this area which led to the publication of various floras and monographs concerning the natural plant wealth. In sharp contrast to the indigenous flora, exotic flora has remained relatively unnoticed till date. Thus the present endeavour has been undertaken to analyse and evaluate the extent of exotic wealth in this state. As many as 320 genera representing 534 species belonging to 105 families have been covered in this publication. The present study provides a glimpsis about their morpho-taxonomy, economic uses and extant links with adjoining regions. It also points out their varied aesthetic significance and acclimatization potential vis-à-vis native locations. In their charming glory the on lookers and nature lovers seek a soothing therapy which is very beneficial under the prevailing stressful times. Above all the exotic wealth has added to the gene pool of this area and contributed to the bounty of nature in its true colour.

Bibliography

Anonymous, (1982) Ladakh Expedition Report, 1980. University of Southampton.

Ara, S. and Naqshi, A. R. (1993) Contribution to the botany of Gurais Valley, Kashmir. *J. Econ. Tax. Bot.* **17**(3): 657 – 678.

Azad, A. R. (1978) Taxonomic studies of the family Asteraceae of Kashmir with particular reference to tribe Cardueae. Ph. D. Thesis, Kashmir Univ., Srinagar.

Bailey, L. H. (1949) Manual of Cultivated plants.The Mac-Millan Co., New York.

Bamber, C. J. (1916) *Plants of Punjab. A descriptive key to the flora of the Punjab, North West frontier provinces and Kashmir.* Lahore

Bentham, G. and Hooker, J. D. (1862 – 1883) Genera Plantarum. Vol. I – III. London.

Bhellum, B. L. and Magotra, Rani (1992) New additions to the flora of Jammu and Kashmir state. *J. Econ Tax. Bot.* **16**(2): 295 – 303.

Bhellum, B. L. and Magotra, Rani (1996) A contribution to the flora of district Doda of Jammu and Kashmir state – Apiaceae. *J. Econ. Tax. Bot.* **20**(1): 143 – 147.

Bhellum, B. L. and Magotra, Rani (2007) Additions to the flora of Jammu and Kashmir state – New reports. *J. of Phytol. Res.* **20**(2): 243 – 245.

Bhellum, B. L. and Magotra Rani (2008) *Nervilia gammieana* (Hook. f) Schltr. – An addition to the flora of Jammu and Kashmir state. *Indian J. For.* **3**(4): 619 – 620.

Blatter, E. (1927 – 29) *Beautiful flowers of Kashmir*. Ser. I – III. London.

Colthurst, I. (1937) *Familiar flowering trees in India*. Thacker's press & Directories Ltd., Calcutta.

Coventry, B. O. (1923 – 1930) *Wild flowers of Kashmir* Ser. I – III. London

Dainelli, (1922-35), G. Italian Expedition to the Himalaya, 1-13. Bolonga.

Dar, G. H., Bhagat, R. C. and Khan, M. A. (2002) *Biodiversity of Kashmir Himalaya.* Srinagar.

Dar, G. H. & Kachroo, P. (1992) Floristic diversity in Sind Valley (Kashmir) *J. Econ. Tax. Bot.* ***16***(3): 647 – 657.

De Terra, H. and Peterson, T. T. (1939) *Studies on the ice age in India and associated human culture.* Carnegie Institution Washington, D. C.

Destreich (1906)

Dhar, U. and Kachroo, P. (1983) *Alpine flora of Kashmir Himalaya.* Scientific Publishers, Jodhpur.

Dhar, U. and Kachroo, P. (1983 a) Some remarkable features of Endemism in Kashmir Himalaya In : Jain, S. K. and Rao, R. R. (eds.) *An assessment of Threatened Plants of India.* pp. 18 – 22.

Dhar, U., Vir Jee and Kachroo, P. (1987) Endemism in Kashmir Himalaya – A retrospect In : Pangtey, J. P. S. and Joshi, S. C. (eds.) *Western Himalaya (Environment, Problem and Development)* Vol. I. pp. 413 – 420.

Dhar, U., Vir Jee and Kachroo, P. (1994) Ladakh : An update on natural resources. In : Y.P.S. Pangtey and R.S. Rawal, High Altitudes of the Himalaya (Biogeography, Ecoplogy and Conservation). Gyanodaya Prakashan, Nainital : 102-114.

Duthie, J. F. (1893 – 94) A report of a botanical tour in Kashmir. *Rec. Bot. Surv. India* **1**: 1 – 28; 25 – 47.

Fotidar, A. N. (1970) Exotics in Kashmir. Proc. State For. Conf. J & K ; 6 – 15

Fotidar, A. N. (1970) Silviculture and management of willow in Kashmir. Ibid. 25 – 31.

Gondwin-Austen, H.H. (1862). On the glacier phenomena of the Valley of Upper Indus. *Britt. Assoc. Rept.* **32** : 67.

Gondwin-Austen, H.H. (1880). On the post Tertiary abnd more recent deposits of Kashmir and upper Indus Valley. *Geol. Soc. London Quart.* Jour. **50**, 589.

Hamal, I. A., Karihaloo, B. A., Wafai, B. A. and Wakhlu, A. K. (1990) Additions to the flora of district Doda of Jammu and Kashmir state. *J. Econ. Tax. Bot.* **14**(1) : 205 – 213

Hartmann, H. (1984) Neue und wenig bekannte Bliitenpflanzen aus Ladakh mit einem Nachtrag zur Flora des Karakorum. *Candollea* **39**(2): 507 – 537.

Hartmann, H. (1987) Pflanzengesellschaften Trockener Standorte aus der subalpinen und alpinen stufe im sudlichen Und Ostliichen Ladakh. *Candollea* **42** (1): 277-326.

Hooker, J. D. (1872 - 1897) *The Flora of British India* vol. I – VII. Reeve and co. London.

Hutchinson, J. (1964) *The Genera of Flowering plants* Vol. I Clarendon Press, Oxford.

Jindal, S. L. (1970) *Flowering shrubs in India*. Pub. Div. Ministry of I & B., Govt. of India.

Kachroo, P. Sapru, B. L. and U. Dhar (1977) *Flora of Ladakh* Bishen Singh and Mahendra Pal Singh, Dehra Dun

Kachroo, P. (1980) *Floristics and morphology*. Kalyani Publishers, Ludhiana, India.

Kak, A. M. (1990) Aquatic and wetland vegetation of Kashmir Himalaya *J. Econ. Tax. Bot.* **14** (1): 1-14.

Kanth T.A. (1985) Stratigraphic profile of Jammu and Kashmir State in : Majid Hussain, Bupinder Zutshim, Mondira Dutta, Mohammad Siddique and Tasawoor A. Kanth. Geography of Jammu and Kashmir (Some aspects) Ariana Publishing House, New Delhi, pp. 1-11.

Kapoor, L. D., Sarin, Y. K and Dutt, A. K. (1963) A Botanical tour to Trikuta hills. *Jour. Bomb. Nat. Hist. Soc.* **60**(3): 533 – 545.

Kapur, S. K. and Sarin, Y. K. (1990) *Flora of Trikuta Hills* (Shri Vaishno Devi Shrine).

Bishen Singh and Mahendra Pal Singh, Dehra Dun

Kaul, M. K. (1986) *Weed flora of Kashmir Valley. Scientific Publishers,* Jodhpur.

Kazmi, S. M. A. (1970 – 1971) A revision of Boraginaceae of West Pakistan and Kashmir. *J. Arn. Arb.* **51**: 133 – 184; **52**: 110 – 136; 666 – 690.

Khoshoo, T. N. (1974) Prospects of Ornamental horticulture in India. *Ind. J. Hort.* **31** (4): 295 – 300.

Khoshoo, T. N. (1993) Himalayan Biodiversity Conservation – An overview in U. Dhar (ed.) *Himalayan Biodiversity – Conservation Strategies*. pp. 35. Nainital.

Koul, A. K. (1977) Evolution of Kashmir Landscape. *Inquiry* 4(5): 1-39.

Lambert, W. J. (1933) List of trees and shrubs from Kashmir and Jammu Forest circles, Jammu and Kashmir state. *Forest Bull. No.* 80. Calcutta.

Lydekkar, R. (1883) The Geology of Kashmir and Chamba Territories. *Rec. Geolog. Surv. India.* 22.

Meher-Homji, V. M. (1971) The climate of Srinagar and its variability. *Geogr. Res. India.* **33**(1): 1 – 14.

Munshi, A.H. and G.N. Javeid (1986) *Systematic studies in Polygonaceae of Kashmir Himalaya.* Scientfic Publishers, Jodhpur.

Naqshi, A. R. (1977) *Taxonomic studies of Kashmir Crucifers*. Ph. D. Thesis Kashmir Univ., Srinagar.

Naqshi, A. R., Dar, G. H., Javeid, G. N. and Kachroo, P. (1988) Malvaceae of Jammu and Kashmir state of India. *Ann. Missouri Bot. Gard.* **75**(4): 1499 – 1524.

Naqshi, A. R., Singh, G. and Koul, K. K. (1984) Plants of Gulmarg. *J. Econ. Tax. Bot* . **5**(3): 709 – 741.

Naqshi, A. R. and Ara, S. (1996) Taxonomy of genus *Draba* L. (Brassicaceae) in Kashmir Himalaya. *Orient. Sci.* **1**(1): 35 – 43.

Parker, R.N. (1918) A Forest Flora of Punjab, Haryana and Delhi, Rep. ed. 1973 Bishen Singh Mahendra Pal Singh, Dehradun.

Randhawa, M. S. (1976) *Gardens through the ages*. The Mac-Millan Co. India Ltd.

Rao, T. A. (1960) A botanical tour in Kashmir. *Rec. Bot. Surv. India* **18**(2): 1 – 67.

Rao, T. A. (1961) Further contribution to the flora of Jammu and Kashmir state. *Bull. Bot. Surv. India* **2**(3-4): 387 – 423.

Rau, M. A. (1975) *High altitude flowering plants of West Himalaya*. BSI. Howrah

Royle, J. F. (1839) *Illustrations of the Botany and other branches of natural History of the Himalayan mountains and of the flora of Cashmere*. Vol. I & II. London.

Sanjappa, M. (1991) *Legumes of India*. Bishan Singh and Mahendra Pal Singh, Dehra Dun

Seybold, S. and Kull, U. (1985) A Contribution to the floristics and vegetation of Zanaskar (Kashmir). *Bot. Jahrb. Syst.* **105**(2): 263 – 277.

Sharma, B.M. (1981) *Flora of Jammu and Plants of neighbourhood*. Vol. I Bishan Singh and Mahendra Pal Singh, Dehra Dun.

Sharma, B.M. (1983) *Flora of Jammu and Plants of neighbourhood*. (Illustrations), Vol. II Bishan Singh and Mahendra Pal Singh, Dehra Dun.

Sharma, B.M. and Jamwal P.S. (1987) *Emex australis* Steinh. A new record for India from Jammu. *J. Econ. Tax. Bot.* **11**(1): 77 – 79.

Sharma, B.M. and Jamwal P.S. (1988) *Flora of Upper Lidder Valley of Kashmir Himalaya*. Scientific Publishers, Jodhpur.

Singh, G. and Gohil, R.N. (1972) Some new records to the flora of Ladakh. *J. Bomb. Nat. Hist. Soc.* **73**(3): 487 – 490.

Singh, G. and Wafai, B.A. (1973) An exploration of Phanerogamic elements along Kishtwar – Duksum route, Jammu and Kashmir state. *Ind. For.* **99** (4): 310 – 319.

Singh, G. and Misri, B. (1974) Some exotic onrnamentals of Kashmir. *Ind. J. Hort.* **31**(1): 91 – 94.

Singh, G. and Kachroo, P. (1976) *The Forest flora of Srinagar and plants of neighbourhood.* Bishen Singh and Mahendra Pal Singh, Dehra Dun.

Singh, G. and Kachroo, P. (1983) Exotic trees and shrubs of Kashmir. *Ind. For.* pp. 60 - 76

Singh, J. B. and Kachroo, P. (1994) *Forest Flora of Pir Panjal Range*. Bishen Singh and Mahendra Pal Singh, Dehra Dun

Stewart, R. R. (1916 – 17) The Flora of Ladakh, Western Tibet. I. Discussion of the flora. *Bull. Torrey Bot. Club* **43**: 571 – 590.

Stewart, R.R. (1967a.) The Cyperaceae of Kashmir – India. A Check List. *Bull. Bot. Surv. Ind.* **9**(1-4): 152 – 162.

Stewart, R.R. (1967b.) Grasses of Kashmir. *Bull. Bot. Surv. India.* **9**: 114 – 133.

Stewart, R.R. (1972) Annotated Catalogue of Vasculara Plants of West Pakistan and Kashmir In : Nasir E. and Ali, S. I. (eds.) *Flora of West Pakistan*. Fakhri printing Press, Karachi.

Stewart, R. R. (1979) The first plant collectors in Kashmir and Punjab. *Taxon* **28**: 5 – 11.

Stewart, R. R. (1982) History and exploration of plants in Pakistan and adjoining area In :Nasir, E. and Ali, S. I. (eds.) *Flora of Pakistan*. Islamabad.

Swami, A. and Gupta, B. K. (1988) Plants of Udhampur District (J&K) – A preliminary List – I. *Indian J. For.* **2**(2): 150 – 157.

Swami, A. and Gupta, B. K. (1988) Plants of Udhampur District (J&K) – A preliminary List – II. *Indian J. For.* **2**(3): 244 – 249.

Swami, A. and Gupta, B. K. (1998) *Flora of Udhampur* Bishen Singh and Mahendra Pal Singh, Dehra Dun.

Van Soest, J. L. (1961) New species of *Taraxacum* from Himalayan region. *Bull. British Mus. (Nat. Hist.)* Bot. **2**(10): 261-273.

Van Soest, J.L. (1963) *Taraxacum* species from India, Pakistan and neighbouring countries. *Wentia* **10**: 1 – 91.

Vir Jee, Dhar, U. and Kachroo, P. (1989) Cytogeography of some endemic taxa of Kashmir Himalaya. *Proc. Indian Nat. Sci. Acad.* B. **55**: 177 – 184.

Vidyarthi, O. P. S. (2003) *Plants of Parks and Gardens*. Manvi Prakashan Publishers, Panjthirthi, Jammu.

Vishnu Swarup (1971) *Gardens and Flowers*. National Book Trust, India.

Wadia, D.N. (1953) Geology of India (Rep. ed.) Mac Millan & Co., London Trinkier, E. (1932), Geographische Forschungen in West-lichen Zentralasien und Karakorum – Himalaya Wissenschaftlche Zentral - Asian - Edpedition Berlin.

Wali, M. K. and Tiku, S. N. (1964) Contribution to the flora of Lolab valley. *Bull. Bot. Surv. India.* **6**(2 - 4): 306 – 312.

Index